Back to Vṛndāvana

Srila Prabhupada's final lila

Other titles by the author.

Transcendental Diary series is planned to cover seven volumes, and at the present moment, five are available.

A Transcendental Diary: *Travels with His Divine Grace A.C. Bhaktivedanta Swami Prabhupada*

(A seven-part daily diary series planned to cover November 1975 to March 1977)

Volume 1 - November 1975 – April 1976

Volume 2 - April 1976 – June 1976

Volume 3 - June 1976 – August 1976

Volume 4 - August 1976 – October 1976

Volume 5 - October 1976 – November 1976

Back to Vṛndāvana

Srila Prabhupada's final lila

Hari-sauri Dasa

Bookwrights Press
Charlottesville, Virginia

Paperback edition published by
Bookwrights Press
Charlottesville, VA
www.bookwrights.com

ISBN 1-880404-36-2 paperback

For bulk orders contact: Mayapriya devi dasi, publisher@bookwrightspress.com

Cover Design & Layout: Raivata Das

cknowledgments

My heartfelt thanks and gratitude go to the following devotees, without whose skills and enthusiastic service this book could not have been published:

Special thanks to *Sriman Krishna Candra dasa* for his generous financial support and friendship and *Kanti dasi* and *Jack Baldwin* for their unstinting support over many years.

Foreword and editing — *H.H. Giriraja Goswami*

Graphics and layout — *Raivata dasa*

Editing — *Mayapriya dasi, Braja-sevaki dasi, Vishakha-priya dasi, Kalachandji dasa, Krishna Rupa dasi.*

Graphics and photos — *Bhaktivedanta Archives, Ranjit dasa, Nitya-tripta dasi*

Computer work — *Srisha dasa*

Website creation and maintenance — *Gopinath Prasad dasa*

Endless encouragement and assistance — *my wife Sitala dasi, and daughter Rasarani-priya dasi*

Along with deep thanks to our sponsors *Sakhi Rai dasa,* and *Krishna Madhuri dasi.*

I also thank wholeheartedly all the many devotees and well-wishers over the years who have read my diaries about Srila Prabhupada and given me the impetus to publish them. May we all, as Prabhupada once said, have "another ISKCON in the spiritual sky."

My deepest apologies if I have forgotten to include anyone who's help I have received. Please forgive me. I pray to Srila Prabhupada that he bestows his full blessings upon you all.

Foreword

Back to Vṛndāvana is Hari-sauri Prabhu's riveting, poignant account of Srila Prabhupada's last weeks in Vrindavan. The narration begins on September 29, 1977, when Hari-sauri landed at the Bombay airport, in India for his one-month stint as Prabhupada's visiting GBC. When Hari-sauri arrived in Juhu, he found Srila Prabhupada in his quarters, emaciated and bedridden. Even in that condition, however, Prabhupada inquired about Hari-sauri's health—and how his books were selling in Australia, where Hari-sauri was GBC.

Later that day, Tamal Krishna Goswami called a meeting to discuss whether Srila Prabhupada should try to remain in Juhu for the temple opening or proceed to Vrindavan. The conclusion was that he should go to Vrindavan, and Hari-sauri flew to Delhi to make arrangements for Srila Prabhupada's arrival in Vrindavan.

Hari-sauri Prabhu served Srila Prabhupada in Vrindavan from October 2 to 27, and in *Back to Vṛndāvana* he describes the events of each day, based on the detailed diary he kept during that period.

The title, *Back to Vṛndāvana* has great significance. Srila Prabhupada went back to Vrindavan to spend his last days, Hari-sauri went back to Vrindavan to serve His Divine Grace there, and after Srila Prabhupada's departure, Hari-sauri went back to Vrindavan for Srila Prabhupada's disappearance festival. And beyond the events described in the book, Prabhupada went back to Vrindavan after having lived there from 1960 to 1965, translating *Srimad-Bhagavatam* and preparing to go to the West, and in 1975 Hari-sauri went back to Vrindavan, where he first became Srila Prabhupada's personal servant. By his preaching, Srila Prabhupada brought us all back to Vrindavan, and now we want to follow him back to Goloka Vrindavan, the Vrindavan in the spiritual world.

Hari-sauri Prabhu's last published volume (Vol. 5) of the *Transcendental Diary* series took us to November 1976, and considering that he did not know how much time he had left to finish that series and wanting to cover this most important period, he jumped ahead to September 29, 1977—to our great benefit.

Reading Hari-sauri's book brought me closer to Srila Prabhupada—and to him, Srila Prabhupada's dear, devoted servant. And I imagine the book will have the same effect on every reader, making us all feel closer to Srila Prabhupada and more committed to his service, his mission, and his followers.

Hare Krishna.

-Giriraj Swami

reface

After leaving the personal service of His Divine Grace Srila Prabhupada in mid-March 1977, I travelled back to Australia as his official *ad hoc* representative, and in April was subsequently appointed by him as his GBC for the South Seas zone (Australia, New Zealand and Indonesia).

The following month, May 1977, Prabhupada, who had gone to Rishikesh for recuperation after serious illness, suddenly declared that he wanted to return to Vrindavana immediately, to leave his body. He legally registered his Will and all the GBCs were called to Vrindavana for emergency meetings.

He consulted with his leaders and clarified how things were to proceed without him, especially in three important aspects of ISKCON –the structure of management, initiations, and the printing of books through the BBT (Bhaktivedanta Book Trust).

However, the immediate crisis receded and His Divine Grace seemed to successfully pass through the emergency.

I stayed on in Vrindavana for a few extra days after most GBCs had returned to their preaching fields, and while doing so I approached Prabhupada's secretary, Tamal Krishna Goswami, with a request to be Prabhupada's visiting GBC secretary for the month of October. This was a system Prabhupada had established right from the beginning of the creation of the GBC body in July 1970—any GBC man could travel and preach with Srila Prabhupada for one month to learn both how to manage the world-wide Society, and for personal purification.

Although I had just completed a year and half as Prabhupada's personal servant, as a new GBC I was still eager to get more personal association with him while it was still possible to do so. Thus I arrived in Bombay on September 29, 1977 to fulfill that opportunity.

As I had done throughout my tenure as servant of the servant, I kept another hand-written diary to record the events of what turned out to be Srila Prabhupada's last six weeks on the planet.

This small book, *Back To Vṛndāvana* a is a fusion of my diary, and other recorded materials, presented for the edification and pleasure of what we hope will be all the many millions of readers for generations to come.

Readers should note that this diary records events from September 29 1977 to October 28 1977. It does not cover the final two weeks of Prabhupada's visible presence. It does however present an epilogue to that period.

Readers who wish to access the transcripts and recordings from October 28 to the *tirobhāva-tithi*, November 14, 1977 [disappearance day] can contact Bhaktivedanta Archives in North Carolina U.S.A. and get a copy of the Bhaktivedanta VedaBase.

May my beloved spiritual preceptor Om Visnupada A.C. Bhaktivedanta Swami Srila Prabhupada be pleased with this small contribution to the ever-growing testimonials to his pure devotion, compassion and mercy, and bless this fallen soul with His Divine Grace.

Hari Sauri Das

Completed Nṛsiṁha Cāturdaśī 2021
Śrī Māyāpur-dhāma

Table of Contents

ℬack to Vṛndāvana
Srila Prabhupada's final lila

SEPTEMBER 29, 1977

I arrived at Bombay airport at 1:35 a.m. and made it to the temple by 2:15. The lift wasn't working, so I climbed the stairs of the guesthouse to the top floor, Prabhupada's level. I took rest for a short while and then took bath at 3:30. Tamal Krishna Maharaja, Brahmananda Swami, Upendra, Abhirama, Giriraja and Kuladri are all in Bombay. Prabhupada has been here since September 13. The opening of the temple is now being organized and Prabhupada is waiting for that. He is staying permanently in his bedroom now, and his condition is very bad. Tamal Krishna told me he hasn't eaten anything solid for one and a half months. Now he takes a glass of *mung jal*, one of grape juice, and another of Complan, a protein drink. A few days ago he took a few spoonfuls of fruit and a piece of *sandeśa* over a half-hour period, but this caused so much difficulty that they had to give him an enema, which relieved the situation.

At around 6 a.m. I peeked through the doorway to see Srila Prabhupada in his bed. He was resting, with one leg bent, his knee raised. I was amazed to see how

1

much his body had become reduced. His leg was so thin.

At 7:30 a.m. I went in, and Tamal Krishna Maharaja was there, as was Abhirama. Tamal Krishna was very gently massaging Prabhupada's leg and arm as he lay with his eyes closed. As I came in, Tamal Krishna informed Prabhupada of my arrival. Prabhupada didn't react at first, and then after a short time he opened his eyes and looked over to me. I offered my obeisances. I was shocked to see how much Prabhupada's bodily condition had deteriorated. He is much worse than in May-June when the emergency GBC meeting was held with Prabhupada here in Vrindavan. Practically he has no fat or muscle in his body, it is just skin and bone. You could see his heart beating as the skin on his ribs moved up and down with every beat.

Still, he is the same Prabhupada, and I was simply surprised how he is maintaining his bodily existence. Only by will power—nothing else. All external activities are now almost stopped, and Prabhupada spends all day resting and being fully absorbed in *samādhi*. His body is so weak he requires assistance even to turn on his side in bed.

He asked, "How is your health?" He is in such a condition, yet he is asking for the welfare of others. I replied that I was all right and that things were going on nicely in Australia. Then he asked, "Books are selling?" His first thought is always for the books. "Yes, now we have the India-printed books, and we distribute more than ever before," I replied.

"Which one sells most?"

"The *Bhagavad-gītā,* Srila Prabhupada." He smiled slightly. This news brings him transcendental pleasure. I told him how on the farm we had just shaved three new boys, but now his eyes were again closed and he did not speak more. Even to say just a few words is a great strain. I sat for some time, and as Tamal Krishna

2

Maharaja massaged his head with some oil, I massaged his left arm. Tamal Krishna made some nice comment about how Prabhupada could enjoy all the devotees massaging him, and Prabhupada smiled. After about ten minutes we stopped, and Prabhupada rested. Then Upendra took over and I left.

I rested after lunch, then Tamal Krishna Maharaja woke me around 5:30 p.m. and requested that several of us meet together. He spoke about Prabhupada leaving immediately for Vrindavan instead of after the opening of the Bombay temple scheduled for the 22nd. Previously, Prabhupada had told them he wanted the devotees to take him on parikramā around Vrindavan-dhāma after the opening. Now there may be some change. He instructed that the GBC and servants should consider everything and meet together to decide. After a few minutes, Tamal Krishna Maharaja called us all into Prabhupada's room and we sat at his side. Tamal Krishna began by offering various comments in favor of going to Vrindavan. He spoke to Prabhupada and pointed out that even if Prabhupada were in Bombay for the opening he would not be able to attend any function in his present condition. Also, he was known as "Nṛsiṁha Guru" for his powerful speaking and preaching, and it would not be fitting for the public to see him in his present condition. He also pointed out that the temple could still be opened and Prabhupada could come back later to visit it if he wanted.

Then Prabhupada said that each of us should comment. Brahmananda Swami gave the opinion that Prabhupada should go back to Vrindavan. I said it was difficult to give any comment, because it was difficult to understand how strong Prabhupada's desire was to be in Bombay for the opening as opposed to the consideration of his health. Prabhupada asked what I was saying, so Tamal Krishna Maharaja repeated it, and Prabhupada replied, "It is for health." So I also was in favor of Prabhupada returning to Vrindavan. Gopal Krishna thought that perhaps it would be better, if possible, for Prabhupada to remain for another three weeks and then go after the opening. Then Giriraj spoke, saying that each day is very difficult for Prabhupada and that each successive day will be increasingly more so. There is constant noise from the construction, and he felt that three weeks waiting would be too long. As he spoke, Prabhupada moved his head to affirm and give his agreement. Abhirama and Kuladri were also in favor of Vrindavan, and Upendra couldn't decide. So, by majority we were in favor of an immediate return to Vrindavan, and Prabhupada appeared pleased by the decision.

Tamal Krishna Maharaja also brought up the question of whether the other GBCs should come, and whether it should be compulsory. Prabhupada said that it is just like they have to come for the Mayapur festival. He said he wished to go on *parikramā* after October 15, and agreed to the proposal that the GBC come first to Vrindavan for one week and then go to Bombay for the opening ceremony. Then Tamal Krishna Maharaja gave one opinion in favor of staying. He said that as long as Prabhupada is in Bombay waiting for the opening, then that is reason for living. But now if he returns to Vrindavan, then it means one goes there to die, so perhaps Prabhupada should remain in Bombay and that will help give him motivation to live. Prabhupada smiled and said, "That is sentiment." His desire to return to Vrindavan was clear, so immediately after the decision, we met and it was decided that I should go immediately to Delhi and arrange for the necessary items needed for Prabhupada to stay in Vrindavan. Since the bedroom there is small, it required a good double bed to be set up in the darshan room, along with a first-class double-thickness cotton mattress, as Prabhupada also indicated that he wanted that kind of mattress and not a spring mattress.

4

I would also make other arrangements, such as borrowing the Mercedes car of Mr. Laxman Agarwal—who is the owner of Laxman Sylvania, a big company manufacturing light bulbs—with whom Prabhupada has stayed several times.

After offering my obeisances to Prabhupada, I left and caught the last flight out to Delhi, arriving at about 11:15 p.m.

SEPTEMBER 30–OCTOBER 1, 1977

In Delhi, temple president Bhagavata Asraya prabhu took me to see one of the friends of the temple, Mr. Dawan, who had recently started a business called WoodAge, which sells handmade wooden furniture. We explained the situation of Srila Prabhupada's imminent return to Vrindavan and our urgent requirement of a double bed. As Krishna would have it, he had just completed a large double bed, the only one he had, which he sold to us at cost price. Along with that we bought various other accoutrements:

Double bed and mattress	Rs. 650.00
Bed sheets and pillow cases	Rs. 465.00
Transportation of bed to Vrindavan	Rs. 400.00

We sent them by road with Radha Mohan dasa, an American from Atlanta. The road to Vrindavan was reported as being impassable due to flood damage, so he went via Aligarh—a six-hour journey.

I phoned Bombay and told Tamal Krishna Maharaja that the road was out, so we booked tickets for Prabhupada to fly to Delhi and then take the Taj Express from Delhi to Vrindavan. Later, Tamal Krishna Maharaja rang and said that now Prabhupada would not fly to Delhi but travel by train directly to Mathura Junction and then drive from there to Vrindavan. He

5

would set off at 11:30 a.m. on October 1, and arrive 7:30 the next morning.

In the evening we visited Mr. Agarwal, but for various reasons he was unable or unwilling to loan us his Mercedes.

On October 1, Bhagavata Asraya and I drove to Vrindavan and made arrangements with devotees there for fixing Prabhupada's rooms and getting vehicles arranged.

OCTOBER 2, 1977

At 6:30 a.m. we arrived at Mathura Junction with Prabhupada's Ambassador car, rigged out with a foam mattress from our guesthouse for Prabhupada to lie on, and a wheelchair for him to cross over the platform bridge to the car. About twenty men, including four *gurukula* boys, were present.

The train came at 7:35 a.m. First the luggage was unloaded, and then Upendra, Abhirama, and Kuladri got down, followed by Tamal Krishna Maharaja and a good number of Bombay devotees. Then Brahmananda Swami appeared at the door, cradling Prabhupada in his arms as one carries a small child, and sat him gently in the wheelchair. Yasodanandana Swami and I wheeled Prabhupada to his car as the devotees all chanted around us, simultaneously ecstatic to see their spiritual master and distraught at his condition.

At the car, Upendra lifted Prabhupada up onto his feet and then lowered him down onto the edge of the car seat. From inside I supported Prabhupada under his armpits and Upendra lifted his lower half until he was completely inside and laying on the mattress. Then we all left in procession. The short ride was difficult for Prabhupada. Any manhandling causes distress, his body is so weak and fragile. I felt very clumsy and offensive as I lifted him into the car.

6

It was a small motorcade: I travelled in the front car with Yadubara, Brahmananda Swami, Yasodanandana Swami, and Bhagatji. Aksayananda Swami, Tamal Krishna Maharaja, Upendra, and Prabhupada came next in Prabhupada's car, which was followed by the minibus with the rest of the devotees. We drove slowly and arrived at the side gate of the temple at 8:15 a.m. We were greeted by 50–60 devotees and *gurukula* children.

Tamal Krishna Maharaja lifted Prabhupada out of the car and lowered him into his palanquin, and Yasodanandana Swami and I carried him aloft into his quarters. The devotees were very upset to see his weakened condition, but they gave a loud reception with chanting.

Inside, we lay Prabhupada on his bed and closed all the curtains to dim the light. A few of us sat around Prabhupada's bedside. For about five minutes, Prabhupada didn't say anything. Tamal Krishna Maharaja commented, "Now you are home, Srila Prabhupada." But he lay very quietly, hardly moving. Then after about five minutes, he moved his hands up to his chest and clasped them together and said, "Thank you." It was as if it was a great relief that he had now returned home. Tamal Krishna Maharaja said, "Now you are in the care of Krishna and Balarama." Prabhupada smiled and slightly tipped his head and said, "Yes." Then he quoted a verse in Sanskrit, *kṛṣṇa tvadīya-pada-paṅkaja-pañjarāntam.*" We sat a minute more and then left Prabhupada to rest.

At around 11 a.m. I was sitting with Prabhupada when he woke and tried to move some pillows. I leaned forward, and he said he wanted to lie on his side, but I didn't know how to assist him. Prabhupada spoke so softly I could hardly hear him, and due to being so weak, he couldn't move over himself. I felt very offensive that I couldn't fully understand his intention, and I called Abhirama, who was at the door, and he showed me how to turn Prabhupada onto his side by grasping his hips and turning them and then adjusting his legs and arms. Then Prabhupada rested again. Practically he has enough strength only to move his arms, and Brahmananda Swami told me this morning that a short while ago Prabhupada had asked Tamal Krishna Maharaja whether his legs were paralyzed.

His servants change the sheets and wash him. Now he doesn't even go to the bathroom. A bottle is used for urination, and when he evacuates they lift him up at the waist, wash him with a wet cloth, apply some disinfectant powder, give a change of cloth, and slide a clean sheet under him.

In Bombay, he was leaving his bed only once a day for a few minutes so that they could change the sheets. He would sit in his wheelchair, and they would wheel him around the room for a short time and then put him back on the bed.

Another difficulty was due to an operation Prabhupada had in London. His urinary tract was blocked and he couldn't pass urine, so his bladder swelled right up. They rushed him to the hospital, and the doctor came to see him. As he inspected him, all of a sudden the passage opened up and the fluid gushed out, and Prabhupada gave a big heave of air and said, "Now I am relieved." However, they consulted with the doctor, and he advised that he should still have an operation to open up the passage, because it could easily happen again. Tamal Krishna Maharaja insisted on being present as they operated. They ended up doing a complete circumcision, as there was scar tissue causing the blockage. Now that is gradually healing, but it causes some difficulty for cleansing, etc.

During the morning, Prabhupada asked Tamal Krishna Maharaja what he was doing. He replied, "Writing notes—recalling when we decided to come to

Vrindavan. We all decided to come, and now we can see it was the right conclusion. Here is home; Krishna and Balarama are here." Prabhupada agreed with a short "Hmm." Then he rested for three hours. When he awoke, he was a little surprised that it was now 12:45 p.m.

Tamal Krishna said, "I've heard it said when great personalities arrive everything is always cleansed, so I see on your coming Krishna has cleansed everything. The atmosphere is cool, and the sound of rain is very pleasing."

Prabhupada asked if the sun was there, but there was no sun, just clouds and rain.

Tamal Krishna Maharaja asked Prabhupada if he wanted the *kavirāja* (Ayurvedic physician). Tamal Krishna suggested he should come tomorrow and let Prabhupada relax today, saying "As you said, for better or worse 'some husband must be there.' " Prabhupada laughed. "So we should have some doctor. Is that all right?" Prabhupada nodded in agreement.

Tamal Krishna:	"It is so nice to be with you in Vrindavan."
Prabhupada:	"Do the needful."
Tamal Krishna:	"Do the needful?"
Prabhupada:	"Yes. You all consider. Is that all right?"
Tamal Krishna:	"In what regard, Prabhupada?"
Prabhupada:	"Everything."
Tamal Krishna:	"Oh, yes. All you have to do is think of Krishna and Balarama."
Prabhupada:	"Yes. Give me that chance. Is that all right?"
Tamal Krishna:	"Yes."
Prabhupada:	"Gurukripa should also remain here."
Tamal Krishna:	"Yes. Actually, he is quite devoted to

9

	Krishna and Balarama, as well as to Your Divine Grace. He likes the two brothers very much."
Prabhupada:	"Very much." (He expressed his positive agreement and appreciation with his face.)
Tamal Krishna:	"Sometimes he likes to go out and collect for Them. Is that all right?"
Prabhupada:	"Hmm, hmm."
Tamal Krishna:	"So, starting tomorrow we will go in front of Krishna and Balarama for a half hour every day?"
Prabhupada:	"Or less than."
Tamal Krishna:	"Or less time—as you feel comfortable."
Prabhupada:	"Let us try."
Tamal Krishna:	"Yes. Maybe Balarama will give you the strength to sit for half an hour there. Are you comfortable here? This new bed is okay. It is jumbo size—very good size."
Prabhupada:	"Where is Visvambhara?" [Visvambhara Dayal, popularly known as Bhagatji]
Tamal Krishna:	"I was going to call him now. I felt it better to let you rest. Now I can call him?"

Prabhupada agreed.

Later, after a sponge bath, Prabhupada met Bhagatji. Prabhupada was seated in his wheelchair. He asked how everything was going on. Bhagatji told him about the construction of the gate, which will straddle the front road, recently renamed from Chatikara Road to "Bhaktivedanta Swami Marg". Now there is a lack of

10

cement, but Prabhupada was satisfied things are going on.

Prabhupada asked about the rain. Bhagatji described how too much rain has ruined crops. Now wheat is seventy rupees, compared to forty last year. Barley was ten, now fifty. New grain has not been coming for seven months.

As they talked, Tamal Krishna Maharaja put tilak on Prabhupada.

Bhagatji said, "Road is clear on day before yesterday." Prabhupada asked if buses are also stopped. He gave a look like perhaps they could have come by plane and car instead of train, but Tamal Krishna pointed out the planes were stopped anyway and said he thought the train journey wasn't so bad. Prabhupada agreed.

Prabhupada asked for a drink. Pranab's wife had prepared mung *jal* and spinach *jal*. Prabhupada was not so keen for spinach when Tamal Krishna Maharaja asked if he wanted to try it.

He asked, "Is there fresh milk? Half water, half milk."

"Right now there is mung and spinach *jal*. Milk we'll keep for later on", Tamal Krishna replied. Bhagatji offered to keep a cow ready for milking all the time. Tamal Krishna Maharaja told Prabhupada, and hearing this his eyes opened wide and his eyebrows raised in delight and surprise and he laughed, "Hmm!?" Tamal Krishna suggested milk in two hours. Prabhupada agreed, and after a minute Prabhupada said, "That's all right," and everyone left. Then Prabhupada took half a glass of mung *jal* and a little spinach juice, and thereafter he lay on his bed.

I asked him if he wanted his beads (he has been wearing his beads around his neck), and he said yes and began to chant silently on them. After a minute he asked for a picture of Krishna and Balarama, and I passed one to him, and he sat for a few minutes looking

11

at Them and chanting. Then I put the picture back, and Prabhupada took rest.

In the afternoon, around 3:50 p.m., Tamal Krishna Maharaja was reading the *Bhāgavatam* to Prabhupada, starting with *kirāta-hūṇāndhra-pulinda-pulkaśā* (2.4.18). He also read 2.4.12, *sri-śuka uvāca namaḥ parasmai puruṣāya bhūyase.* Prabhupada asked him to read slowly, first Sanskrit, then translation and purport.

At five minutes to four, Prabhupada asked what time it was. Then he inquired whether the bell had been rung. He heard a bell and thought it might be the "time" bell that is supposed to ring on the hour, every hour, at the front of the temple, but Tamal Krishna Maharaja explained there was also a bell in the temple.

The reading continued for a little while, and Prabhupada again asked about the bell—he didn't hear it being rung. He was concerned that everything should go on nicely here. I went for Aksayananda Swami, but then the bell rang so he wasn't required.

After some more reading, Prabhupada again inquired about the bell. Tamal Krishna Maharaja gave assurance that we would see that things go on. Prabhupada said, "Yes, give me that chance." But then Prabhupada said we had not asked about the bell. Tamal Krishna replied it was because it had rung so there was no need.

Prabhupada: "What kind of ringing is going on? It is going on whimsically. That is my concern, that such huge establishment is properly managed— if not properly managed, then everything will be finished."

Tamal Krishna: "I don't think that's going to happen, Srila Prabhupada. We are too much indebted to you to allow what you

	have established to become spoiled."
Prabhupada:	"Hmm. Please see to that. In this condition..."
Tamal Krishna:	"All you should have to do is just think about Krishna and Balarama."
Prabhupada:	"Yes. Kindly give me that chance. In this condition, even I cannot move my body on the bed. Only chance if you give me... Let me lie little peacefully, without any anxiety. I have given in writing everything, whatever you wanted. My Will. Disaster will be if you cannot manage this."
Tamal Krishna:	"Yes, we do not want any disaster to happen. Our only business as your sons and servants is to maintain what you have established. Even if we can't increase—if we just maintain it."
Prabhupada:	"Yes."
Tamal Krishna:	"You have done so much. If it is even maintained, it will be great credit. We shall be proud if people will say, 'These men are fit sons of their Guru Maharaja.' "
Prabhupada:	"I must thank you that you took me to London and again brought me without any difficulty. That is a great credit for you. That, I am thanking you, in this condition, a bundle of bones. Still, you did it. Krishna will... Yesterday I saw that Central Railway station in Bombay

13

was so much crowded. Unexpectedly, is it not? You marked it? Because they have introduced this train, twenty-four hours this deluxe train is running."

Tamal Krishna: "There's a train that's even faster than the Rajdhani—seventeen hours."

Brahmananda: "Also there was an air strike, so people who normally take plane took train."

Tamal Krishna: "Giriraj made a life member on board the train—a nice gentleman living on Marine Drive, quite wealthy. He says he never takes the train, only flies, but he went to the airport at 4 p.m. and the airport said 'no flights—all flights cancelled.' They didn't even have the courtesy to call the people to tell them the flights were cancelled, although they have the phone numbers of the ticket purchasers. So, the man had to take the train."

Prabhupada: "This strike instrument invented by modern civilization, so dangerous."

Hari-sauri: "It means the government becomes completely controlled by the lowest working class."

Prabhupada: "Naturally. Without hands and legs, how one can function? Therefore Vedic civilization is that everyone is engaged."

Tamal Krishna: "Just like in our temples. Everyone is

14

engaged in some service. We don't reject anyone."

Prabhupada: "No. The system should be made in such a way that everyone can be engaged."

Hari-sauri: "With these farms, that is very easy to do. No unemployment. Everyone can work. Next to our farm in Australia the man has 500 acres of land but he sends his wife out to work. He is so lazy. He doesn't work the land. Simply they put some cows there to become fat and then kill them. He has 500 acres of land."

Prabhupada: "Husband does not work?"

Hari-sauri: "This is the modern disease. Everyone is so lazy. You have always pointed out that there is so much land unused. Now no one wants to work. It is much simpler for them to go work eight hours in the office, get some paper money, and buy from the grocery store."

Brahmananda: "Or even if they're farmers, all they do is just graze cows. They don't do any work. They just have the cows eat, and then they sell them."

Prabhupada: "And maintain slaughterhouse."

After a pause Prabhupada asked for kirtan, so I chanted Śrī-guru-caraṇa-padma prayers and then full kirtan.

Later Prabhupada called Aksayananda Swami about the bell again, and took assurance from him that it was ringing on time.

Then Prabhupada asked some questions about banking. Prabhupada has given Tamal Krishna and Giriraj power of attorney on all his accounts. Prabhupada has given instructions to the bank to transfer fixed deposits to total four lakhs. They have come from the bank four times to try to change his mind about it. They came at 7 a.m. this morning but Tamal Krishna spoke with them and they again left. Prabhupada said if they want to see him he will allow it. Tamal Krishna said we want to relieve Prabhupada of all that now. Then we continued kirtan.

Later Prabhupada was speaking about how nice the milk was. By drinking the milk twice a day he could avoid any fruit juice—milk is better. "By simply drinking this milk I can live healthy."

Tamal Krishna Maharaja mentioned how the saintly people in the past had that policy. He said Prabhupada looked happy and natural to be in Vrindavan. Prabhupada agreed.

Prabhupada had a good restful night with Abhirama and Kuladri attending him.

OCTOBER 3, 1977

Prabhupada had a quiet morning, and at 9 a.m. the *kavirāja* came to see him. Sometimes they spoke in Bengali and sometimes English. After some discussion, Tamal Krishna asked about drinking milk. He feared it would cause mucus and coughing and prevent sleep. The *kavirāja* said the cough would clean out the body so he thought cough was good. He said Horlicks was okay, and also Complan. Prabhupada decided to take the Complan and not the milk. The *kavirāja* said the milk could be taken once a day.

As a treatment for the swelling in Prabhupada's legs and hands, they have been using some powder mixture (kaolin, French chalk, and calcium carbonate) which draws out the liquid, and the *kavirāja* recommended it be continued. He said there was nothing specifically wrong, but that Prabhupada's body was very exhausted.

Hamsaduta Swami arrived from Sri Lanka in the middle of the meeting.

Prabhupada sent for Sacidananda dasa, a Bengali devotee, to instruct him on the medicine. For bathing, the *kavirāja* advised no water, just a wrung-out *gamchā* and cold water for the head. He said grape juice was all right, mixed with honey. We had been giving it with sugar water but he said not to. Pomegranate juice was also advised, and *kismis* (large raisins) mashed with honey into a paste was advised for strength. When they asked about darshan of the Deity, he said "Radharani *caraṇa-padma*" was very good.

Then Prabhupada went in his chair to the temple to have darshan. He stayed only long enough to hear the "Govinda" recording and then asked to be taken straight back.

Later Prabhupada and Tamal Krishna Maharaja were talking, and Prabhupada asked for Bhakti Charu Swami to come from Mayapur so that he could look after Prabhupada's medicine. He began by saying, "The *kavirāja* said that my life is finished; now by the grace of Krishna... So under the circumstances, whatever medicine and instruction he gives, strictly follow cooperatively. So you cannot understand Bengali, Bhagatji can understand Hindi and Bengali, and Sacidananda also."

Then Tamal Krishna Maharaja said, "Yes, but they are not as qualified as Bhakti Charu."

Prabhupada agreed and said, "Call him immediately."

Tamal Krishna asked how they could recommend milk when Prabhupada's cough is so bad. Prabhupada replied that it is counteracted by *adrak* (ginger).

17

Prabhupada: "He said that life is finished and you are simply still living by the grace of Krishna. And while there is still life let us try it [medicine]."

Tamal Krishna: "So you feel a little hopeful?"

Prabhupada: "For me, either live or die, I don't mind, but if you are trying for my life, try it very seriously. That is my point. Don't be negligent of whatever he advises."

Prabhupada is coughing on and off, and he is also getting bed sores.

Tamal Krishna told Prabhupada that he (Prabhupada) knew him (Tamal) very well and therefore he had called him to tell him to cooperate together in following the *kavirāja's* instructions (Tamal Krishna had been complaining about Sacidananda, that he was not very competent). So he will see that is done, but he said his cooperation is immediately there when he sees there is someone competent to do the job. Therefore he wants Bhakti Charu to come. Prabhupada said, "Call him, then."

Tamal Krishna went on that it was a miracle that Prabhupada was still here. In Bombay he appeared to have become hopeless about living but here in Vrindavan he appears to have become more hopeful.

Prabhupada replied, "That *kavirāja* was also hopeless," meaning the Bombay one.

Tamal Krishna Maharaja mentioned that this local man appears to be a genuine *kavirāja*, and Prabhupada said, "I think so."

Prabhupada asked him to send a telegram to Bhakti Charu, and asked for Hamsaduta, so I went to fetch him. I couldn't find him, but when I got back, he was already there telling Prabhupada of his preaching in Sri Lanka,

18

as Prabhupada sat up with elbows resting on a pillow on his lap. Hamsaduta had been having some public challenge going with one Dr. Abraham T. Kavoor. Dr. Kavoor had challenged anyone who believes in God to substantiate the claim and he would give Rs.1,00,000. Hamsaduta counter-offered Rs.10,00,000 in foreign exchange if he could prove life comes from chemicals by making a mosquito or a mouse. Hamsaduta told Prabhupada that due to political unrest it had fizzled out. When we tried to revive the challenge, Dr. Kavoor backed down because he had gotten cancer and was expected to die within two months. Hamsaduta said he thought we could use the same offer technique to challenge university scientists, and scholars, and draw public attention that way.

Prabhupada said, "Yes, their idea [of life coming from chemicals] is accepted by all scientists and Nobel Prize winners."

Then he asked how everything was going on there in Sri Lanka.

Hamsaduta explained that they want their government established on dharma but they have gambling, meat eating, etc., so he is getting an article published in the paper criticizing this.

Prabhupada asked if we had status to stay there yet, but Hamsaduta explained we had none. We can only stay six months at a time and have to change $3 foreign exchange each day to be able to stay. The government there is pushing Buddhism, trying to make it the official religion. He said we could preach freely, because we are not identified as Tamils or Hindus since we are white. We hire public halls. He said that the three million Tamil population there mainly worship demigods Durga, Ganesa, and Shiva, and there is hardly a single Krishna temple there. Prabhupada remarked that demigod worship means followers of the Vedas.

Hamsaduta mentioned that once he heard that

Prabhupada had suggested we could buy a church in America and keep the altar and pulpit and simultaneously lecture from the *Gītā* and Bible. He asked if he might be allowed to install a *mūrti* of Buddha and speak from *Gītā* and *Dharmapada* to establish that *Gītā* is beyond the stage of nirvana. He asked if it were a good idea or not.

Prabhupada replied, "Good idea provided you can present properly."

Hamsaduta said people come and ask that if Buddha was a Vishnu incarnation, why didn't he teach about God, the soul, etc. He replies to them that it's like teaching ABCs before advanced literature; Buddha was teaching ABCs, he didn't go into higher subject matter.

Prabhupada:	"First of all, he wanted to make them sinless, 'Don't kill. You [meaning the people] are not following that even.' His business was to stop sinful life. In sinful life one cannot understand God."
Hamsaduta:	"Once Lord Buddha, they say, was sitting under a Bodhi tree and a leaf fell down. He picked up the leaf and said, 'The knowledge I am giving you is like a leaf compared to the tree of knowledge.' I always quote that. They appreciate that: 'Oh yes.' That beyond nirvana there is *brahma-nirvāṇa*, and beyond that there is Paramātmā, and above that there's Bhagavan."
Prabhupada:	"Nirvana means '*sarva-dharmān parityajya.*' That is nirvana. Krishna says *sarva-dharmān parityajya;*

parityajya means 'giving up' and that is nirvana. It requires expert presentation."

Hamsaduta: "In all the temples there is a Vishnu deity; all the Buddhist temples have a Vishnu deity. They have a saying that Vishnu promised Buddha to protect the Buddhist religion in Sri Lanka for 5,000 years in this age."

Tamal Krishna Maharaja asked if he should go to Radha-Damodar temple to check how Prabhupada's rooms are being maintained. But Prabhupada said not today.

Then Prabhupada started speaking about Punjab National Bank. "As soon as I got the sentiment that this bank was interested to keep our money in their pocket I was very careful not to increase deposits."

Tamal Krishna said he had spoken with the manager this morning, and the manager had complained that now our fixed deposits were being withdrawn and deposits being kept to a minimum.

Prabhupada: "Yes, because you are harassing us."

Tamal Krishna: "They think our money is now theirs and that is giving us fear."

Prabhupada: "They think like that. We cannot free our money."

Tamal Krishna mentioned how they had come four times to try and dissuade Prabhupada from withdrawing deposits. He felt they were taking advantage of Prabhupada's ill health and merciful nature. Therefore he suggested Giriraj could deal with them. Prabhupada agreed.

Prabhupada mentioned that the Central Bank is very straightforward.

Tamal Krishna told Prabhupada he didn't want Prabhupada to have to deal with them again.

Prabhupada: "Therefore I say, do the needful."
Tamal Krishna: "Now you have to allow us to give you some relief, Srila Prabhupada."
Prabhupada: "Hmm!" [Yes.]

After seeing Hamsaduta and Tamal Krishna, Prabhupada took some medicine and then asked about milk. Upendra said, "If you like we can supply now."

Prabhupada became agitated and asked, "Where is it and who will prepare? It is not a question of liking: instruction is there, who will follow them?"

I explained I had taken a list; milk was not due until morning.

Prabhupada spoke loudly, "That's all right, but where is it? Who will prepare it? What is this 'if you like?' Instruction must be followed strictly."

Upendra promised that we would keep very strictly to the times.

Prabhupada replied, "But you are saying 'if you like.' "

He sent for Sacidananda, who had given me the list and purchased the medicine. After some discussion, Prabhupada took 100 ml. of Complan, which the doctor said was okay.

After Prabhupada had his bath and took some drink, I read to him from the new *Back to Godhead* brought by Satsvarupa Maharaja.

In the afternoon he took some of the medicines prescribed by the *kavirāja*—some powders mixed with the juice of various leaves.

In the early evening Tamal Krishna Maharaja was with Prabhupada, so I came in and sat down. I was waiting to go to Delhi to make some phone calls and try to contact the Sydney temple, so I sat for a while. I told Prabhupada how in Auckland I had seen the new movie *Audrey Rose* [which is about reincarnation], and then the devotees got the cinema to put up a display board in the foyer showcasing *Bhagavad-gītā*.

Then I told him how the deprogrammers were almost finished in Australia. A devotee's mother had kidnapped her and hired a psychiatrist to prove her daughter had been brainwashed. But after testing me and two other devotees using an electro-encephalography (EEG) machine, we got such high alpha readings compared to a news reporter and the psychiatrist himself, that the man went on television and declared we were perfectly sane. Prabhupada enjoyed hearing all this and was smiling at the descriptions.[1]

After Tamal Krishna Maharaja went out and I was alone with Prabhupada, I asked if I could purchase a small deity of him to worship. Prabhupada screwed his face up a little and said that it wasn't necessary. I explained that I wanted just to do a little puja in the mornings, so he said there could be a deity on the altar then all devotees could worship. I said that I had a few items of his clothing and he replied, "That you can do after my leaving, but for now you are doing greater service."

Hari-sauri: "I enjoyed very much when I was

---

1   The mother of one of the devotees had her daughter locked up for a month to try to make her "normal." It became a big court case with much national coverage. In an effort to prove her daughter had been brainwashed, the mother hired a psychiatrist to test her with an electroencephalography machine, which records alpha brainwaves. The higher the recorded response, the more sane and mentally healthy the subject was supposed to be. Our public relations devotee, Cittahārī prabhu, arranged with the psychiatrist to have several devotees tested (including me), a reporter, and even the doctor himself. The results showed that the devotees were far more mentally healthy than even the psychiatrist. Consequently, the doctor appeared on a TV show with Cittahārī and declared that the devotees were perfectly sane.

giving you personal service."

Prabhupada: "Now you are giving greater service in Australia. I am very much pleased by your service. You are serving me very nicely by being there."

Then Upendra came to give Prabhupada a damp-cloth bath, and it was time for me to go to Delhi.

In Delhi I purchased some items for Prabhupada—a water heater, mosquito net, and some powders for his dry bath. Also I informed Adi-kesava Swami by phone that only the GBC should come to see Prabhupada at present. Tamal Krishna Maharaja had previously informed the US temples that Prabhupada's leaving was in sight and whoever wanted to come should do so. Then afterwards we considered that in Vrindavan, Prabhupada was showing more animation. If so many devotees came, there would be no program for them and they may stay around for weeks and not be able to see Prabhupada either. Therefore I phoned to tell them only GBCs and sannyasis should come. The call was just in time. Hundreds of devotees were preparing to come.

In Delhi we tried to get pure musk oil (good for the heart), but it is difficult and costs around Rs. 1,000 for 20 mg, and we need half a tola (approximately 6 grams). So, one Life Member will try to get it for us.

Svarupa Damodara and Madhava prabhus are now here to organize a science conference, "Life Comes from Life," to be held in Vrindavan from October 14–16.

OCTOBER 4, 1977

During the night, Prabhupada coughed a lot due to too much mucus. The *kavirāja's* medicine increased the cough, so Prabhupada didn't rest much. Also the swelling in his legs and arms increased tremendously. The *kavirāja* came to see him. He prescribed hot ghee and ginger juice to be applied externally to his chest. After some discussion, the *kavirāja* explained the medicine was meant to bring out mucus. Prabhupada said that the medicine caused havoc. He eventually decided not to take any medicine until he felt a little better. The *kavirāja* also recommended musk for Prabhupada's heart and to help to clear any cough.

Later on, Hamsaduta Swami came in and talked with Prabhupada, and then Bhagatji also came. They told Prabhupada that ex-Prime Minister Mrs. Gandhi had been arrested and then released on bail. She is becoming popular again because prices have gone very high since the Janata Party gained power. She had announced that the government didn't have the guts to arrest her, but then they did, and now she is becoming more popular. They described how the ex-prime minister for Sri Lanka is an old school friend of Gandhi, and whatever Gandhi does, she repeats.

Hamsaduta: "Sometimes when preaching I tell them that 'what kind of country is this? The land of the *rājarṣis* and some lady is running the government.' "

Prabhupada: "Hmm. Don't touch politics!"

Hamsaduta: "We should stay clear of the government. They're too dangerous."

Prabhupada: "Hmm; cultural. Our [approach], cultural and philosophy. To be arrested is not new thing for politicians."

Hamsaduta came again later and told Prabhupada

25

he had a book in Singhalese ready for composing.

Prabhupada discussed the Punjab National Bank with Giriraj and Tamal Krishna Maharaja. He said if things were not clarified on their policies, then we should gradually shift our money out from them.

Prabhupada also had Upendra crush four *kismis*—large raisins—which he took mashed with an equal amount of honey.

OCTOBER 5, 1977

More devotees are arriving daily. Adi Kesava and Tripurari Swami, along with Sridhar Swami from Hyderabad, all arrived in Delhi, and travelled together to Vrindavan by Taj Express.

Gurukripa Swami also had arrived in Vrindavan at 1 a.m., and Surabhir Abhipalayantam Swami and Gopal Krishna came from Bombay. Bali Mardan and Giriraj had come with Prabhupada, and Jagadisa is also here in charge of the *gurukula* with Yasodanandana Swami.

I arrived back in Vrindavan in the morning around 9:30 a.m., after finishing some shopping errands in Delhi and a consultation with Ashu Tosh Ojah, the astrologer.

Prabhupada had a restful night, but in the morning Upendra and Abhirama gave him an enema in the bathroom and it weakened him, although it cleansed his system out a good deal. Prabhupada said he felt better after it.

Most of the day he rested and didn't say much. Around midday he asked for Sacidananda, but he wasn't available, so he called for Tapamaya dasa ("Any Bengali"). After some talk, Tapamaya left and appeared a little later with some chunks of slaked lime and dry turmeric root. Prabhupada sent me with him to make a preparation of the two. He crushed the turmeric then soaked the slaked lime, which made it very soft, like paste. It went dark red. He then mixed equal quantities

26

of each. Then we heated it and took it to Prabhupada. Prabhupada's feet and hands were very swollen since last night. The hot paste was applied externally to those parts of Prabhupada's body after first applying a little ghee to protect his skin. Then Prabhupada rested.

During the afternoon and evening, some of the GBC and sannyasis came in to chant softly for Prabhupada.

At 4:45 p.m., he awoke and asked me to make some Complan for him. Then he sat up and drank about 175ml and ate one and a half teaspoons of butter. Afterwards, I helped him urinate. Now Prabhupada can't go to the bathroom, so he uses a bottle. Then afterwards, his circumcision wound has to be cleaned to prevent infection. A cotton swab dipped in Savlon solution is used and then some antibiotic powder called Cicatrin is applied. This was the first time I had done this, but there was no difficulty for Prabhupada. Now Prabhupada is so weak that every little thing has to be done for him, and I can understand that to do this intimate personal service is great mercy for fools like me. Prabhupada is very mercifully remaining here, even though he has the power to leave any time.

Now he has entered into his final *līlā* of retirement and complete *samādhi*, and he is allowing his most intimate disciples to come and offer their worshipful service to him. Actually he relishes the association with his disciples very much, and when Tamal Krishna Maharaja told him that soon all the GBC would come to Bombay, he said he had no objection; and again, on the evening just before I left for Delhi, Tamal Krishna mentioned their coming again, and Prabhupada was very satisfied to know that.

Prabhupada gave garlands to Gurukripa, Hamsaduta, and Satsvarupa when he sat up for his Complan.

Between 6:30–7:30 p.m., we again applied the solution to Prabhupada's hands and feet. He asked if the swelling had reduced, but I said it had not by any

27

significant amount, and suggested we try the treatment several times. He agreed.

At 7:30 p.m., Tamal Krishna Maharaja felt Prabhupada's forehead and thought his temperature was up. Prabhupada was very still and quiet. He spoke a little to Giriraj before this, but he has not been very active today.

At 9:30 p.m., Prabhupada called me in and asked me what the astrologer had said. Ojah had previously done a chart for Prabhupada. This time I went with Bhagavata Asraya and requested him to give us a detailed chart, especially for the next month. He gave us a mantra, prayers to Lord Shiva for increased health and longevity, and gave instructions that it should be chanted by ten brahmans for twenty-one days and it would produce an immediate result of better health.

I told Prabhupada that the chart would take a couple of days to make, and that he had given a mantra. Prabhupada immediately said, "We have the maha-mantra." Then I related the details of it and he again said, "The maha-mantra is sufficient, there is no need of others." He was smiling when I told him about the astrologer's suggestions. I mentioned how he had thousands of disciples chanting for him already.

I told Prabhupada that the astrologer had repeated his earlier statement that until next March would be a very difficult time, but if Prabhupada went over that period, then for the next three to four years his health would return. Prabhupada was silent.

Then he asked me to scratch his back because it was itching.

Hari-sauri:	"Are these astrological charts very much applicable for a devotee, Srila Prabhupada?"
Prabhupada:	"No."
Hari-sauri:	"Because Krishna can do anything."

28

Prabhupada: "Yes."

After a pause, Prabhupada asked for Tamal Krishna.

Tamal Krishna: "Yes, Srila Prabhupada?"

Prabhupada: "Hmm. Don't waste money on this astrology."

Tamal Krishna: "In London when we were going to get this astrologer to do it, when I heard it was expensive, then we cancelled. How much money is he asking?" (to me)

Hari-sauri: "He didn't say a price. He said it would take two or three days to do a detailed chart."

Prabhupada: "It is useless. We can arrange as many hours as possible to chant kirtan. That is..."

Tamal Krishna: "Srila Prabhupada, today we did kirtan starting in the afternoon until the evening, so do you want more than that?"

Prabhupada: "I can hear day and night."

Tamal Krishna: "So should we arrange starting in the morning going until the night?"

Prabhupada: "That is according to your convenience; but kirtan is very sweet."

Hari-sauri: "Last June, we were doing twenty-four hours."

Prabhupada: "That is real business. (short pause) These astrologers are *karmi*. We have nothing to do with the *karmi*."

Hari-sauri: "Their measurement of happiness and distress is how much nice wife

29

and children they get and how much
money they get."

Prabhupada: "Yes, [do] *Bhāgavata* reading;
sankirtana."

Hari-sauri: "They don't understand that the real
happiness is giving everything to
Krishna."

Prabhupada: "Yes. [Pause] Don't waste time and
money on any..."

Tamal Krishna: "Sometimes I find that you are
sleeping, Srila Prabhupada, so I was
just wondering at night when you do
most of your sleeping whether we
should still do kirtan. I was thinking
that we could stay up till 9 p.m. at
night and begin in the morning
again."

Prabhupada: "No."

Tamal Krishna: "You'd like it to be throughout the
night?"

Prabhupada: "Hmm, hmm."

Tamal Krishna: "Okay. We'll have enough people
so that we can do it. We'll start it
tomorrow, Srila Prabhupada, in the
morning, because it's difficult to
arrange now. Most of the devotees
here have begun to take rest."

Prabhupada: "Yes."

Tamal Krishna: "They'll definitely like it, though,
because they like to be with you."

Prabhupada: "Yes, I also."

Hari-sauri: "Within one or two days every GBC
and sannyasi will be here to come
and do kirtan."

Tamal Krishna:	"They've come to take care of you, Srila Prabhupada. So many fathers."
Prabhupada:	"Please do that."
Hari-sauri:	"That is our greatest pleasure."
Prabhupada:	"Yes."

Then Tamal Krishna Maharaja read Prabhupada some telegrams from London, Berkeley, and others, asking him not to leave. London had distributed 70,000 books in one week in a special *saṅkirtana yajña* marathon to please Krishna and plead for Prabhupada's health. Prabhupada was very pleased. Then he rested.

OCTOBER 6, 1977

This morning Tamal Krishna Maharaja told me and Upendra that we should cleanse Prabhupada because the lime and turmeric mix had made a big mess. There was powder everywhere on the bed and Prabhupada was lying in it. When Prabhupada woke at 8:30 a.m., we sat him up and carefully cleaned his body. Upendra wiped his face first, then his chest, arms, and legs. Prabhupada then cleaned his teeth with a bowl on his lap, and afterwards Upendra shaved him once, and then again, applying cream to make a good job. Then we sat Prabhupada in his wheelchair and changed all the bedding. During the night, he had passed stool after drinking milk and Horlicks, and so his system is cleared out now. Then we cleaned the room.

Rupanuga, Jayadvaita, and Paramananda arrived. Tamal Krishna Maharaja brought Paramananda in to see Prabhupada and they presented to him a gift of a woolen shawl that was entirely produced by the women on our Pennsylvania farm, Gita Nagari. Prabhupada was very pleased to receive it. Paramananda explained

31

that because Prabhupada couldn't come to see them, they had come to see him.

Prabhupada: "So organize these farm projects, simple living. Human life is meant for God realization. Try to help them. This is my..."

Paramananda: "We are always feeling your presence very strongly, Srila Prabhupada. Simply by your teaching and instruction. We are always meditating on your instructions."

Prabhupada: "Thank you. That is real presence. Physical presence is not important."

Then Tamal Krishna read a short note to Prabhupada from Paramananda's wife, Satyabhama dasi, to offer the shawl to Prabhupada. Prabhupada thanked her for it.

Prabhupada then took rest after requesting that the shawl be spread over his feet.

Tamal Krishna: "Is it warm?"

Prabhupada: "Hmm, hmm. Very nice, very comfortable. Hare Krishna, Hare Krishna...."

Hamsaduta Swami led a soft kirtan and Prabhupada rested, looking very contented as he pulled the shawl up under his chin.

At 11 a.m., Prabhupada sat up and requested to be carried in his palanquin to the temple. The palanquin has fold-up legs and the seat hangs from a horizontal pole; it is carried by two men, front and back. Brahmananda Swami and I helped Prabhupada into it and then we carried him to the temple. Prabhupada had darshan and decided to sit for a few minutes, and

Gurukripa led kirtan. After a minute or so, Prabhupada turned to the assembled devotees and moved his hand, palm open, up and down, urging them to stand up and chant and dance. He was smiling very nicely and he enjoyed the kirtan for 10–15 minutes before signaling us to carry him out. Then we carried him once around the temple on *parikramā* before returning.

After a little while, he called in Gopal Krishna and asked him, "For printing, in Australia there is good field, so why you are not printing more books and send there?"

Gopal Krishna: "We'll print more. Now we are printing more books for them. We are printing as many books as they order. So, as they increase their order, we'll increase our print."

Hari-sauri: "He's just sending. There's a ship leaving on the 10th with 15,000 *Gitas.*"

Gopal Krishna: "And 15,000 *Raja Vidyas.*"

Hari-sauri: "That's for our Christmas distribution. That will arrive just in time for the month of December."

Gopal Krishna: "As he orders, we print."

Prabhupada: "And you can send to Europe, America."

Gopal Krishna: "Yes, England. For America, we are talking of printing small books for them, because for America to get lower price on books, they have to print many hundreds of thousands, and so many books of yours are out of print, out of stock with BBT LA. But we can get the same price on a lower run. This means that on a lower investment we can print the same books and this way at least they would have some books in stock of every title you have published. So, if somebody wants some book they won't say that they don't have it, but that they can supply it. So, I've been writing about this to Ramesvara Swami."

Prabhupada: "My point is, I don't wish to keep money in the bank. Invest in printing."

Gopal Krishna: "And now we are making a big godown in Bombay, a professional godown for BBT."

Prabhupada: "Where?"

Gopal Krishna: "In Bombay."

Prabhupada: "In our..."

Gopal Krishna: "Yes, in our Hare Krishna Land. In that building, because now we have so many books and we don't have enough space. So we're going to start work on the godown. We just need three lakhs, so when Ramesvara comes I'll talk to him."

Prabhupada: "Three lakhs we have got."

Gopal Krishna: "Okay. Because this will be a professional godown. Also New Zealand is ordering books from India, and the second print of *Bhagavad-gītā*, which is going out on the 10th, has come out even better than the American, the color work. I'm going to show it to Hari-sauri.

Actually, we should print some *Śrīmad-Bhāgavatams* also, because many *Bhāgavatams* are out of print and I have been using this mail-order company. We are advertising our *Gītā*, and we have already sold more than 1,000 in two months. And the mail-order company is paying for the ads. They're very keen to also promote the Bhaktivedanta Encyclopedia, but before I do that I must have all your *Bhāgavatams* in stock, because as the order comes we have to fulfil it right away. This is working out to be very, very big— this mail order technique. That is, we advertise and people..."

Prabhupada: "And print Hindi books; Gujarati books also."

Gopal Krishna: "Yes, the Gujarati *Gītā* will be ready in one month. We're finished printing the color pictures for the Hindi *Gītā*, the Gujarati *Gītā*, and Telegu *Gītā*. It's already completed. The Telegu *Gītā* is being printed in Hyderabad, and the Gujarati *Gītā* is also at the printers, and the Hindi *Gītā* is being composed. Plus we are doing a Kannada *Gītā* in Kanarese language."

Prabhupada: "Is it necessary?"

Gopal Krishna: "Yes. We have a temple in Bangalore, and they need it for distribution in Bangalore. But this will be just your

	verses and translation, like they have done in Telegu, two years ago. A small book which they can sell for one or two rupees."
Prabhupada:	"Don't keep money unnecessarily. Invest."
Gopal Krishna:	"No. There's no money, BBT is... I'm always asking Hari-sauri to make payment quickly because we have invested everything into printing."
Prabhupada:	"Now we have sent four lakhs."
Hari-sauri:	"Prabhupada just transferred four lakhs from matured fixed deposits to Bombay."
Gopal Krishna:	"Should we use that four lakhs for printing? We can use it for the godown."
Prabhupada:	"Whatever it may be, there is no need of keeping money in the bank."
Gopal Krishna:	"Because we can print more books and keep them in stock. And now we are finding out that this mail order is selling thousands of books. Like in two months, I sold more books than Gargamuni's party did in one year, by this mail-order technique."
Prabhupada:	"Hmm. It is very good. So, follow this policy, don't keep idle money in the bank."

Later, at noon, Prabhupada took some Complan. He rested most of the afternoon. Then he called Tamal Krishna Maharaja and complained that he couldn't drink and that still he was coughing mucus. Tamal Krishna asked why he wasn't drinking, and Prabhupada replied that firstly, there is no inclination, and secondly, when he drinks, there is cough. We discussed a little about doctors.

Prabhupada was sitting up, and then he lay down and said how pleasing the soft massage was to him. Prabhupada also asked me to make him Yogendra Rasa. This was the only medicine that remained. He said to soak some rice and make it with the water. He said to soak it two hours and then give it to him.

Prabhupada told Tamal Krishna to send another telegram for Bhakti Charu Swami to come, as there has been no reply.

Prabhupada said he didn't like the mentality of the *kavirāja*. He charged five rupees the first time and then because we went a second time, he charged ten. Tamal Krishna added that it was also fifty-five rupees for the medicine.

Prabhupada:	"We are not hesitating to pay, but this mentality is bad."
Tamal Krishna:	"Yes. The point is, if this man has this mentality, then how much can we trust him? This is becoming dishonest. Still, some husband must be there, you said. We should have a doctor—I still believe that—if possible. After all, we are not doctors."
Prabhupada:	"No, we are taking the help of doctor by this Yogendra Rasa."
Tamal Krishna:	"You are just beginning that now, but tomorrow you might give it up, then what will be our position?"

Prabhupada paused and then said humorously, "Then I'll be widow!" We all laughed, and Prabhupada laughed so much his teeth showed, and he exclaimed,

"Krishna is the ultimate husband!"

Prabhupada had Tamal Krishna massage him with the calcium carbonate/kaolin/French chalk mix.

Later Prabhupada called Sacidananda in and requested him to call another doctor. He asked Tamal Krishna for his opinion, but he was negative about the whole thing, having become disgusted after so many doctors. Still Prabhupada told him to bring the man. Then afterwards he sent for Tamal Krishna again and told him not to go today, as Thursday is inauspicious, and to wait until tomorrow.

Gurukripa came in and read aloud *Srimad-Bhāgavatam* Sixth Canto for a while and then led kirtan.

Upendra also gave Prabhupada some mint tea to try, but he didn't like it.

Prabhupada has been more lively today. Yesterday he spent almost all his time lying down, but today he sat up several times.

Hamsaduta Swami came in and chanted for almost four hours. Prabhupada likes his kirtan very much. At one point Sacidananda came in and began to lead, but Prabhupada stopped him and asked Hamsaduta to continue. He listens very intently to the chanting, and when Hamsaduta missed out a word, Prabhupada immediately corrected him. He appears to be asleep, but he is very intently hearing. When Adi-kesava was chanting the second verse of *Gurv-aṣṭaka* prayers, he sang *romāñca-kampā śru-taraṅga-bhājo vande guroḥ sri-caraṇāravindam* [with a break between *kampā* and *śru*], and Prabhupada immediately corrected him, saying that it should be *romāñca-kampāśru-taraṅga-bhājo*; he also noted that Adi-kesava was trying very hard to get it correct.

Around 10:15 p.m., Prabhupada suddenly raised his palm as a sign to stop so that he might rest. When Hamsaduta came up to the bedside, Prabhupada very quietly said, "Thank you." It was a very intense moment with Prabhupada expressing his love and gratitude to his devotee for assisting him in his remembrance of Lord Krishna.

Throughout the night, there are men coming in to sit with Prabhupada.

At one point in the evening, Prabhupada had called in Tamal Krishna Maharaja and discussed with him again about the doctors and told him not to send for any. He had written to invite Dr. G. Ghosh, his friend from his early adulthood in Allahabad, to come. The doctor wants to open a clinic here in Vrindavan and also suggest some treatment for Prabhupada.

Prabhupada: "These doctors will come and give something to try and save. I don't want to be saved. Dr. Ghosh may come for the clinic he wants to develop, but not for treatment."

Tamal Krishna asked if the two Vrindavan doctors should come and Prabhupada said, "No. Better to take your advice for kirtan."

Tamal Krishna said that was best, because then we can ask Krishna for His saving.

Prabhupada: "Better you don't pray to Krishna to save me. Let me die now."

He lay for a short time and then asked to sit up. As he sat up, he said suddenly, "Anything to ask before I depart?" Tamal Krishna said, "No, you have already told us everything." Then Prabhupada said, "If Hamsaduta is not tired, he may continue singing."

OCTOBER 7, 1977

Hamsaduta again came in the early morning to lead kirtan from 4:45 until 7:45 a.m.

Prabhupada slept very soundly throughout the night. I went in about 8 a.m., and after Prabhupada had rested for an hour, Upendra began to bathe him. Prabhupada asked for Tamal Krishna, and when I brought him, he said, "I thought you wanted to bathe me." Prabhupada has complete reliance on Tamal Krishna. He sends for him whenever there is any decision to be made about doctors, food, banks, books, etc. Tamal Krishna is very affectionate to Prabhupada and strokes his arms or feet whenever he speaks with him. He always speaks so as to glorify and encourage Prabhupada, and he has become very purified over the last few months due to the intimate service being performed.

Tamal Krishna asked Prabhupada if he would go for darshan, and Prabhupada agreed.

Tamal Krishna: "Yesterday you did not drink very much."

Prabhupada: "Due to that coughing."

Tamal Krishna: "Today, no coughing yet. So if there's no coughing, you can increase a little bit today."

Prabhupada: (humorously) "Survive!"

Tamal Krishna: "We're not ready to let you go yet, Srila Prabhupada. We can't resign ourselves to it."

Prabhupada: "Hmm."

Earlier, Kirtanananda Swami had arrived and he came in to see Prabhupada. As he knelt by his side, Prabhupada said, "There is nothing to lament about."

He asked Kirtanananda what was the special news from New Vrindaban. Kirtanananda told him how his palace was almost finished and now up to thirty persons a day were coming to see the place. Prabhupada said, "Yes, such things are unknown in that quarter." He was very pleased to hear and see Kirtanananda.

Then we showed Srila Prabhupada a nice life-size bronze bust of himself, made by the famous sculptor Peter Hawkins. He sat up and liked it very much. These busts are put into libraries and other public places. Prabhupada tapped it with his fingers to see if it was solid.

Later, after Prabhupada bathed and just before he went out to the temple for darshan, Bhakti Prem Swami came in. Gopal Krishna had gone to Govardhan to bring him to see Prabhupada. He left our company a couple of months ago. He came in with clean-shaven head, and garlanded Srila Prabhupada as he sat in his wheelchair. Prabhupada was glad to see him. As he knelt down, Prabhupada called him forward and affectionately rubbed his hand over his head. He looked as though he was going to cry but checked himself.

Bhakti Prem Swami was offering some reason why he had gone away, but Prabhupada stopped him, dismissing it as a small thing, and continued, "You have come. And whatever comfort you want, you will get here—these Americans and Europeans. When I was in London, I was thinking of getting you here. Anyway, by Krishna's grace you have come; good for us, good for you. Thank you very much."

41

Then Prabhupada went out in his palanquin, which had been made bigger for him. Paramananda and Vakresvara Pandit from New York carried him around the *parikramā* path and through the main entrance doors. Then, after sitting in front of each Deity, he sat under the *Tamala* tree in the courtyard and we had kirtan for twenty minutes. Then we walked around the temple once and then back into the house.

Tamal Krishna Maharaja and I then spent half an hour rubbing Prabhupada's arms and legs with the powder again, which seems to have had some small effect on reducing the swelling.

Prabhupada rested until noon while kirtan went on. Then Kuladri came in with some gifts for Prabhupada from New Vrindaban. He gave him $8,000 in *dakṣiṇā*—Kirtanananda Swami had collected $111 from each person he had initiated as one of Prabhupada's *ritvik* representatives, and this was the total. Then he showed him a silver-threaded crocheted bead bag one woman had made. Prabhupada liked it very much. Then he opened two onyx jewelry boxes inset with precious stones in gold, and gave him a ring of sapphires laid into gold. Prabhupada put it on. Also, there was a gold medallion inset with rubies, emeralds, opals, and sapphires. He gave him some cloth too.

Prabhupada smilingly received the opulent gifts and, with a laugh and deep appreciation, declared, "So, we will have to find out some bride!"

Prabhupada said the jewelry could be given to Krishna and Balarama, but he was concerned that it should be looked after.

After Kuladri finished the presentation, he submitted a prayer on behalf of Kirtanananda Maharaja. "He said you asked us to pray to Krishna before, but he doesn't feel qualified to pray to Krishna. But he asks that you please pray to Krishna for us, because we can't pray to Krishna directly. We don't know Krishna, but if you ask Krishna, Krishna must be sure to fulfil your desire. So would you please pray to Krishna to stay with us? Because you are His pure devotee, Krishna will surely grant whatever you pray for—so on our behalf."

Prabhupada was silent and looked deeply moved as Kuladri continued, "I think he must want you to come to the palace, Srila Prabhupada, if it is possible."

Prabhupada was choking up with emotion and after a short silence said, "I wish..."

Kuladri: "You wish? I think that will make him very happy."

Prabhupada: "But unless I become a little strong, I can't go."

Then Prabhupada tried a little ice cream that they had brought all the way from New Vrindaban, a very small amount on his spoon. He appreciated it very much and announced, "First class!"

Then he picked up the silver-threaded bead bag and asked Kuladri to list everything and keep it in the bag, checks included. Even in this condition, Prabhupada is still giving us instruction on how carefully we should look after whatever Krishna has provided for us.

Vakresvara Pandit, who has a very sweet voice, led kirtan. Prabhupada had previously commented how nice his voice was. At the same time, I scratched Prabhupada's back for over half an hour. He showed me with his hand, moving his fingers like a claw, how I should use my nails to scratch. After ten minutes, he told me to scratch hard. Then after another ten minutes, he said, "Scratch very hard!" I was scratching so hard, I was scared of cutting. White marks appeared on his back, but Prabhupada didn't stop me. I carried on for about fifteen minutes and then he lay back and rested. While I was scratching very hard, I reminded him that when I used to massage him he sometimes complained

43

because I was scratching. Prabhupada smiled. Later we tried to persuade His Divine Grace to drink something, but he wouldn't, due to cough. Upendra told him that the doctor in London had said that if he doesn't keep his body cells strong by drinking in proteins, then they won't be able to handle the water build-up and his lungs will gradually fill up and cause more cough. And gradually his heart will become blocked. Prabhupada still chose not to drink anything, although we are making mung *jal* with the hope he will drink later on.

Gurukripa sat with Satsvarupa Maharaja and read *Bhāgavatam* Sixth Canto during the afternoon.

Later on, Tamal Krishna Maharaja was trying to persuade Prabhupada to drink something. Prabhupada wouldn't do it and complained of mucus. Nor did he want medicine. He said he was taking Yogendra Rasa and that is the strongest Ayurvedic medicine.

Prabhupada told us, "I want strength for hearing the prayers. Otherwise, if my senses become weak..." When Tamal Krishna said we wanted him to live, Prabhupada said, "I have no objection." But then he said that now it was too difficult to make the effort anymore.

At 3:45 p.m. Tamal Krishna knelt by Srila Prabhupada. He mentioned Kirtanananda Swami's prayer for Srila Prabhupada to petition Krishna on our behalf to remain here. He said that because Prabhupada is a pure devotee, then Krishna can make it happen. Prabhupada lay very quietly and replied, "You are all pure devotees, because you have no other desire."

They discussed about Prabhupada not drinking anything. Prabhupada still wouldn't, and complained about so much coughing.

Then Prabhupada turned the conversation to the gifts Kirtanananda Swami had brought. He had me go and get them and discussed with Tamal Krishna what to do with them. He would give the jewels to Krishna and Balarama, but there is danger of theft.

Therefore he decided that they could be given back to Kirtanananda for Radha-Vrindavan-chandra, and Tamal Krishna suggested the money could go into Prabhupada's personal account. Then Prabhupada sent me to get Kirtanananda Swami. When he came in, Prabhupada immediately told him that he could take the jewels and money and use it all for developing New Vrindaban.

Prabhupada: "Kirtanananda Maharaja, these presentations may be utilized in New Vrindaban, and the money also may be used for developing. I have accepted. Now you can utilize for developing."

Kirtanananda: "Thank you very much, Srila Prabhupada. If it pleases you, I'd like to save it for the *mūrti* in your palace and utilize it there."

Prabhupada: "Yes. You take back and utilize it there. That is my wish."

Kirtanananda: "First of all, we want you, though."

Prabhupada: "Yes. I shall come, and if I survive, I have a strong desire to go and live there. It will be a great pleasure."

Kirtanananda: "All the devotees feel you are already living there, Prabhupada. They are already having puja there, every day, twice a day."

Prabhupada: "Yes, that is the way."

Kirtanananda: "And everyone feels when they come in there, it is a very holy place."

Prabhupada: "You are worshipping Radha-Vrindavan-chandra very intelligently, and the place is being developed very nicely."

Then Kirtanananda asked Prabhupada if he would like to see pictures of his palace. Prabhupada agreed and sat up. He donned his glasses and looked on as Kirtanananda described each picture, and Prabhupada made comments.

Prabhupada:	"Very, very nice. The unique is coming. It will be a tourist attraction."
Kirtanananda:	"It will. Already it is."
Prabhupada:	"We have got so many artists. How they learn this art?"
Kirtanananda:	"We all thank you very much because it is only by your grace we have gotten this inspiration."
Prabhupada:	"Whenever you require money, you can ask, he will give"—indicating Tamal Krishna Maharaja.
Kirtanananda:	"Thank you, Srila Prabhupada, I prefer to give."
Prabhupada:	"No, give and take."

Prabhupada's voice quivered, and he almost cried. He has so much affection for his devotees, and he was overcome with love for his dear disciple. He stretched his hand out, and choked, "Thank you," as he stroked Kirtanananda's head several times. Now practically every meeting with his older disciples, whenever one of them arrives, is very emotional and intense, as though he is finally calling them to his lotus feet for the last time. Each man that comes, he thanks him for his service and remembers all the nice things he has done for him to help spread Krishna consciousness.

Prabhupada told the small group gathered by his bedside, "You are fulfilling my dreams, New Vrindaban. I dreamt all this. Wonderful things have happened.

He [Kirtanananda] is the first student. From the very beginning, when I was in the storefront, he was bringing carpet, bench, some gong, some lamp—in this way."

Tamal Krishna: "He's still bringing gifts."

Prabhupada: "*Sevā*, service attitude. *Jaya!*" [Pause] "Live long, serve long!"

Another pause. Prabhupada was choking with emotion as he recalled all the wonderful service Kirtanananda Swami had done.

Prabhupada: "You are all so nice that, whatever *prasādam* they get... from New Vrindaban. That is devotee. So for the time being, you utilize the money and checks—everything—for developing." (Turning to Tamal Krishna Maharaja) "So you have returned [the gifts]?"

Tamal Krishna: "Yes, Srila Prabhupada."

In the evening, Prabhupada asked Upendra, "Call Tosan Krishna."

Upendra: "Tosan Krishna, Prabhupada? Tosan Krishna isn't here."

Prabhupada: "He was my secretary."

Upendra: "He was your secretary? He's a grihastha."

Prabhupada: "He was a grihastha."

Upendra: "With an Indian wife?"

Prabhupada: "No."

Then, again, a few minutes later.

Prabhupada: "Call Tosan Krishna."
Upendra: "Tosan Krishna?"
Prabhupada: "He's my secretary."

Then Upendra realized he was asking for Tamal Krishna. Also, he asked Hamsaduta Swami what his program in Sri Lanka was. Hamsaduta told him, and Prabhupada said he wants him to make a program like New Vrindaban there. Hamsaduta asked Prabhupada if there was something special he wanted him to do.

Prabhupada replied, "No, there is every chance of making it successful. Just as Kirtanananda Swami has developed New Vrindaban, similarly you can do there." Prabhupada commented also how the atheist Dr. Kavoor's position was now lost.

Bhakti Charu Swami arrived. He saw Prabhupada at about 10:30 p.m. Prabhupada asked him how Mayapur was going, and then sent him to take rest.

OCTOBER 8, 1977 - EKADASI

I went in at 8:45 a.m. Prabhupada was sitting in the center of the bed after having had his bath. Brahmananda Swami knelt, leaning over one side of the bed, and Tamal Krishna Maharaja sat at the right-hand corner with some written notes in his hand. It was Prabhupada's horoscope by Ashu Tosh Ojah, which had arrived from Delhi. The astrologer had not charged anything, so Tamal Krishna thought that this indicated an honest and reasonable report. As he read the description of the different planetary movements into the different houses, the whole chart gradually revealed that the entire period from now until mid-March and early April 1978 is very negative for Srila Prabhupada.

He listed the particularly inauspicious days. Immediate ones are today, tomorrow, and the 11th. Then others, later this month, and going through November and December: October 24–25; November 20–22; and December 3–4.

Prabhupada sat and listened in silence. Then the astrologer mentioned the mantra which he had given to me a few days before. He recommended this as the most effective means for counteracting the bad influences.

Prabhupada immediately said, "So, we have got the *mahā-mantra.*" He requested us to chant Hare Krishna and asked for a kirtan party.

This morning Prabhupada appears depressed and completely resigned in himself. He appears to have given up any attempt to fight for continued bodily existence. Now he is simply leaving it to Krishna. All we can do is chant and pray to Krishna that He will relieve Prabhupada from any difficulty, and hope that he will be allowed to stay with us. We know that Prabhupada has to leave us sometime, but still it doesn't seem that it should be so soon. We have such a long way to go on the path of devotion to Krishna, and we have always had the benefit of Prabhupada's personal presence to give us insight and correction, and most of all, enthusiasm. Everyone is a little fearful for a future without his presence, although all instructions are there and actually Prabhupada is always with us. In this final *līlā*, the spiritual master shows us how we should spend our final days: fixing the mind, intelligence, everything on Krishna, and not remaining bound by obligation to anything else.

Hamsaduta Swami came in with Sridhar Swami, Bali Mardan, Jayadvaita, Svarupa Damodara, and Gurukripa, and began chanting. Prabhupada lay back very quietly and was quite still. Then he began to say out loud, "*Jaya rādhe, jaya kṛṣṇa, jaya vṛndāvana*" and indicated he wanted this to be sung.

Yesterday he had only one big drink in the morning

49

and then nothing the rest of the time. Today, after hearing his horoscope, he drank a full glass of grape juice and then asked for more. Because it wasn't immediately available, he lay back and didn't take anymore.

About 11 a.m. Prabhupada again spoke with Hamsaduta about Sri Lanka. Hamsaduta had asked him exactly what he meant by developing it like Kirtanananda Swami.

Prabhupada responded, emotions not fully in check. "Now you are serving, live very simple life and at same time chant Hare Krishna." He began crying at this point. "Don't waste time for bodily comforts. You have got this body, you have to eat something, you have to cover yourself, so produce your own food and produce your own cloth. Don't waste time for luxury, and chant Hare Krishna. This is success. In this way organize as far as possible. Either in Ceylon or in Yugoslavia; same time, chant Hare Krishna. Don't be allured by machinery civilization. There is enough land, especially you Americans. Anywhere you can inhabit, it's not very difficult. A cottage, you can produce your own food anywhere. Am I right?"

Hamsaduta: "Yes, Prabhupada, we will do it."

Prabhupada: "And money, spend for Krishna and Krishna palace, Krishna temple, for Krishna worship, for Krishna glorification. Not for personal. This is human life. And organize this varnashrama, divide the society, brahman, kshatriya—as there is division in the body. That is help. Don't waste the human form of life by sinful living. I wanted to introduce this; I have given the idea. You can read—you are all intelligent, all of you. Chaitanya Mahaprabhu said, 'para-upakāra,' so do good to others; not exploit all others. Any human being who has been bestowed with this body has the capacity to chant Hare Krishna. Give them chant and make the situation favorable. Is that clear?"

Hamsaduta: "Yes it's clear, Prabhupada. You have made everything very clear."

Later, Prabhupada called Brahmananda Swami from the back of the room and started to talk about Africa.

Prabhupada: "Distribute *prasādam* and kirtan. Go to the interior. Develop Africa. With Nava-yogendra—both of you. There also gradually they are taking. Who is going there?"

Brahmananda: "Jayatirtha."

Prabhupada: "And Tosan Krishna?"

Brahmananda: "In South Africa? Tulasi dasa?"

Prabhupada: "No, before that, when I was going."

Brahmananda: "Pusta Krishna."

Prabhupada: "Yes. Try to bring him back. He is very competent. So jointly organize Africa; have *sankirtana*, all Europeans, Americans, Africans. Tulasi dasa is very competent also. United Nation under Chaitanya Mahaprabhu's flag. It is possible. This is the real United Nations."

Brahmananda: "You said that when you first came to New York. You went to the United

51

Nations. The very first time I came to your kirtan in New York, the next day you went to that peace vigil outside the UN and you were chanting Hare Krishna and saying that this Krishna consciousness is the only method for making United Nations."

Prabhupada: "Hmm. It is fact. If you try under the protection of Chaitanya Mahaprabhu things will be successful. Others will simply waste time and be disappointed—and change his body and suffer. Today is Ekādaśī?"

Brahmananda: "Yes."

Then Prabhupada asked for two songs especially to be sung: "Cintāmaṇi-prakara-sadmasu and Hare Krishna mahā-mantra should be continuously chanted here in this room."

Tamal Krishna: "You want to drink something now, Srila Prabhupada?"

Prabhupada: "When I shall want, you will give me caraṇāmṛta."

Tamal Krishna: "We can give you some now. Would you like it now?"

Prabhupada: "I am not thirsty now. A little can be given.... But don't take me to the hospital."

Tamal Krishna: "No, Prabhupada, under no circumstance. Even if you're unconscious we'll simply chant."

Prabhupada: "Yes. I'm quite all right here."

Tamal Krishna: "That we can see."

52

Prabhupada: "I came back from London on account of fearing this hospitalization."

At this point, the cassette player being held by Upendra close to Prabhupada's head to record his faint voice, dropped out of its case and hit Prabhupada's shoulder.

Prabhupada: "Oh, be very careful!" Then, "You can go on chanting Hare Krishna."

The kirtan began again. A few minutes later, Prabhupada asked that after his departure his watch be given to Upendra.

Prabhupada rested throughout the day, completely peaceful and quiet, hearing the kirtan. Gurukripa chanted for three hours in the afternoon.

Now there is no difficulty and no struggle for bodily existence. During the afternoon, he took another 100 milliliters of grape juice, the second time today.

Prabhupada called Tamal Krishna Maharaja in the middle of the afternoon to again ask what the most critical times were. Before they discussed, Tamal Krishna asked Prabhupada if he would like to lie with his head toward the Deities. Prabhupada agreed. Up until now he had been lying with his head toward the door, but now ten men lifted the bed and turned it around so that Prabhupada's head pointed toward the Deities, his body parallel to the windows. Then Prabhupada had a small sip of *caraṇāmṛta* from his spoon, and Upendra massaged his head with oil.

Prabhupada: "So, how many critical days?"

Tamal Krishna: "Critical days—today, tomorrow, and then on the 11ᵗʰ, three days from today. Today, tomorrow, then one day is not so bad, then the next day after that becomes bad again."

Prabhupada: "In this way, how long prolonged?"

Tamal Krishna: "Well, those three days are the worst. Then the whole month is not very good. In fact, for another two to three months it's not very good, but these two to three days mentioned are very bad."

Prabhupada: "And then again?"

Tamal Krishna: "Then there are some critical days in the following month. At the end of this month there are a couple of critical days, and then in the next month there are two or three, and in the following month there are some. The whole period is not very bright looking."

Prabhupada: "Hmm."

Tamal Krishna: "I think this program of kirtan and just taking very little drink whenever you're thirsty is the right program, because I'm seeing now how peacefully you're resting, more than in many days, and now you should not struggle very hard. If Krishna wishes, then He will do."

Prabhupada: "Hmm."

Tamal Krishna: "We're prepared to stay here and sing for you for one year in a row."

Prabhupada: "That's nice."

Tamal Krishna: "It is our greatest pleasure to come and sing for you. Actually, I was thinking how your whole life is so perfect, Srila Prabhupada, and you have so many nice disciples, nice sons, and they are all gathered here to be with you, and everything is perfect by our chanting."

Prabhupada: "Yes, go on chanting."

Tamal Krishna: "Shall we go on chanting?"

Prabhupada: "Oh, yes."

Then Gurukripa carried on with kirtan.

Tamal Krishna Maharaja sent Bhakti Charu to Narayana Maharaja's Kesavajī Gaudiya Matha in Mathura. He is one of Prabhupada's "God-nephews," and he helped Prabhupada when he first came to Vrindavan-Mathura in 1956 and served him nicely. Prabhupada had a Lord Chaitanya Deity at that time, and he gave Him to Narayana Maharaja's *maṭha* to worship. This last June-July, Narayana Maharaja sent one of his men every day for over a month to massage Prabhupada.

Now Tamal Krishna Maharaja has sent Bhakti Charu Swami to find out the details for the burial ceremony of Vaishnava acharyas. Later in the day when he returned, he and Bhakti Prem Swami related the details and they were typed up. Tamal Krishna Maharaja, Brahmananda Swami, and I each have copies.

About 6:30 p.m. Tamal Krishna, Adi-kesava, Brahmananda, Giriraj, and I were all sitting in the front office discussing about the banking problems with the Punjab National Bank. Then Upendra came in and said, "Prabhupada is asking for Krishnadasa Babaji." We immediately got hope; we thought of the Krishnadasa Babaji from Radha-kuṇḍa, who is a *paṇḍā*, a tour guide of Vrindavan. *Parikramā!* We all went in, thinking that perhaps Prabhupada wanted to make *parikramā* arrangements, that still he was thinking of staying with us for a while longer. We crowded around

Prabhupada, leaning close to catch his faint voice.

Tamal Krishna: "I don't think you're feeling any pain."

Prabhupada moved his head very slightly to confirm this.

Tamal Krishna: "Srila Prabhupada, do you want to see that Krishnadasa from Radha-kuṇḍa? The *paṇḍā?* The man who takes people around?"

Prabhupada's slight shake of his head showed us he was thinking of someone else.

Tamal Krishna: "Not Niskincana Babaji?"
Prabhupada: "Yes."
Tamal Krishna: "From Mayapur. The one who always laughs a lot?"
Prabhupada: "Who comes to me."
Tamal Krishna: "Yes, your godbrother." [Prabhupada affirms this.] "Okay. I'll make sure that he comes."

Then Tamal Krishna informed Prabhupada that as per the astrologer's reading, there were two difficult days, then a one-day break; so, that day is Govardhana-pūjā. We wanted to see if that would encourage Prabhupada, but there was no significant reaction from him. This turned out to be wrong information anyway, because Govardhana-pūjā is next month.

Tamal Krishna: "Srila Prabhupada, have you been thinking about *parikramā?*"
Prabhupada: "Do you think in this state it is possible?"
Tamal Krishna: "I think it would be difficult; I

56

think it would be better if we go
on *parikrama* around our temple,
Krishna-Balarama Mandir. That's a
little easier. Don't you think that's
better?"

Prabhupada: "Hmm."

Tamal Krishna: "If you get a little stronger, then it
may be possible. That will depend on
Krishna. So Krishnadasa, we should
bring him here. Anyone else you
want to see? Narayana Maharaja?"

Prabhupada again affirmed with a slight movement of
his head.

Tamal Krishna: "Yes? We went to see him just
to inquire about the necessary
ceremony, and he gave us
instruction. I sent Bhakti Charu
Swami and Bhakti Prem Swami,
and they wrote down everything.
But Narayana Maharaja was very
concerned. He said he would try to
come see you tomorrow. That's all
right, isn't it? So Krishnadasa can be
called for, any time? Okay. He stays
at Radha-kunda. Does he stay at the
Gaudiya Matha here? He does. We'll
inquire."

Prabhupada: "Narayana Maharaja comes, then
everything will be all right."

Tamal Krishna: "So if I call Narayana Maharaja, is
there any need for Krishnadasa to
come?"

Prabhupada: "He can arrange."

Tamal Krishna: "Narayana Maharaja. Actually, he wanted to do that. He gave us instructions, but he also wanted to take part. So better I call Narayana Maharaja than Krishnadasa. He was saying he would like to come tomorrow, so I'll send a car and say that Prabhupada says he requests that if it's convenient, that you come this morning. Is that all right? Jaya Srila Prabhupada."

Half an hour later, Bhagavat dasa arrived. He has lost 115 pounds weight due to his *cāturmāsya* fast and looks very weak and thin. He went straight in to see Prabhupada, who was lying down and so could not see Bhagavat directly. Prabhupada asked him when he had come. Upendra told Prabhupada that Bhagavat was "real skinny". Prabhupada was a little concerned.

Prabhupada: "Why?"

Bhagavat: "Because I'm following *cāturmāsya*. I've reduced to 160 pounds. Before I was 260; now 160."

Prabhupada: (smiling) "Very nice!"

Then Bhagavat led the chanting for a while. A few of us were sitting in Prabhupada's room. Kirtanananda was leading. Then Prabhupada called for Bhagatji and started to ask him about the managing of our Vrindavan temple in his absence.

Prabhupada: "Nothing can be said about that; if He [Krishna] wants, then everything will be all right."

Bhagatji: "You mean about Vrindavan?"

Prabhupada:	"Yes!"
Bhagatji:	"Yes, everything will be all right by your blessing."
Prabhupada:	"One thing is, after my disappearance there should be festival in every temple."
Bhagatji:	"Should I call Ramdas Shastri tomorrow?"
Prabhupada:	"Why?"
Bhagatji:	"Just to consult. Should there be some *Vaishnava-seva* afterwards?"
Prabhupada:	"Yes, in the temples. Visvambhara Maharaja [from Radha-Ramana temple] is there, Atul Krishna is there."
Bhagatji:	"Yes, I'll go tomorrow."

Prabhupada indicated his room and asked, "Who is there?" Tamal Krishna Maharaja identified himself, "Tamal Krishna." "Chant!" Prabhupada said.

Then after a few minutes Prabhupada called Bhagatji again. "Do you think everything will run smoothly?"

Bhagatji:	"Vrindavan. I believe that everything will run smoothly, if everyone works earnestly, honestly."

At that point, Brahmananda Swami gave some news.

Brahmananda:	"Krishnadasa Babaji is not here. He has gone to Madras. Should I call Narayana Maharaja, Srila Prabhupada?"
Prabhupada:	"Didn't Panditji come?"
Brahmananda:	"I looked for Krishnadasa Babaji, but he has gone to Madras."

Prabhupada:	"No, I meant the small man who comes here at times, don't you know him? Who told you about Krishnadasa Babaji?"
Brahmananda:	"I heard his name, and when you wanted to get that man from Chaitanya Matha, I thought it was him."
Prabhupada:	"Will Narayana Maharaja come tomorrow?"
Tamal Krishna:	"If Bhakti Charu goes with the car, Narayana Maharaja may come now."
Prabhupada:	"Okay."

During this whole conversation everyone was feeling very depressed. The atmosphere was filled with resigned despair. Prabhupada was talking about his *samādhi*, and everything from the last few days has pointed more and more definitely to one conclusion—that Prabhupada will leave us soon.

We have gotten details of the ceremony for burial, and now he is calling his Godbrothers. Every meeting seems to be like a final goodbye. Brahmananda Swami was sobbing at the side of the bed for some time. Gopala Krishna also.

Eventually Narayana Maharaja arrived with a few men. I had been sitting and stroking Prabhupada's right arm and hand for half an hour or more. Tripurari was massaging his feet, Bhagatji his right leg, and Tamal Krishna his left arm. When Narayana Maharaja came we gave him a seat at the side of the bed, but Prabhupada was talking so low that he had to lean over very near to his head to hear him. It was intensely affecting, with Prabhupada opening his heart and thoughts to his spiritual siblings in a way we had never seen before.

Prabhupada: "Srila Prabhupada wanted that we should preach in Europe, America; that was my desire, and my other desire was that you all will work together, jointly, to preach."

Narayana Maharaja: "Yes, that's right."

Prabhupada: "I didn't waste a single moment. I tried my best, and it has been successful to some extent." At this point, he was almost crying, his voice cracking with emotion. "If we work jointly, then as Sri Chaitanya Mahaprabhu said, *'pṛthivīte āche yata nagarādi-grāma'* has great possibility. My life is coming to an end. It is my desire that you all will forgive me for my mistakes. My Godbrothers, when you are preaching, at times there are some disputes, some misunderstandings; maybe I also committed some offences, like that. Please ask them to forgive me. When I am gone, you all sit together and decide how you can arrange for some utsava [festival] for me. How much we should pay. What do you think of this?"

Narayana Maharaja: "Whatever instructions you give me, I'll follow them with absolute sincerity. I consider you as my guru."

Prabhupada: "Do you think there is any wrong with this proposal?"

Narayana Maharaja: "It is very nice! This should be

61

done. You have created something, and it is everybody's duty to protect it. You have taught them yourself. But in future, if everyone is co-operating with them, then there will be something great all over the world."

Prabhupada: "They don't have anything hereditary; they are born in mleccha and yavana families. Whatever I could, I taught them, and they are also doing with their full capacity. If you all work jointly, then the whole world is there. Many big temples have been built. There is no dearth of money, there is no want of people. So if the work is done with the right spirit..."

Narayana Maharaja: "Yes, everyone should co-operate. And if they are also humble, then it will be so nice. Whatever I can do, I'll do. Whatever help they need from me, I'll always be there to help them. If they call me, if they want my advice, if they want me to go somewhere, I'll do everything according to my capacity. But my capacity is very limited. Still, whatever I can, I'll do."

Prabhupada: "In Vrindavan how many of our Godbrothers are there?"

Narayana Maharaja: "Bon Maharaja may be there. And Indupati prabhu."

Prabhupada: "I was thinking of him, Indupati."

Narayana Maharaja: "No one else is here now."

Prabhupada: "Call these two, Indupati prabhu and

Bon Maharaja."

Narayana Maharaja: "This is a very nice proposal."

Prabhupada: "You can sit down for a while. Let him also come. All these misunderstandings and disputes."

Narayana Maharaja: "They are all trivial things. In this worldwide preaching, if some little things go wrong here and there, what difference does it make? It is all right. Whatever you have done, you have done for the wellbeing of the entire human society. There is no individual interest; everything was done in the interest of God."

Prabhupada: "All these have been done by your blessings."

Narayana Maharaja: "You have achieved an enormous thing. Now it has to be maintained properly."

Prabhupada: "I can't talk. You explain it to them. How are you?"

Narayana Maharaja: "I'm all right. They are all very efficient and worthy. You don't worry. Now you think of the Lord."

Prabhupada: "There was a big trouble in Mayapur."

Narayana Maharaja: "They will all become all right. Some evil persons, due to their personal interests, have done that. These kinds of obstructions will come, but that is nothing."

Prabhupada: "Twenty thousand people came to the protest march. Have you heard anything?"

Narayana Maharaja: "Yes. I heard about, and I was very sad. That was done by the Communists. They have committed a great wrong. You don't worry about anything now; they will take care of everything efficiently. Now you think of the Lord peacefully."

Prabhupada: "You have your affection for me."

Narayana Maharaja: "How can I have affection for you? I respect you as my guru."

Prabhupada: "Yes, I know that."

Narayana Maharaja: "If we have committed any offence, please forgive us. Bless us that we develop the attraction for the lotus feet of the Lord."

Prabhupada: "Where is Sroti Maharaja?"

Narayana Maharaja: "He's in Bengal now."

Prabhupada: "When did he go?"

Narayana Maharaja: "About a month ago. Sheshashayi has come with me."

Prabhupada: "That brahmachari?"

Narayana Maharaja: "Yes, Sheshashayi Brahmachari; he used to cook for you at times."

Prabhupada (to us): "Give them some prasādam."

Narayana Maharaja: "'Sri rūpa mañjarī pāda'— sing that."

Sheshashayi Brahmachari at this point sang very sweetly, and then Narayana Maharaja sang, and then everyone sang *"Jaya* Gurudeva" and *"Jaya* Prabhupada."

Prabhupada: "Where is Tamal?" (Then to Narayana Maharaja) "I have only these bones left."

Narayana Maharaja: "It has been very nice that you

64

came to Braja-bhūmi from the West."

Prabhupada: "Yes, I told them that my condition was very bad."

Tamal Krishna Maharaja came forward, and Prabhupada asked him, "You have consulted with Narayana Maharaja?"

Tamal Krishna: "Yes, this morning. Bhakti Charu Swami and Bhakti Prem Swami and Sridhar Swami went to see him, and Narayana Maharaja described the ceremony after the departure of a Vaishnava."

Narayana Maharaja: "I told them all that is to be done. And I told them that whenever you need me, I'll come and I'll go with you."

Prabhupada: "Is it the right side of the entrance?"

Tamal Krishna: "Left side; when you enter to the Deity, it is on the left side."

Prabhupada: "You put salt on the body."

Narayana Maharaja: "Yes, I told them everything. I'll make all arrangements."

Tamal Krishna: "It is on the same side as the vyāsāsana, facing east."

Prabhupada: "Flowers should be sent to Mayapur for *puṣpa samadhi.*"

Narayana Maharaja: "Yes, I told them about that also. During that time I'll be here personally to see to everything. You let me know."

Prabhupada: "Has Sheshashayi taken sannyasa?"

Narayana Maharaja: "No, he is still a brahmachari." [Pause] "All the work of your life is very well performed; nothing is

65

left to be done. There is nothing
to worry about. You have fulfilled
everything.... They should be
told that they should never get
motivated by their own self-interest.
They should make your mission
successful."

Prabhupada looked at us all and lifted his hand, palm open, as an appeal, and said, "Don't fight amongst yourselves. I have given direction in my Will." Then again to Narayana Maharaja, "Today is Ekādaśī. Mahaprabhu *sevā* is going quite well?"

Narayana Maharaja: "Yes."
Prabhupada: "My Mahaprabhu from Jhansi?"
Narayana Maharaja: "Yes. Mahaprabhu is with us.
We are worshipping Him very nicely."
Prabhupada: "There was a good chance in Jhansi,
but then I felt that Bhagavan's desire
is to build something greater than
that."
Narayana Maharaja: "That has been better. Why
should you stay at narrow limits?
Bhagavan wanted you to preach all
over the world."
Prabhupada: "I thought that I would stay in
Vrindavan as a *niṣkiñcana*, but
Bhagavan gave me the inspiration to
go to the West at the age of seventy,
and His will has been fulfilled.
Something very great has been
done."
Narayana Maharaja: "Srila Rūpa Gosvami's special
mercy has been showered upon

you. Special mercy of Sri Sri Radha-
Damodara."

Prabhupada: "That is something—a pauper like
me! How things happen!"

Indupati prabhu arrived at this point. He asked, "How
are you?"

Prabhupada: "I called you just to tell you that my
end is nearing."

Narayana Maharaja: "He is finding it a little
difficult to speak, but he told me
everything—I'll tell you. He said,
'You all come together and preach
the words of Mahāprabhu.' "

Prabhupada: "First of all, I want to say, forgive me
for all my offences. I didn't want to
hurt anyone, but while preaching
one has to sometimes say something
that may offend others. Will you
forgive me?"

Indupati: "Yes, yes."

Narayana Maharaja: "Maharaja, you didn't commit
any offence. We never thought that
you did anything wrong. On the
other hand, you bless us. We need
it. You never did anything wrong. If
someone is offended by any of your
actions, then it is his fault."

Indupati: "He just came back from London.
Why did he go to London in such a
condition?"

Narayana Maharaja: "That's all right; good that he
came back to Braja-bhūmi."

Prabhupada: "The program was to go around the

world, world tour. But after going to
London my body's condition became
very bad."

Narayana Maharaja: "Whatever you told me, I'll
tell that to all the disciples of
Prabhupada. I'll tell just as you told
me. And I'll see that everyone helps
these boys. You don't worry about
anything, just think of God only."

Prabhupada: "Just make a list of how much money
will be needed, so that in every
Maṭha and temple an utsava is
observed with due honor."

Narayana Maharaja: "Did you all understand?"
Bhakti Charu: "Yes, I understand. Everything will
be done."

Narayana Maharaja: (to Indupati) "I'll tell you what
he said. He wants *utsava* should
be observed in every temple and
whatever money is needed, they
will pay." And to Prabhupada, "You
don't worry about anything. All your
disciples are very efficient, and they
will take proper care of everything.
Now they have got to know about
your desires and they will take care.
The way you have inspired the whole
world with the holy name of Krishna,
everything will be successful for
you. Let us go now."

Prabhupada: "Give them some *prasādam*."

Even at such a time, Prabhupada was immediately
thinking of the comfort of others and concerned to
show due respect.

Then Hamsaduta Swami began kirtan.
Narayana Maharaja felt Prabhupada's pulse.

Narayana Maharaja: "The pulse is all right. Your consciousness is perfect; your pulse is perfect. If you have to go, by the will of the Lord, then you will go perfectly. Maharaja, allow us to go now. I'll come again."

Prabhupada: "Bless me." To Tamal Krishna, "Are you sending them by car?"

Tamal Krishna: "Yes, Prabhupada. Bhakti Charu, you take them."

Indupati: "All is Prabhupada's desire!"

Prabhupada: "Who is in Imlitala?"(a temple where he once lived for a short while.)

Narayana Maharaja: "None of Prabhupada's disciples is there."

Then they all left, and Prabhupada lay back, resting in the now nearly-vacant room.

I gave Prabhupada his beads. When Indupati arrived, I changed my position from the right side of the bed to kneeling on the bed at Prabhupada's left side. Fifteen to twenty devotees were all crowded around, and the atmosphere was surcharged with expectancy. The general feeling of the last few days has been gradually more and more hopeless for Prabhupada staying with us. Gradually he has cut down what little bit of fluid he was taking, and now he wants only *caraṇāmṛta*. Preparations for samadhi and performance of the funeral ceremony are now openly discussed, and Prabhupada himself seems to have given up any idea of trying for improvement. I continued to massage him for a little while.

At around 11:30 p.m. Harikesa, Jayatirtha, Balavan-

ta, and Hridayananda Goswami all arrived and immediately went in to see Prabhupada. As they sat by his
bed, Prabhupada asked Jayatirtha, "What is the news
of South Africa?" Jayatirtha told him 15,000 people had
come for Janmastami and everything was becoming
very successful there. Prabhupada thanked him and
rubbed him affectionately on the head.

Later on, about 2 a.m., Bhagavat felt Prabhupada's
pulse. Tripurari Maharaja was leading kirtan. Prabhupada asked who was leading, then he asked Bhagavat
what was going on in Orissa.

Bhagavat told him he had sent $6,000 and they
were already constructing in Orissa, and described
the basic plan—a *kuṭirā* for Prabhupada, a guesthouse,
a brahmachari ashram, a water tank, and an Orissan-
style temple, although Surabhir Swami had told him
that Prabhupada's preference was for a Krishna-
Balarama Mandir style. Prabhupada said he would see
the plans. Prabhupada was especially pleased when
Bhagavat said he was going to distribute books in all
the villages of Orissa.

OCTOBER 9, 1977

Tamal Krishna Maharaja felt Prabhupada's pulse
and thought it was a little weaker and slower, around
60 beats per minute. Gurukripa was leading kirtan
softly when suddenly Prabhupada said, "*Yaśomatī-
nandana, yaśomatī-nandana.*" I couldn't understand
what he meant, but Gurukripa immediately broke into
*yaśomatī-nandana, braja-baro-nāgara, gokula-rañjana
kāna.* Prabhupada smiled slightly.

We bathed him this morning, because yesterday he
didn't have a bath or a change of cloth. However, we
had to do it all with Prabhupada practically lying down,
as he is feeling very weak. There is no possibility of
darshan now, as Prabhupada can hardly sit up. Still,

once he did sit up, he remained for some time and had me scratch his back quite vigorously for fifteen minutes. Then he lay back again. Tamal Krishna asked Prabhupada if he would drink something, but he refused. He had already had three spoons of *caraṇāmṛta*, and that was sufficient.

As Gurukripa continued singing, Prabhupada declared, "Let me drink *amala harināma amiya-vilāsā!*" and gave a big smile.

Hari-sauri: "That is the sweetest nectar."
Prabhupada: "Hmm."

As Prabhupada lay quietly, he said something out loud. I leaned forward to catch it, and Prabhupada again said *"yaśomatī-nandana"* and then fell silent again.

Just after breakfast, Prabhupada spoke with Tamal Krishna Maharaja, Brahmananda Swami and Gurukripa Swami.

Prabhupada: "Nivṛtta-tarṣair upagīyamānād
                 bhavauṣadhi [SB 10.1.4]. This is
                 bhavauṣadhi, hari-kirtan."

Jayadvaita prabhu completed the Sanskrit quote: "Bhavauṣadhāc chrotra-mano-'bhirāmāt."

Prabhupada: (smiling) "Yes. And caraṇāmṛta,
                 paṭha—diet. Diet and medicine. Let
                 me depend on these."
Tamal Krishna: "Very pure. Pure diet, Srila
                 Prabhupada. Transcendental. Not
                 feeling any discomfort?"
Prabhupada: "Same discomfort or same comfort.
                 No change. Some discomfort. Lots of
                 cough in my chest."

71

Tamal Krishna:	"So, you're bathed a little bit now."
Prabhupada:	"Hmm? You bathed the head? No."
Tamal Krishna:	"No. Your face was bathed and your eyes. Tilak is put on fresh."

Prabhupada asked what *prasādam* was being supplied for the devotees' breakfast.

Tamal Krishna gave a detailed report: "What they supplied? You mean *prasādam?* Of course, today is the day after Ekādaśī, so they had some cereal made with *gūr* and some guava fruit salad, with guavas and bananas. That was all this morning. Lunch is usually substantial, very good. It's the best *prasādam* that we have had in many years in India here. This boy Ayodhya-pati is doing very nicely. He cooks usually. Do you want to know what he cooks for lunch? He cooks *ālu sabjī* with dahi sauce, and he makes *bindī*, very nicely spiced, and *ḍal*, rotis, rice, apple chutney, and dahi-raita. Every day."

Tamal Krishna told him that people staying in our guesthouse come and eat also.

Prabhupada was happy. "Yes, that I want."

Tamal Krishna:	"They give a chit. They pay at the guesthouse."

He said the price was only three rupees and explained that we don't charge much because we are an ashram, not a hotel. Prabhupada agreed with that. He was smiling to hear how everyone takes *prasādam* together, and he rolled his eyes up to the top of the bed towards Jayatirtha and asked him what he thought. Jayatirtha said he thought it was good, and Prabhupada asked, "Everyone else liked?" Everyone gave their agreement.

As he has become accustomed to doing, Tamal Krishna Maharaja expressed his and our love and appreciation, encouraging Srila Prabhupada.

Tamal Krishna: "You're the perfect father, Prabhupada. You've provided everything for us, a place to live, food to eat, everything. And you trained us up in spiritual knowledge."

Prabhupada: "Hmm. Chant, all together!"

So all the devotees chanted the *mahā-mantra* together for Prabhupada.

Later on I sat in his room transcribing a tape, and Prabhupada coughed. I brought the spittoon to him. He spat out a thick, heavy glob of mucus, not the usual thin, frothy, watery stuff. Prabhupada was disappointed to see it and commented, "Without drinking, cough is coming?"

"That's what the doctor said would happen," I said. "Without strength, the body cells weaken, and then blood turns to mucus and the lungs clog up."

"And if I take [drink], the cough will stop?" Prabhupada asked.

I suggested the Complan could help, but Prabhupada said it was already tried, so I mentioned the high-protein drink from America. Prabhupada curled his lips a little in distaste and said, "We shall see later on." Then I helped him onto his side, and he slept for a while.

At about 11:15 a.m., Prabhupada woke and asked where Tamal Krishna Maharaja was. I told him he was at a meeting, so Prabhupada had me bring him. When he came, Prabhupada asked him, "What meeting going on?"

"A very interesting meeting," Tamal Krishna told him. "Paramananda, Vamanadeva, Tripurari Swami, Adi-kesava, and myself, discussing our Gita Nagari community and talking about varnashrama. We were trying to reflect on all of the teachings in your books and what we had read about Krishna's life in Nanda

Maharaja's community, trying to see how Nanda Maharaja, how the vaishya community, lives. How the different varnas and ashramas function together and what their responsibilities are to one another. We will try to set up our Gita Nagari community based upon the teachings you've given in your books. It is a very enlivening and stimulating meeting. Dhṛṣṭadyumna Swami will be coming tomorrow with his brother, and he has designed a very ideal plan for all of the varnas and ashramas to live together."

Prabhupada: (smiling) "Do it! Go on!"

Tamal Krishna: "*Jaya* Prabhupada. We're going on your teachings, Prabhupada. You're always the center of our lives."

Prabhupada: "Let us make some community."

Tamal Krishna: "Show the world how to live ideally— go back to Godhead. Raise your own food, make your own clothes, make your own buildings, and chant Hare Krishna, worship Radha Krishna. People are working so hard, yet they don't have a nice home, they don't have nice clothes, they don't have nice food, and they don't have any love for Krishna. We have to show how to do everything very nicely, and you've given us... We just have to understand what you've given us, Prabhupada—your teachings."

Prabhupada: "Thank you."

Tamal Krishna: "We have nothing new to find out, no research to make. You've given us everything. We only have to carry out exactly how you've trained us up."

Prabhupada: "Very nice. Hmm. So you can go on with your business."

Tamal Krishna returned to his meeting, kirtan began again, and Prabhupada rested.

Later, at about 12:30 p.m., Upendra tried to persuade Prabhupada to drink something, but he wouldn't. He complained about the mucus. Upendra explained that at present he is losing more fluid than he is taking in and he will become dehydrated, but Prabhupada still wouldn't take anything. "I feel no inconvenience." Then when Upendra went out, Prabhupada turned to Abhirama and said, "I am afraid of cough." Abhirama asked about taking water. Prabhupada thought for a moment and then told him, "So you discuss amongst yourselves and decide what you want me to do."

Abhirama: "About recovery, Prabhupada?"
Prabhupada: "I don't want."
Abhirama: "You don't want recovery, Prabhupada?"
Prabhupada: "Yes."

Abhirama came out into the front office of Prabhupada's rooms, where a small group of us were meeting. He told us what Prabhupada had said, that "You decide what you want me to do." But the significance of his words didn't immediately impact us, in view of Prabhupada's decreasing attempts for carrying on.

We have become resigned to accepting that Prabhupada wants to leave now and die peacefully. We have tried to encourage him to drink, but now he seems determined to simply fast until the right time comes. For myself, I can't really accept it is happening, but it is. It doesn't seem the right time—too soon. But we can't see how Prabhupada can go on with his body in its present condition. We were talking in the morning, and we all felt like this. Everyone seems down and depressed. I feel vaguely agitated and drained—like being in maya, but not.

Then at 1:25 p.m., Prabhupada called for Tamal Krishna Maharaja. He was half way through eating lunch but came in with Brahmananda, followed by Upendra, Tejiyas, Harikesa, myself, and several others. Our small group circled Prabhupada's bed, drawing close to him to hear his weak voice.

Prabhupada told us, "If I want to survive, of course I'll have to take something. It is not possible to survive without taking any food. But my survival means so many complications, one after another. Therefore I have decided to die peacefully in Vrindavan."

Prabhupada's voice trailed off. His speaking was very, very low—just a whisper. We were all stunned. No one could speak. All we could do is just look at Prabhupada blankly as he lay with his eyes closed. Occasionally he made some noise, "Hmm," but it was two and a half minutes—very, very long minutes—before Tamal Krishna Maharaja managed to ask if we should go on with kirtan. By this time, Gurukripa, Bhagavat, and others had come in. Hamsaduta started singing. My voice was choked and eyes full of tears. I heard Harikesa sniffle behind me. We couldn't take our eyes off Prabhupada.

Then Tamal Krishna told Prabhupada that when some postal receipts in his ex-family's name came due they would be given to them. He assured him that they will be satisfied and won't be sorry in any way. "You've provided for everyone, Srila Prabhupada."

Then after another minute or so I sniffled again, and Prabhupada heard me. He said softly, "Why do you want me to survive?"

I couldn't speak. I felt that if I asked him to stay it would be offensive if he has decided to leave, but I couldn't keep my emotions under check. I didn't want to say "stay and struggle," but none of us wanted him to leave either. Tamal Krishna didn't immediately catch what he said and leaned forward more.

Tamal Krishna said half questioning, "They want you to survive?" Then there was another short pause. The kirtan had stopped as soon as Prabhupada spoke, and everyone strained to catch his voice. The atmosphere was incredibly intense.

Prabhupada whispered, "If I want to die, this is the way of peaceful death."

I couldn't keep my composure anymore, and the tears rolled out from my eyes. I had to sink my head into my *dhoti*. I couldn't stop shaking or crying, and I couldn't sing when Prabhupada said, "Go on chanting."

After a short time, Tamal Krishna told Prabhupada that he was going out for about fifteen minutes. Prabhupada asked why, and Tamal Krishna told him he was going for a discussion.

Prabhupada, lying peacefully with his eyes closed, rejoined, "For discussion. They want me to survive, and I want to die peacefully. I cannot make miracles. The physical body has to be maintained if I am to survive, but without taking food, how the physical body will go on? That is fanaticism."

There was a long pause. Tamal Krishna told Prabhupada, "Everything is in the hands of Krishna." Then after another pause, Prabhupada opened his eyes. "Krishna wants me to do as I like. The choice is mine. Krishna has given me full freedom."

Then Brahmananda, who was standing at the foot of the bed, voice choking but wanting to reassure Prabhupada, said, "It doesn't matter whether you live or die, you'll always be with Krishna and we will be with you because we'll follow your instructions."

Prabhupada: "Whether I live or die, I'll always be Krishna's servant. If Brahmananda has assured me that this movement will go on, then better let me die peacefully."

Tears were rolling down Brahmananda's cheeks as he realized his words of loyalty were taken by Srila Prabhupada as a further confirmation that he could now leave.

After a few more minutes, Hamsaduta began chanting. He was singing the *Brahma-saṁhitā* prayers. When he got to the verse *advaitam acyutam anādim ananta-rūpam*, Prabhupada opened his eyes and said, "This one, *yaśomatī-nandana*, and Hare Krishna. Chant these three."

Then there was a little confusion whether he meant the whole Govindam prayers or just that particular verse. But then he again spoke. "*Advaitam acyutam anādim ananta-rūpam*," and it was clear he meant that particular verse.

After a few minutes, Tamal Krishna, Brahmananda, and a few others left, leaving just the small kirtan party. After a while, Prabhupada suddenly asked, "Kirtanananda has left?"

Hari-sauri: "No, Prabhupada, he's still here."
Prabhupada: "Where is he?"
Hari-sauri: "He's right here in the room."

Then Prabhupada softly said, "Oh," and went back to rest.

Meanwhile, outside, everyone went for *prasādam*. Brahmananda felt very low that he had told Prabhupada that everything will go on, and thus Prabhupada had said, "Okay, I will die then."

After *prasādam* there was a meeting of some GBCs and sannyasis in the secretary's room. We began to discuss what was our understanding of Prabhupada's statements; that although he was saying he should die peacefully, he had also informed us that Krishna had given him the choice to do as he desires. Kirtanananda concluded that therefore actually the choice was ours. If we want Prabhupada badly enough, then we should go in and beg him to stay. He is giving us the choice.

Tamal Krishna Maharaja also pointed out that Prabhupada used the word "survive." Did that mean we should ask him to survive as he has been doing for the last two months? In that case, no. But if we mean he should survive to finish the *Bhāgavatam*, then we should all request him to stay for that. Everyone agreed. It must be done.

Kirtanananda Swami also brought up the point that why should we think there's no hope for him to become fit again. Jesus brought people back from the dead, even mundane yogis can do it, so Prabhupada certainly can if he wants.

In this way, the depressive mood of increasing helplessness that we had been feeling for the last few days was suddenly reversed as we got the determination to request Prabhupada to stay with us. I mentioned to the group that previously, after everyone had gone out of the room, Prabhupada had asked where Kirtanananda was, and so it was agreed that he should make the presentation. We waited for a few minutes, and then Prabhupada stirred, so we all went in and crowded around the bed. It was 3:30 p.m.

Kirtanananda came forward to the bed, at the side near Prabhupada's head, with the rest of us encircling the bed. Prabhupada lay silently, waiting to hear from our delegation. But as Kirtanananda leant over to speak, his lips trembled and his eyes filled with tears and he broke down sobbing, his head on the side of the bed. He was so overcome he couldn't speak. As he sobbed, Prabhupada, his eyes still closed, raised his arm up in the air and tried to feel who it was, but he had a little

79

difficulty twisting his arm around and down. As he did this, he asked, "Who?"

"Kirtanananda."

He lay his hand on his disciple's head and gently rubbed. "Hmm? So, what you want?"

No one could say anything. We were all waiting for Kirtanananda. Brahmananda was rubbing him on the back to soothe him, and Tamal Krishna was encouraging him to say something. Finally, after another minute, he got a little control and raised his head. He looked at Prabhupada and implored him with great emotion, "If Krishna gives you the choice—don't go! We need you!"

Prabhupada moved his hand around in the air to indicate us all. "This is your joint [decision]? You have discussed?"

Then Brahmananda spoke, full of emotion, but this time trying to be positive about Prabhupada staying: "We have all met together, Prabhupada. We want you to remain and lead this movement and finish the *Srimad-Bhāgavatam*. We said you *must* remain at least for another ten years. You've only done 50 percent work."

Prabhupada listened carefully without any movement, his eyes still closed. At the final part, about 50 percent work, he screwed up his face a little, "Nooo." Then he gave a loud "Hmm," as if he were considering our proposal. Again "Hmm," several times. We were all held in suspension, not able to speak, think, or do anything except look intently at Prabhupada.

Then, still with eyes closed, he began to yawn. As his mouth stretched open and his gold teeth showed, he assented: "All right."

It seemed the most completely casual decision on life or death ever made. At that moment we understood Prabhupada's supremely independent position. He can stay or go as he chooses, but we had become so faithless that we had actually been thinking that Prabhupada's leaving was inevitable and could not be prevented, that his body was finished and no one could do anything about it. Now he displayed his wonderful transcendental nature. A simple yawn, "All right." As if it were the most unimportant thing in the world. Immediately Harikesa gave out a short laugh, the sort he saves only for when Prabhupada has done something completely outrageous from the material standpoint and fooled everyone, and proved himself to be completely beyond any understanding. Everyone else laughed short, nervous laughs. It was out of relief and joy at such a wonderful thing, but stopped short because we weren't sure whether it was appropriate or not. We didn't know whether to laugh or cry, and we fell silent again to see what Prabhupada would say or do next.

Prabhupada:	"So, give me something to drink."
Devotees:	"*Jaya* Prabhupada!" Now it was confirmed. Great relief everywhere.
Kirtanananda:	"All glories to Srila Prabhupada!"

Prabhupada, commenting about our request, declared, "That is real affection!"

The entire atmosphere completely changed. Prabhupada completely changed. Now he was helped up to a sitting position so that he could drink, and as we watched, he drank a full glass of grape juice. Now, instead of withdrawing his energy as he had done steadily for the last few days, he came to life again. He lay back, "Thank you very much. Hare Krishna!"

Devotees:	"Hare Krishna!"

Then after a long pause, he asked, "Strawberries, they have brought?"

Tamal Krishna:	"Yes, Prabhupada, very nice strawberries."

Prabhupada:	"I'll take some strawberries."
Tamal Krishna:	"You want by juice or plain strawberries?"
Prabhupada:	"Plain!"
Devotees:	"Jaya!"

Then Prabhupada asked what was the value of strawberries. None of us seemed to really know. Finally, Tejiyas suggested that they were beneficial because they had sugar. Prabhupada seemed satisfied with that. Then he questioned Tejiyas. Had he come from Hyderabad? What was the news?

Tejiyas told him that mung and rice were being harvested, corn also.

Prabhupada:	"From corn you can make two things—roti and *bhat*. The villagers will like it very much. You smash it by *ḍheṅki*. You know that machine?"
Tamal Krishna:	"The ladies jump on it."
Prabhupada:	"Yes. So, as much as is powder, make it roti, and the hard portion, rice. It is very nutritious."

After a short pause, Tamal Krishna spoke, "Actually, Prabhupada, you gave your word to Krishna in Bombay that you would see Him sitting in His new big temple, and you have yet to keep your word fully to Him."

At this, Prabhupada began to smile very brightly.

Brahmananda:	"We have fixed a date for the opening of Bombay temple—January 1, 1978.
Prabhupada:	"Oh." (he was very pleased).
Brahmananda:	"So we would like to invite you to come, Prabhupada. It is your temple. You have asked Krishna to come there. When we all gave up, you

	carried on the fight."
Prabhupada:	(smiling even more) "Yes. There was a great fight. After fighting, to construct such a big temple is a great triumph."
Tamal Krishna:	"I don't think Krishna will come into the temple unless you are personally there, Prabhupada, to open the door up."

Prabhupada was smiling. Then after a pause: "All right, but chanting should not be stopped. Things should go on naturally." Then after another pause, "Kirtanananda's palace? When it will be ready?"

Kirtanananda:	"Early spring, as soon as the weather is a little warmer. It just gives you a little time to recuperate and then go to Bombay and open up the temple there and then come to open your palace. I have about 50-75 letters from all the devotees in New Vrindaban, and they're just about begging you to come. They say their life is finished if you don't."
Prabhupada:	"So let me take a little rest, and then I shall take strawberry."
Devotees:	"Prabhupada *ki jaya!*"

Then Prabhupada called in Giriraj to discuss the banking situation. We are having difficulty with the local branch of PNB, so Tamal Krishna and he have decided to transfer the fixed deposits to the head office in Delhi. Prabhupada listened to everything and then rested a little.

In the afternoon, Ramesvara Swami arrived

83

and immediately went in to see Prabhupada. He told Prabhupada how Parivrajakacharya Swami is preaching to the royal family in Iran. The Shah sends a car to him every day, and he preaches to the prince and princess and other family members. Prabhupada was very pleased. Because it is a Muslim country, other religious books are difficult to publish, but the princess has ordered the minister in charge to print our first book. She has visited the Los Angeles temple and was greatly impressed by the doll museum.

She also has a Tenth Canto painting of Krishna stealing butter hanging on the wall in her palace. Ramesvara took it to Tehran before he came here.

As they talked, Prabhupada asked for someone to scratch his back. Kirtanananda was doing it. Then Prabhupada asked, "Anyone can scratch very hard?" Kirtanananda said, "I'm afraid you'll have no back left!" Prabhupada laughed. "Oh, Kirtanananda, you are doing?"

Ramesvara went on to say that the royals want to meet Prabhupada. Prabhupada was pleased and commented that they have money, so if they take our instruction they can do much good.

After hearing from Ramesvara how the three European zones were top in the world last week for book distribution (London did 70,000 books in a week, a world record), Prabhupada commented, "Vedic civilization is *sarve sukhino bhavantu:* everyone be happy. This is Vedic civilization, and this is the way— Chaitanya Mahaprabhu's mission."

Ramesvara described the restaurant in Iran, how many important people were coming for lunch. Prabhupada said Atreya Rishi was very expert. He also asked about Dayananda.

Ramesvara told Prabhupada how a local man was translating *Bhagavad-gītā* into Parsi. Prabhupada said, "Do like that. *Pṛthivīte āche yata nagarādi-grāma* [CB Antya-khaṇḍa 4.126]."

Tamal Krishna: "You are doing that, Prabhupada."

Prabhupada: "You are helping me."

Later, at 9:15 p.m., Yasodanandana Swami was chanting *Brahma-saṁhitā*, but Prabhupada stopped him and began to preach.

Prabhupada: "That will be our excellent achievement. This is our mission. Whatever we have got—teach others. Distress, the whole world is... Did you recite these verses in Fiji [at the temple opening]?"

Yasodanandana: "Yes. We recited all these verses in Fiji, Prabhupada."

Prabhupada: "They appreciated?"

Yasodanandana: "Yes. They liked very much. They had never heard before."

Prabhupada: "The *gurukula* is meant for this purpose. Teach them and let them go around the world to teach. *Taroho e bhava-sindhu. Durlabha mānava-janama sat-saṅge, taroho e bhava-sindhu re [Bhajahu Re Mana].* This is our mission. [Pause] *Īśopaniṣad? Jijiveso?* What is that verse?"

Gurukripa immediately responded with the verse Prabhupada wanted: *"kurvann eveha karmāṇi jijīviṣec chataṁ samāḥ evaṁ tvayi nānyatheto 'stina karma lipyate nare [Īśopaniṣad Mantra 2]*

Prabhupada: "How many things we have to do for preaching, for teaching. And live hundreds of years. [devotees chuckle] That is *jijīviṣo śataṁ yaḥ?"*

Yasodanandana: "*Jijīviṣec chataṁ samāḥ.*"

After a short pause, Prabhupada informed his men, "We are receiving very good reports from Iran."

Tamal Krishna: "The royal family is taking to Krishna consciousness. I think even your Guru Maharaja would have been surprised to hear that, Prabhupada."

Prabhupada: "Everyone! If one is actually gentleman. So, we have this *gurukula*—good chance for teaching future preachers. Here is Yasodanandana Maharaja, and others. He can do. Prepare and send out. How much tremendous work we have to do!"

Brahmananda: "The whole world, Prabhupada."

Hari-sauri: "It's unlimited."

Prabhupada: "It is unlimited."

Tamal Krishna: "And you have to lead us, Prabhupada."

Prabhupada: "Yes, I am prepared—provided Krishna allows me."

Tamal Krishna: "Today you said Krishna is giving you the choice."

Prabhupada: "Hmm."

Hari-sauri: "In the *Bhāgavatam* you mention that Narada Muni has the free will to travel anywhere in the material and spiritual universe, so you must also have the same ability."

Tamal Krishna: "Today we were discussing how nice a devotee you are, Srila Prabhupada, that you are so faithful a servant and devotee of Lord Krishna that He

	allows you to do whatever you want, because He knows that you'll do everything for Him."
Prabhupada:	"*Viṣaya* means material activity. So one side is *viṣaya chāṛiyā, se rase majiyā* [*Sri Gaura-Nityānander Dayā*, 2]. One has to give up material activities and engage himself in Krishna consciousness. This is one side. Another side, my Guru Maharaja said, *kṛṣṇa sevāi yāṅhā kahe anukūla, viṣaya boliyā tāṅha haya bhula.* Anything which is favorable for *kṛṣṇa-sevā,* if we give up that business as *viṣaya,* that is mistake."
Tamal Krishna:	"Your life, Srila Prabhupada, is the most favorable thing in this whole world for spreading Krishna consciousness. You should not give it up."
Prabhupada:	"Anyway, Krishna has given us so many innocent boys. Yasodanandana Maharaja, teach them."
Yasodanandana:	"Yes, Prabhupada."
Prabhupada:	"Like you, superexcellent!"
Tamal Krishna:	"We are your innocent boys, Prabhupada."
Prabhupada:	(after a pause) "Let there be struggle for existence, for this purpose! What is the time?"
Tamal Krishna:	"9:15 p.m."
Prabhupada:	"*Nānā-śāstra-vicāraṇaika-nipuṇau*" [*Ṣaḍ-gosvāmy-aṣṭaka* 2].

87

Brahmananda:	"Srila Prabhupada? I was thinking that the religion of Jesus Christ has spread all over the world, and you are much greater than Jesus Christ. Your teachings are far, far greater, and your power is far, far greater. So if you remain here more, more years, then certainly this Krishna consciousness movement will spread all over the entire world."
Prabhupada:	"I am willing."
Brahmananda:	"Actually we could make this whole world Krishna conscious."
Prabhupada:	"Yes. It is not difficult."
Tamal Krishna:	"You said that you still want to see the world overflooded with Krishna consciousness. You said you wanted to see that happen."
Prabhupada:	"We can do that."
Tamal Krishna:	"As you instruct us, Srila Prabhupada, we will carry out your orders exactly."
Prabhupada:	"Two things: *viṣaya chāṛiyā*. Material motive should be given up, and everything should be engaged for Krishna's... whatever favorable. Then it will be..."

After a short break, Prabhupada again commented on how well his preachers in Iran were doing.

Prabhupada:	"Atreya Rishi is doing nice. Who is that Maharaja?"
Tamal Krishna:	"Parivrajakacharya Swami."
Prabhupada:	"Very nice. Good combination."

88

Tamal Krishna:	"He's been there now, Parivrajakacharya Swami, for, I think, two or three years. He's worked pretty faithfully there. He tricks them. In the guise of teaching a little *haṭha-yoga*, then he teaches bhakti."
Prabhupada:	"That is preaching."
Brahmananda:	(laughing) "You also tricked us, Srila Prabhupada, when you came to New York. You were just chanting Hare Krishna and speaking on *Bhagavad-gītā,* and we came and we listened, and then you took everything. You took our lives, took all of our money. [Devotees chuckle.] We left our families."
Prabhupada:	"There is a Bengali word, 'Enter like a needle and come out like a plough.'" Everyone was laughing, appreciating Prabhupada's transcendental trickery.
Prabhupada:	"If you say in the beginning, 'I am a plough,' he'll not allow you to enter. Say 'I am needle.' Let us try to serve Krishna. He'll give all intelligence. *Buddhi-yogaṁ dadāmi tam* [*Gītā* 10.10]. Now go on. Take rest."
Hari-sauri:	"*Jaya,* Srila Prabhupada."
Prabhupada:	"*Jaya ho.*"
Hari-sauri:	"Would you like some chanting?"
Prabhupada:	"Chanting I like always."

OCTOBER 10, 1977

This morning Bhavananda Goswami, Satadhanya

89

Swami, and Subhaga prabhu arrived. Prabhupada talked with Subhaga about Mayapur for a while. He's always anxious to hear what the news is there since the attack by the Muslims. Bhavananda Maharaja came in at about 7 a.m. with Tamal Krishna Maharaja. He informed Prabhupada about Mayapur. Prabhupada asked for details. They said everything was nice at Mayapur. Bhavananda told him that they were released by the magistrates for travelling and preaching within India. Previously they were restricted to Nadia. The next court hearing is set for November 29, and we are expecting that charges will be brought against the Mohammedans for attacking us.

Prabhupada:	"*Rākhe kṛṣṇa māre ke.*"
Bhavananda:	"As soon as we were released, Srila Prabhupada, I immediately came here. I'm free to stay here with you. When we heard that your health had gotten worse and worse, I realized that I'm totally dependent upon you for my very life and soul, Srila Prabhupada. "If you should leave, I don't..."

Bhavananda described how his men are distributing thousands of books, and at Haridaspur, 5,000 people took *prasādam* on Haridasa Ṭhakura's disappearance day.

Prabhupada asked what was the attitude of his Godbrothers.

Bhavananda responded positively, "Favorable and helpful." He described the monsoon floods—the Ganga came within fifteen inches of Bhaktisiddhanta Road. Our residents have reduced now, after the attack. We lost 20-25 devotees. We have 160, including 86 *gurukula* children. Older children are distributing many books

90

now, going out in the vans. In Calcutta they sell 100–150 books a day from a stall in Park Street.

Prabhupada listened carefully and with satisfaction. At the end he said that on the whole, everything was favorable. Then after a slight pause, "For myself, I will live or not live, it doesn't matter."

Tamal Krishna:	"Actually, Prabhupada, it may not matter for yourself, but it matters too much for us and for the world."
Prabhupada:	"Hmm."
Tamal Krishna:	"We don't want... You can't leave us now."
Prabhupada:	"I don't want, but if there is force..."
Tamal Krishna:	"But you said that Krishna would let you choose now. That you can live or go. Krishna has given you that choice."
Prabhupada:	"I am living still."

Tamal Krishna, as he so often does now, tried to encourage Prabhupada, listing all the many reasons why he should stay with us, "There's so much to be done, Srila Prabhupada. Your activities are not completed yet. We have to install the Deities in Bombay, you have to live in your palace in New Vrindaban, you have to show *varnashrama*, you have to complete the *Bhāgavatam*, you have to live in a new house in Mayapur, and we have to at least make a good start to begin the big temple in Mayapur. Everything is still incomplete, what to speak of the fact that we are all very much still neophyte. We need you more than anything else. This movement has to last ten thousand years. We're not ready yet. We're still very much conditioned and contaminated. If you stay with us for another ten years at least, then there's a chance that we can become more purified. And it's within you to be able to do that. Krishna will allow you to do that."

The talk of Mayapur piqued Prabhupada's interest, so Bhavananda continued painting an almost idyllic vision of our world headquarters. He said that the flood waters have receded and busloads of respectable people are coming, some offering service.

Bhavananda:	"Everyone at Mayapur is expecting you to come for the winter season. The sweet sunshine in Mayapur in the winter is the nicest, and the *prasādam* is the nicest. Everything is."

Tamal Krishna saw it as yet another reason for him to carry on with the struggle. "Actually, Srila Prabhupada, if it gets very cold here, it might be a good idea to go there."

Prabhupada:	(brightening up) "Yes."
Bhavananda:	"That sweet sun."
Subhaga:	"Yes, so nice, Prabhupada."
Tamal Krishna:	"Then January 1, we can go to Bombay for opening the temple. Then, if the temple is open, there should be not much work left, hopefully."
Bhavananda:	"The women at Mayapur are busy making *nimbu ācār.* The flowers will be blooming, wintertime flowers, so many nice flowers, so many nice *sabjīs.* But without Your Divine Grace's presence, Srila Prabhupada, it's not complete."
Tamal Krishna:	"Everything we've done there is for

92

you, Srila Prabhupada. Actually, everything we've done in this movement is for you. We don't know Krishna at all, Srila Prabhupada. We only know you."

Prabhupada was enjoying the loving exchange. He reciprocated their sentiments, "But I know you."

Subhaga: "If you, Prabhupada, stay, you can give us so much encouragement, simply your very presence."

Tamal Krishna: "I remember when we were last in Mayapur, Srila Prabhupada, before going to the Bombay pandal. Every morning we would take you upstairs, and you would sit in the sun, and Bhavananda Maharaja would massage you for two hours. Remember? You said you were getting your strength from that sun and the massage. And it's also very nice to take you around. Even as you say it's wonderful how we do it, but we like to take you in any condition, travelling.

"Actually, Srila Prabhupada, the motive behind everything we do is to please you. You must be present to accept whatever service. We are not very good servants, but whatever little we do, we do for you. Without you being present, we would lose our very reason for working hard and serving."

A little later, Prabhupada asked Tamal Krishna what he should eat. He said he didn't know.

Tamal Krishna: "At least in my mind it's a perplexing question which I don't know the answer to. In all of these events I have to face the reality I'm simply a completely bewildered fool. I can understand... I mean, I know you have to, if you're to get better, you have to be able to eat something. I don't know what to suggest, though."

Upendra: "Srila Prabhupada, I think that just as you gradually decreased your eating and drinking and became very weak, so you should increase gradually, very carefully. Yesterday you drank barley water and grape juice, and you didn't come down with a cough. So if you increase just a little barley water and mung water, then after a few days thin milk, maybe some Complan, and then gradually increase the resistance."

They had a slightly prolonged discussion on the merits of milk, barley water, and Complan, and even that exchange tired Prabhupada. "I want to sleep."

Tamal Krishna: "Should I massage you a little to help you sleep? Okay. Where should I massage you especially? Which part?"

Prabhupada: "Any part."

Tamal Krishna: "But I think it's very important that you take something to drink. By

drinking something it'll give you
a little reason to sleep better. The
program this morning should be
that you drink something now, then
take rest, and then, after resting,
then we'll bathe you."

Eventually he took some barley water and Complan. Then he coughed up for ten to fifteen minutes. The drink had immediately turned to mucus. Prabhupada complained of weakness and went to sleep to try and recuperate. Actually, he spends most of the time resting and hearing the chanting. Conversations tire him very much.

When he awoke, Prabhupada took a sponge bath. Later on his Godbrother Dr. O.B.L. Kapoor, came. He offered to call a doctor for Prabhupada. He knows a man from Agra, Dr. Vyas. Prabhupada agreed to see him. Also, one old Ayurvedic doctor, Raj Vaidya Pandit Lakshmi-Narayan, was called. He keeps *mauna* and writes on a slate with chalk to communicate. He prescribed a few things and left after half an hour.

Later, Ramesvara Swami came in, and Prabhupada immediately inquired further about the restaurant in Iran—what do they serve and who does the cooking. Ramesvara said the restaurant is always full. Prabhupada asked if Nandarani was cooking. Ramesvara said yes, and others also. And a special attraction is that they play song tapes of Prabhupada, and people buy his books from a table in the main entrance.

Ramesvara: "For now they are selling *Bhagavad-gītā, Back to Godhead,* and Satsvarupa Maharaja's book. That is also being sold. They are just now printing the first Persian *Back*

95

to Godhead, and in three months'
time the *Bhagavad-gītā* in Persian
translation will be completed."

It was all good news. Prabhupada was very pleased to
hear they were already looking for a bigger place. He
asked about the weather there.

Prabhupada:	"Hmm. Very warm nowadays?"
Ramesvara:	"During the day it is just like here— 80, 85 degrees. In the early morning and in the evening sometimes a little chilly."
Prabhupada:	"At night snowfall?"
Ramesvara:	"No."
Jayatirtha:	"Snow starts around December in Tehran."
Ramesvara:	"This is the best time in Tehran, the fall, autumn season. Parivrajakacharya Maharaja told me that the Indian ambassador to Iran spoke with him and told him, 'You are the real ambassador of India.' "
Prabhupada:	"Why?"
Ramesvara:	"Because he is becoming friendly with the royal family. Actually, he goes every day to the palace. They send a chauffeured Mercedes to pick him up every day. He spends four or five hours every day talking to the royal family."
Prabhupada:	(smiling appreciatively) "It is great opportunity."
Jayatirtha:	"It's the wealthiest family in the world, much more wealthy than

	Rockefeller."
Prabhupada:	"He goes alone or with somebody else?"
Ramesvara:	"For now he's going alone. They are very interested in hatha yoga also, and he knows something of it, so he teaches them. The prince and the princess have already become vegetarian."
Prabhupada:	"And they are not making any *chānā* preparation?"

Tamal Krishna got confused. He thought he meant *chana dal,* chickpeas.

Prabhupada:	"Not chickpeas."
Jayatirtha:	"Cheese."
Tamal Krishna:	"Oh, *chānā.* [Laughs] Yes, cheese; right, cheese."
Jayatirtha:	"Any vegetable?"
Ramesvara:	"Sometimes they make one *sabjī* with eggplant, tomatoes, and fried cheese, very nice wet *sabjī.* Actually, that's one of the *sabjīs* every day in the restaurant."

At this point, Doctor Vyas from Agra came. Dr. Kapoor said he had met him quite fortuitously. "He came here by chance for darshan. Only this morning Prabhupada and I were talking that he should be called from Agra. Accidentally, when I went to bring the *vaidya,* I saw his car on the way. I stopped them."

The doctor was very respectful and reverential to Prabhupada. "I had my desire in my life to see him once, and that God has fulfilled."

Prabhupada said it was Krishna's arrangement.

97

He was a nice man, sympathetic to Prabhupada's aversion to hospitals and injections. After lengthy discussion, he advised that Prabhupada must get some energy and thought Glucose would be very good for that. We showed him some vitamins and the protein drink, and he said they also would be good. He prescribed three syrups: Santivini, Digiplex, and Neurovion. And to increase his protein intake, he prescribed whey.

A little later, Prabhupada discussed with Satadhanya Swami about the communists and the situation in Bengal. Satadhanya was optimistic. He said everyone takes *prasādam*, and they have kirtan. "They are so-called communists. Actually, Bengalis are devotees, Srila Prabhupada. Simply that they know your name is enough to purify all of Bengal, what to speak of if you remain present; the whole world will become completely flooded by *kṛṣṇa-prema*. That is why we are begging you, Srila Prabhupada, that you remain with us for some time longer, because we are very weak and are still attached to material sense gratification. But if you are present, it is like a transcendental ocean."

As they talked, Prabhupada complained about some strain in his left hip, and had some Vicks rubbed into it. Now he keeps his left leg bent and resting on a pillow to prevent the strain.

Prabhupada called for Bhakti Charu and Bhavananda and asked about the reaction to his books in Bengal. Bhavananda replied that they get "huge amounts" of mail every day asking for Prabhupada's books. The Bengali *Gītā* is about to be published.

During the day a general meeting of the GBCs was held to assess the present situation and decide how best to deal with it. Points were made that Prabhupada has called us all here for a special purpose. Now that Prabhupada has agreed to stay, we should not think that we can immediately go back to our zones. He has called us to chant for him.

Eventually it was decided that we should all stay at least one week and then meet again on October 16. Tamal Krishna Maharaja made a proposal that at least four GBC members should be with Prabhupada from now on, with the secretary extra. That proposal was deferred until the next meeting.

After the GBC meeting, Harikesa took in seven new books to show Prabhupada. Prabhupada was ecstatic. Harikesa showed him the Yugoslavian *Īśopaniṣad*. They printed 10,000 copies. It has been highly praised by a famous Yugoslavian professor.

Harikesa: "We made it very scholarly, because I remember last time you said it should be very scholarly. We printed ten thousand copies of this."

Prabhupada: "Selling?"

Harikesa: "Yes, we can sell these like anything, because in Yugoslavia we can pretend we're going to Greece, and we can bring as many as we like, and then we can sell them."

Prabhupada: "So why not print ten million?"

Harikesa: "I only had time to print ten thousand, Srila Prabhupada. We did it in one day, from the flats to this book in one day, just so I could bring it to you."

Then he showed *Śrīmad-Bhāgavatam* Second Canto, First Volume, in German, 20,000 copies. Prabhupada looked through it with obvious appreciation. It had a beautiful photo of Sri Sri Radha-Londonisvara on the front.

Prabhupada: "Finely printed. Everything first-class."

Next he showed *Śrīmad-Bhāgavatam* Second Canto, Second Volume, with a picture of Radha-Govindadevji in Jaipur. Prabhupada thought the pictures were so attractive, they alone would sell the book. He asked the selling price. Harikesa told him,"About 8–9 marks." Next he showed *Śrīmad-Bhāgavatam* Second Canto, Part Three, with the German Deities from Schloss Rettershoff, Sri-Sri-Radha-Madana-mohana, on the front. Then he showed *Kṛṣṇa* in three volumes, 60,000 copies of the first volume and 35,000 of parts two and three.

Seeing the impressive display, Tamal Krishna exclaimed, "Wow. Look at Ramesvara. He jumped at that."

Prabhupada laughed brightly. He has long promoted transcendental competition among his disciples, especially when it involves his books, and declared, "He's defeated!"—meaning Harikesa had defeated Ramesvara in his printing efforts.

Prabhupada: "Ramesvara Maharaja, how do you like?"

Ramesvara was happy to concede.

Ramesvara: "Oh, yes. These books are very good. The most incredible thing. The printer can print them faster than anywhere else in the world. From the day he gives the book to the printer and the day the printer ships it, it is faster than anywhere else in the world."

Harikesa: "The printer has invited all the BBT trustees from all over the world, and he will pay their fare, and he will say he will beat everybody's price in

100

	the whole world for printing."
Prabhupada:	"Then why not print there?"
Ramesvara:	"He wants us to go to do the research next month, in November."
Prabhupada:	"So go. If you get cheaper and nicer, why not?"
Ramesvara:	"We're planning to go and research it very carefully."

Altogether the printings of the seven books totaled 200,000. Ramesvara couldn't resist exclaiming that in America they had printed 1,500,000 copies of just one book. And that next year they planned to double that.

As Harikesa informed him that they were also laying out the Arabic *Bhagavad-gītā* and the Polish *Easy Journey,* Prabhupada couldn't contain his emotion. He started crying, he was so ecstatic. A year ago, Harikesa had been Prabhupada's personal secretary here in Vrindavan, but Prabhupada had sent him back to Europe under what seemed rather fraught circumstances. At the time, Harikesa had taken it as a kind of punishment, but Prabhupada had seen his disciple's greater potential. Now as he saw the fruits of Harikesa's hard work and intelligence, with tears flooding his eyes and voice choking, Prabhupada told us, "He was rotting here, typewriting. I said, 'You go.' I had ten servants. He thought that I am degrading him. No. Now you understand?"

Harikesa began sobbing, "Yes, I understand, Prabhupada."

"So, here is an intelligent boy," Prabhupada went on. "Why he should rot here, typewriting?"

He paused and then continued impressing upon his disciples the same preaching mood and sense of urgency he imbibed from his own spiritual master, to print books at any cost. "Whatever deficiencies are

101

there, that is excused by Guru Maharaja. Go on printing, go on printing. Deficiency will be corrected, next, next, next. I printed *Bhāgavata* in that way, so many defects. 'All right. Whatever is printed, that's all.' But these are first-class. There is no defect. German printing is very pure. They have got the first-class machine. So, we have got so many centers. Wherever cheaper and better printing can be gotten, we may take from there. That's all right. Thank you."

Harikesa could barely speak, his voice was choked with gratitude and emotion. "Thank you, Srila Prabhupada. Now you just have to become better, healthier."

Prabhupada was ironic, "Healthy? I have nothing to do with this body! I have to do with the spiritual world."

A short while later, Bhagavan prabhu gave more good news about how many books his zone was doing; all over Europe, book distribution is booming. They are aiming to distribute over 20,000 big books in one week. Italy is doing 3,000 a week. He said they are doing it to encourage Prabhupada to stay.

Prabhupada was full of gratitude, "Bhaktisiddhanta Sarasvati will give them blessings. He wanted this."

Later in the evening, Tamal Krishna Maharaja was called. Prabhupada asked again what the crisis days were. Tamal Krishna told him, "Tomorrow is the first one."

Prabhupada's response was languid, "I think every day is crisis day."

Kirtanananda Maharaja tried to encourage him, "You're not under the control of material energy, Prabhupada."

But his physical condition remains precarious, and his response was enervated, "Things are coming bad to worse."

Prabhupada did increase his liquid intake, though, to about 450 milliliters, and he is taking some Glucose in his drinks.

OCTOBER 11, 1977

Prabhupada had a restful night, and in the morning Dr. O.B.L. Kapoor again visited with the Ayurvedic doctor, Pandit Lakshmi-Narayan. Prabhupada complained about a feeling of intoxication, but this was explained as being an effect of taking Glucose and protein drink after not ingesting anything for the last few days. Prabhupada hasn't taken any of the syrup prescribed by the allopathic doctor, but today he is taking some of his medicine.

After the doctor left, Dr. Kapoor was asking about the coming scientific conference which is being held here by our scientists. An introductory booklet announced it as "Bhaktivedanta Institute Lecture Series on the Origin of Life and Matter, sponsored by Bhaktivedanta Institute." Over ninety and up to one hundred and fifty Indian scientists are expected for the three-day meet. Madhava, Rupanuga, Brahmananda, and others explained that the main topic to be presented is that life cannot come from matter.

Asked if he felt better today, Prabhupada said overall he was not any better. Nevertheless he began to speak about the scientists. He asked Dr. Kapoor, "On the whole, the nature of the conference, how do you like?"

Dr. Kapoor thought it a good idea. He laughed, "The conference should be interesting at least."

Prabhupada: "Without life, life coming is bogus— Darwin's theory."

He declared as nonsense all different modern theories by Vivekananda, Gandhi, Ramtirtha, and Darwin. He asked if they'd all been discussed in the booklet.

Dr. Kapoor: "The most wonderful thing is that they say life comes from matter, and

103

they don't know what matter is. They confess, 'We don't know what matter is.' Yet they say life comes from matter. Not one scientist till today has been able to say what matter is. Rather, they have confessed. You see, they say, 'I know not what matter is.' "

Prabhupada: "And the person from whom life is coming, He says *aham ādir hi* (*Gītā* 10.2). And they will not accept."

Madhava prabhu orally listed a few of the invited speakers, all scientists, mainly from Delhi and surrounding areas.

Dr. Kapoor noted a little critically that no philosophers had been asked to make a presentation. "Ah, no, but is any of the philosophers going to speak?"

Madhava: "No."

Dr. Kapoor: "So you'll not go to the root of the problem, you see. It will be something superficial."

Madhava: "We consider the philosophers to be superficial. They have no evidence to back up their words."

Dr. Kapoor (laughing) "That can be a subject for discussion by itself. All the modern scientists are taking to philosophy, because there comes a stage in scientific investigation where you cannot but philosophize."

Madhava: "Yes. But the philosophers cannot continue in their own speculations."

Dr. Kapoor: "What is philosophy? Philosophy is

104

not thinking in vacuum. Philosophy is systematic thinking. The scientists must be systematic."

Prabhupada: "The scientists... Without systematic, how it is science?"

Dr. Kapoor: "Yes. And the science is basically unsystematic in the fact that it starts with certain assumptions, which by itself is unscientific. Why should you start with certain assumptions? Philosophy does not commit that. Philosophy... I don't raise the questions. You see? Why do you believe that matter is ultimate? Why do you believe that spirit and time are ultimate? Science believes in assumptions. Philosophy has not taken for granted. Very systematic thinking, really. Therefore, I say you'll not go to the root of the matter. It will be just superficial things."

Madhava: "We are trying to apply both. We are adding the philosophy into this science."

Dr. Kapoor: "Yes, both. As a matter of fact, there is no watertight compartment. They're not simply a part of each. They're dovetailed. Science penetrates into philosophy."

Rupanuga: "But the root of the problem practically is whether life comes from matter or matter comes from life, and that is the basic theme."

Dr. Kapoor: "That is the basic theme, but the philosopher will ask the question, 'You must first be very clear in your mind about these basic concepts, "What is life and what is matter?" You may have some idea about life. Because we are life ourselves, we have some experience, some idea of life. But what is matter? No scientist has any clear conception of matter."

Prabhupada of course had his own basic definition: "Matter has no consciousness."

There was some back and forth, and Prabhupada joined in a little, becoming enlivened in anticipation of the conference and the bold approach being presented by his men.

Prabhupada was speaking with great effort, and Dr. Kapoor thought their philosophical discussion was a strain for him. But Prabhupada was animated by it. "No. It is nonsense that matter gives life. That we want to prove. Matter, I have studied it. Life is superior energy. *Apareyam.* This matter is useless. *Bhūmir āpo 'nalo vāyuḥ khaṁ manaḥ* [*Gītā* 7.4]. They are inferior. *Apareyam itas tv viddhi me prakṛtim.* Another, *yayedaṁ dhāryate jagat* [*Gītā* 7.5]. This is actually governing the whole universe. They are defying this *apareyaṁ me prakṛtim, parā.* They are not accepting. The scientists are speculators, most of them. Philosopher means materially thinking."

Dr. Kapoor took his leave, having made his pitch for philosophy. Prabhupada said he is a *smārta.* Actually, he was a little put out because he hadn't been invited to speak, although he has been given an invite to attend. We were glad to see him leave so Prabhupada wouldn't be further strained.

Around noon, Atreya Rishi and Parivrajakacharya Swami arrived from Iran, bearing with them a plate of sweet lemons, plums, and oranges. Prabhupada was pleased and asked for some of the juice. He had Atreya Rishi sit near him, and Parivrajakacharya gave Prabhupada a copy of the first Persian magazine, called "*Bhakti*." Prabhupada liked it.

Having been prepped by Ramesvara about their amazing preaching, Prabhupada was keen to hear their account firsthand. "I understand that you go to the royal family and talk with them for hours."

Parivrajakacharya: "Yes."

Prabhupada: "This is very good sign."

Parivrajakacharya: "Yes, some people in their family are very good and interested in learning about *Bhagavad-gītā* and Krishna consciousness. They can do very good things for the world if they simply have knowledge what to do. So we're trying to preach to intelligent people."

Prabhupada: "Yes, intelligent. *Yad yad ācarati śreṣṭhas tat tad evetaro janaḥ* [*Gītā* 3.21]. What intelligent man takes up, so ordinary man, ordinary generally follow. *Bhagavad-gītā* is meant for *rājarṣi*, not for foolish. *Imaṁ rājarṣayo viduḥ* [*Gītā* 4.2]. Not for a so-called loafer class. *Imaṁ vivasvate yogaṁ proktavān aham* [*Gītā* 4.1]. That is being mistaken. *Bhagavad-gītā* should be taught to such royal family, and if they take up, others will take up. Hmm?

Atreya Rishi? Do you follow?"

Atreya Rishi: "Yes, Prabhupada."

Prabhupada inquired about the property he had been taken to see last year. "The same building I went to see?"

Atreya Rishi: "*Jaya*, Prabhupada. That building is now a restaurant. Many people come every night and take *prasādam*. Seventy to one hundred come."

Prabhupada: "What do you supply?"

Atreya Rishi: "One *thali*—two vegetables, dal, rice, salad, sweet, then herbal tea and dessert and sometimes fruits."

Prabhupada: "They like it?"

Atreya Rishi: "They like it very much. Nandarani and Dayananda are managing."

Prabhupada: "They are both intelligent. What do you charge?"

Parivrajakacharya: "About sixteen rupees for one plate."

Atreya Rishi: "A very reasonable price, but many people give donations, and many of them take your books. They take and read and love it."

Prabhupada's eyes lit up, "Success!"
I asked what kind of people were coming. Prabhupada laughed as if I should have known. "High class!" he exclaimed. "The low class, they purchase a big roti! They cannot come to the restaurant."

Atreya Rishi: "Some people, higher class people, even come and work. They give their service in the restaurant. They wash

dishes; they serve tables. We engage
them in *bhakti- yoga.*"

Deeply satisfied, Prabhupada certified their efforts.

Prabhupada: "So you've made good progress."

Atreya Rishi: (humbly crediting his spiritual
master) "It's your mercy,
Prabhupada. They respect you a lot
in Tehran."

Prabhupada: "Persian civilization, very high Aryan
civilization. Things are going very
nice—slow but sure." He glanced
lovingly at Brahmananda, who
was also preaching in difficult
circumstances, and playfully melded
their efforts. "You have got this
Persian civilization, and he has got
the African. Black and white!"

Prabhupada sat up for a drink and declared that he
was very much pleased by the report from Persia.

Atreya Rishi: "You should come and visit us,
Prabhupada."

Ever-enthusiastic for preaching, Prabhupada smiled, "I
am ready to go immediately."

Atreya Rishi: "Yes, you will come, Prabhupada.
There are millions of people waiting
for you."

Being belayed to his bed made that a sweet dream only.
"Now you have to take a bundle of bones," he answered
sardonically. "That is the difficulty. There is nothing
but a bundle of bones."

Bhakti Charu: "Bone or flesh, your body is divine, Prabhupada."

Prabhupada: (declaring defiantly) "Bone is being separated from life! Here by example, matter is different from life. Matter is inferior, life is superior—from my life example!"

After a moment, Prabhupada questioned Atreya Rishi, "Why do the Persian people love me?"

Atreya Rishi: "They respect your philosophy, Prabhupada. They understand the philosophy. They respect the philosophy."

Prabhupada: "Very good."

Atreya Rishi: "They respect chanting. They see that your boys are pious and they're chanting the names of God, and they see them doing wonderful things, and they respect it. They see your books. Wonderful philosophy, always glorifying God. They respect God, they're religious."

Prabhupada: "Oh, yes."

Atreya Rishi: "And they know that no one else is doing this."

Prabhupada: "Persians, they are Aryans. When they were attacked by the Mohammedans they fled from Persia to India."

Atreya Rishi informed him that now some of the Parsees have returned to Iran and visit the restaurant every night and are respectful. He told Prabhupada that they respect him because he is the only one who is

110

engaging anyone in devotional service. They have high philosophy, but no one is practically engaging them.

Prabhupada was tremendously pleased with his disciples' efforts, which had yielded results far beyond his expectation. "So as soon as I get opportunity I shall go and meet them. Thank you very much." Then they began to chant. Parivrajakacharya Maharaja led, and Prabhupada sat up and listened. He asked for Parivrajakacharya to come over to the bed. As Parivrajakacharya knelt by his side, Prabhupada reached out and lovingly stroked his head back and forth. "Thank you so much. You are a great *rājarṣi!* So do it very nicely. Don't commit mistake. Present the philosophy. Make them *rājarṣi.*"

Prabhupada told him it was a very good chance.

Parivrajakacharya: "These people are the door to rulers all over the world, because they are the closest friends of King Khalid of Saudi Arabia, King Hussein of Jordan, King Constantine and Queen Tina of Greece. They know all over the world this whole set of rulers who have great opulence and great intelligence and who simply lack spiritual knowledge."

Prabhupada: "Guidance."

Parivrajakacharya: "They lack guidance. They lack brahmans. Instead, they have cunning ministers who simply want to have the same opulence as they have. But these are the people who can change the world. If we can only give them philosophy, they can do the..."

Prabhupada agreed, "Raja. And if we turn them rishi, then our mission is fulfilled. Very good." To Atreya Rishi he noted, "Now you have started your own business."

Atreya Rishi:	"*Jaya*, Srila Prabhupada. With your blessing. The business is not important, but it is a medium for Krishna consciousness. My secretary is already a devotee, and the other people are also becoming interested. The goal is to have a Krishna conscious group working in the society."
Prabhupada:	"Go very slowly. Never mind. You are all young men. All right. Go on chanting."

After two minutes, Prabhupada turned his head towards Parivrajakacharya. "So, you take care of your health."

I told Prabhupada, "It's your health we want to take care of." Prabhupada smiled.

At about 6 p.m., Prabhupada called for Tamal Krishna Maharaja. He and several other leaders were again meeting and planning together how to make the Gita Nagari farm successful. Bhavananda Maharaja, Paramananda, Vamanadeva, Dhrstadyumna Maharaja, Tripurari Maharaja, Balavanta, and Rupanuga were all attending. Also present was Dhrstadyumna's brother Bill, an architect, whose firm, Tamal Krishna informed Prabhupada, is doing a big project for the Shah of Iran.

The mention of Iran evoked in Prabhupada further deep appreciation of his disciples' preaching there. "I was very happy when I heard, respectable gentlemen, out of love, they are washing dishes. You know that? Atreya Rishi told me."

Hari-sauri:	"Yes. In Iran. Some important people in Iran, just out of some... to do some service, they're even going in the restaurant and assisting by washing the dishes, and they're bringing things here and there."
Tamal Krishna:	"Phew. It's really devotional."
Prabhupada:	"They are so gentle."

Tamal Krishna Maharaja briefed Prabhupada on their ambitious plans to make Gita Nagari an ideal place for preaching and living, by demonstrating *varnashrama*. But his real concern was to express our heartfelt desire that Srila Prabhupada continue to lead us by remaining present.

"Everything is there, but you have to be there. Otherwise, I don't know if it's actually possible. And it's very important. You have to get better, Srila Prabhupada. We're prepared to stay with you—all of the devotees feel this way—to encourage you to get better. Our plans are there, we're there, but we need you. You have to be there with us to guide us. I think that this disease is simply Krishna testing our love for you, Srila Prabhupada, so that we will learn that we fully need you, because actually we do. Everything we've done in this movement, you've guided us. We're realizing that you have to continue to guide us. We're not self-realized. We are simply able to carry out your instructions. So we have nothing else to do but to be with you here until you get healthy again and then lead us. This is our business now—to be with you.

"It seems like there are so many opportunities now that are beginning to present themselves. When you first went to the West there was nothing at all, and you created a whole world of Krishna consciousness. And now the public is beginning to actually take a real interest in our movement, and people, respectable people from all over the world, are coming forward to want to help our movement. So there's a great facility that's available now even more than ten years ago. So, if we've made so much progress in ten years, in another ten years there's no way to measure how much our movement can be expanded. And we're all just ready to follow each one of your directions. You don't have to tax yourself by... You can just talk to us and tell us, and we'll act. And we're very happy. In the meantime, we will give you the medicine of *hari-nāma*."

Prabhupada:　　(smiling) "Hmm. That is real medicine."

Tamal Krishna:　"I think that our being here and chanting before you is spreading this movement, because the more we chant, the more love and dependence we develop for you, and that's making us strong in our Krishna consciousness, and therefore our movement is getting stronger. Every day that we stay here, we become stronger in our devotion for you and dependence on you."

Tamal Krishna Maharaja did his best to beseech Prabhupada to remain with us. "Actually, you have to get better, Srila Prabhupada. Kirtanananda Maharaja has built this palace. It's only meant for you. We were seeing pictures of it today. It is so beautiful. It is exactly the place that you want to retire in and translate. And this community of Gita Nagari will be just the proper place to give direction how to establish nice spiritual community. These two places are very close to each other—New Vrindaban and Gita Nagari. They're only

114

three hours away from each other. Two very good communities for showing the example of how to spread ideal Vedic life.

"We were discussing that actually it is not anything new that Krishna can make His devotee better, because we were reading before in the *Caitanya-caritāmṛta* how sometimes Lord Chaitanya would bring back to life someone who had even expired. And His associates were able to do that. And there are many cases. I think if we are very determined, then Krishna will surely fulfil our desire."

Prabhupada responded simply and wonderfully, "Without fail."

Tamal Krishna:	"What, Srila Prabhupada?"
Prabhupada:	"Without fail."
Tamal Krishna:	"Without fail." [Chuckles]
Hari-sauri:	"Jaya!"
Tamal Krishna:	"And I can see even though this is a difficult time, actually it's still very sublime, because... This is wonderful, that all of your senior disciples are coming, and we're all chanting, and you're hearing, and we're hearing. And actually, it's a very wonderful... Even though it's critical, it's very wonderful, because we're all chanting the holy name. And then gradually Krishna will answer our prayers. And in the meantime, we're becoming purified by chanting like this, and you're pleased by hearing our chanting. Most people, when they are ill— everything is very horrible. But this

115

is very different. It's all spiritual. So we're very satisfied. Of course, we want you to get better immediately. But still, as long as it takes, we're very satisfied to remain chanting and expecting Krishna's mercy at every moment."

The intimacy of Tamal Krishna Maharaja's exchanges with His Divine Grace has deepened markedly in the last few months in his service as personal secretary. It is no longer simply a question of managerial efficiency and responsibility. Their reciprocations go way beyond the traditional teacher-student formalities; they are often deeply sublime, loving personal interactions, revealing a depth of bonding most of us have not witnessed or experienced before.

During the day, Giriraj had gone to Delhi to arrange to transfer the Vrindavan Fixed Deposits lodged here at the PNB, to their main Delhi branch. He came and gave a report in the evening. His trip was very successful. He met with the chairman and the assistant general manager. They told him that the local manager who is giving us the most trouble will be removed. The assistant Delhi manager will also come here to Vrindavan on Saturday with his family to check everything and take *prasādam*. The fact that Prabhupada is hearing this kind of report is good because it means that he is not thinking of leaving us.

Today Prabhupada took 620 milliliters of juices, the most since September 30. In the night, Kirtanananda Swami had Prabhupada sitting up, persuading him to breathe deeply.

116

OCTOBER 12, 1977

Prabhupada had some more sweet-lemon juice this morning, but now he is coughing much more than usual. We tried sitting him up to prevent the coughing, but he complained of pain around his seat. He has a sore there, so when he sits it is painful, and he needs to frequently adjust his posture.

Lokanath Swami came in mid-morning and gave a short report on his party's distribution of Prabhupada books, selling many in Hindi and a few in Bengali.

Around noon, Dr. Ghosh Sinha from Kodaikanal arrived. He came in and looked quite shocked to see Prabhupada's condition. Prabhupada didn't speak anything. When he went out, Prabhupada called Tamal Krishna Maharaja to ask who had called Dr. Ghosh. Tamal Krishna said he hadn't but he thought it must be one of Hamsaduta Swami's men acting on his own. Prabhupada has already rejected the doctor's treatment last June, so for him to see him again now is a botheration for Prabhupada. Now that he has been called here, Prabhupada is forced to see him so that the doctor is not offended. Perhaps seeing that he could do little to contribute to Prabhupada's treatment, he left after a short time.

Prabhupada's old friend Dr. G. Ghosh from Allahabad was also discussed, and Prabhupada said a man may be sent to see him. Dr. Ghosh wants Prabhupada to go into a nursing clinic, but Prabhupada absolutely rejects that. However, he is willing to receive some personal treatment. Later, at 2:30 p.m., Prabhupada told the devotees to try to contact him by telephone first, as it is quicker.

Kirtanananda Swami offered to take charge of administering Prabhupada's medical care. Prabhupada

117

said it was all right, but as soon as Maharaja hinted that it may mean his admission in a medical facility, Prabhupada reacted emphatically that there must be no hospitalization. He repeated this twice. Kirtanananda is convinced that under some stricter treatment, Prabhupada will recover more easily. He feels that he may be able to get Prabhupada to follow a regular system by being a little insistent with him.

Prabhupada coughed up some mucus and commented that with milk or fruit juice the result is mucus-generating.

Jayapataka Swami came at 1:00 p.m. and gave Prabhupada a detailed report of Mayapur and other centers. Legal restrictions and bail conditions imposed on our men after the attack have been eased, and so he was able to visit two centers in Orissa: Bhubaneswar and Bhadrak, where a disciple of one of Prabhupada's Godbrothers has donated via Lokanath Swami a Gaura-Gopala Mandir, along with twenty-four bighas (about eight acres) of land. Jayapataka told Prabhupada about some success in the preaching there, "Lord Chaitanya went there on occasion. It's in the *Caitanya-caritāmṛta*. It mentions the place. And the people who have given us the temple are descendants of the devotee with whom Lord Chaitanya stayed. They're the same family. So they're very enthusiastic, and they want to give all help. Although it's a small place, they've already made a couple of Life Patron members, and they're trying to collect donations. There's a college there, and some of the professors come regularly to the temple, and they are chanting *japa* and bringing their students and other colleagues."

He said there is also an offer of another one hundred bighas with a goshala nearby, and local people are eager to support us.

In Haridaspur, near the Bengal-Bangladesh border,

Bhakti-prabhava Swami held their Janmastami festival and two thousand people came. They had a huge crowd. Some devotees from Mayapur attended, and all the local villagers helped organize the whole thing.

Apart from that, Jayapataka said the Mayapur *gurukula* was running well, with about eighty students. Some of the older boys went to Darjeeling on book distribution, selling seven thousand books in less than ten days. Another party is still in Bihar, and they did four thousand books in Bengali and Hindi.

Srila Prabhupada was highly pleased to hear how the preaching is continuing to advance. When Mayapur was attacked there was a lot of bad publicity, especially against the "foreign" devotees, but the situation now seems to have reversed. Many more people are inquiring through the mail about our activities, and the Muslims who attacked us have changed their tune.

Jayapataka: "They want that the case be dropped and that they be given jobs, like before. They're sending messengers requesting that there should be some type of agreement whereby the charges against them are dropped, the case is dropped, and that they're given the old jobs back."

We all laughed at the reversal, but Prabhupada was in no mood to be generous. "The charges are made by the government. We cannot drop. Do you follow?"

Jayapataka: "Yes. The charges can't be dropped by us, but if the two parties make a type of compromise agreement and file a petition to the court..."

Prabhupada: "But now the fight is not between them and us. The fight is between

119

government and them."

Jayapataka: "Many barristers in Calcutta say that if due to political pressure, this or that, some people come and ask us to try to file a petition for dropping charges, that there's no need to do that, because the case is well in our favor."

Prabhupada: "Yes. If you drop, they get opportunity."

Jayapataka: "Yes. No, we have no intention to drop the charges. That will not clear our name. The day I returned, the General Secretary of the State Congress Party, Mr. K. K. Sukla, just happened to visit our mandir, and he heard the whole story, and he said that he'll give whatever support he can, and if they get back into any power, then he will see that our programs get full assistance.

"Then our lawyer told us that he has been talking to some ministers in the present Communist government, and they're saying that they're willing to support our Movement if we do some works that are beneficial for the people. They're not saying that we're not doing any now, but for any future other things, like the bridges or the schemes we have, they're willing to give us support. By your mercy everything is gradually changing around."

Jayapataka also said that one tantric astrologer in Mayapur had told Bhavananda two weeks ago that he would soon be called to Vrindavan along with all our society leaders. This man said that Prabhupada was a kind of avatar especially empowered by God, so he was free to choose whether to come or go.

As far as his future prediction went, he said the present illness would end by November 28 (Venus enters another house on this day), and that it could take another month to recuperate, and then there would be no further illness for seven years.

Jayapataka: "He said that he is praying that Krishna will keep you here, because without a pure devotee in the world then everything becomes dark."

Prabhupada listened attentively but didn't comment.

Jayapataka Maharaja brought his report to a close with an optimistic account about our food-distribution program.

"The West Bengal Council for Child Welfare and the West Bengal Government Health Department Inspector came out and inspected our distribution. We have five centers where we distribute five days a week, Monday through Friday, the foodstuffs. We eat another thing given by the government. We prepare that and offer it to the Deity and distribute that from our temple as well as from a nearby village. The local villagers help to distribute. Right now twelve hundred people are taking every day. So they were very satisfied with the arrangement. And one of the centers is Mayapur village, they had been refusing to take, and he said, 'You just change and put into another village. They're not the only poor people in the world. Any other village can take.' They are very favorable to our program. They've given us a full quota that daily 1,846 people can get food, and they'll bear the costs of the grain and oil."

Prabhupada: "What is this preparation?"

Jayapataka: "It's wheat that's chipped. It's called bulgar wheat. It's wheat that's chipped into small pieces. It's like oversized suji, about three times the size of suji, and that's boiled and cooked with oil and some gur and spices. Or it can also be cooked with vegetables and spices. It's supposed to be nutritious, healthy, strength-giving food."

He said our Muslim neighbors had tried to interfere but failed. "Mayapur Muslims tried to get the other Muslims in other villages not to take it, because it was being given by us, but they said, 'Why we shouldn't take? Just because you're giving them trouble doesn't mean we shouldn't take.' So now they've all rebelled, and now they're all taking *prasādam*. He gave us an address where we can possibly get powdered milk also."

Prabhupada: "It is mixed with powdered milk?"

Jayapataka: "What we have right now isn't mixed with powdered milk. We want to mix powdered milk with it, but this department ran out of powdered milk, so another department has it. They give oil to cook it in, like *halavā* type, vegetable oil. It's like a cereal that they have in the West, in America and some places. Like *dalya* they call in Western India."

Prabhupada was listening carefully. Distribution of

prasādam has always been one of his most important preaching programs. "They take it relishably?" he asked.

Jayapataka: "Yes."

Prabhupada: "How much they can take?"

Jayapataka: "Well, the government calculates that each person gets eighty grams of *dalya* and seven grams of oil, and when that's cooked that comes to nearly about four, five hundred grams cooked per head. It's about three clay cups; three, four clay cups."

Overall, Jayapataka's report was very pleasing to Prabhupada, and the upswing in preaching heartened everyone. Hearing such news seems as rejuvenating as any medicines.

In mid-afternoon, as he received his guests and reports, Prabhupada's sister, Bhavatarini dasi, known amongst our devotees as Pisima (Aunty), arrived from Calcutta, and she came straight in to see him. Prabhupada told the devotees to call her son, who is now residing at the Imlitala Maṭha, and give them rooms in the guesthouse.

Prabhupada spent most of the afternoon sitting up despite having a bed-sore, because as soon as he lays down his lungs fill up with mucus.

OCTOBER 13, 1977

After giving his report yesterday on the practical preaching, Jayapataka Swami returned to Prabhupada's bedside this morning and opened his heart and expressed some of his and the other devotees' emotions. "At first some of the devotees were disturbed, but after the Balarama's Appearance and the Jhulan Pūrṇimā procession, that gave everyone new encouragement, because they saw how much the local people were appreciative of your work, Srila Prabhupada."

Prabhupada was visibly pleased with his disciples' efforts and spoke to encourage his men. "Everything will be settled up. Don't be disheartened. So, when you left Mayapur, things were in order?"

Jayapataka replied affirmatively. "Because we are foreigners, when they first came and said that 'The foreigners are firing upon us Indians, although we did no wrong,' rather than take what was the actual situation, they immediately said, 'Oh, yes, foreigners are firing upon our Indians.' They took a national stand, influenced by different reasons. That is why that matter initially went against us. But now the fact that they are such type of guṇḍa and anti-social, they are just showing by their own mistakes. They can't hide their nature."

The group who attacked us are also now facing charges on an unrelated case, Jayapataka told Prabhupada, "So day by day it's becoming more and more apparent, their nature. You gave me the name Jayapataka, Srila Prabhupada, and I hope that by your mercy this name can become true. Then there will be victory in all these efforts."

Prabhupada: "It has become true."

The apparently adverse situation has also worked now in our favor in a different way. There is a sadhu with land adjacent to ours who wants to sell it to ISKCON. On inquiry from Prabhupada, Jayapataka told him, "Actually, right now he's more eager than ever to sell his land. The sadhu next to us, Praphulla Brahmachari, and I met together, and we made an oral agreement that we wouldn't give him any hope for purchasing his land at a high price. And as the result, now because of this incident... Before he had some hope that some outside person would come and buy land, but outside people don't want to purchase land at Mayapur. So now he has no other hope than to sell either to me, to us, or to that brahmachari. So, now he's still asking four thousand. He's come from six to four. But it's even appearing that within a short time he may come down to three thousand."

Prabhupada told him to go ahead and purchase it, "My idea is, it is a land where we shall dig another pond. No building."

Jayapataka:	"Build another pond."
Prabhupada:	"Yes."
Jayapataka:	"The *pukura* [pond]. That land, at least at the front, the whole length is very long and wide."
Prabhupada:	"Long and wide."
Tamal Krishna:	"It sounds like Prabhupada wants a moat."
Bhavananda:	"We could make a moat, a water barrier, so they couldn't attack from the back of the building."
Tamal Krishna:	"Is that your idea, Srila Prabhupada?"
Prabhupada:	(nodding) "You dig the earth and make it like a lake."
Tamal Krishna:	"Right along the building?"
Prabhupada:	"No. Throw the earth this side and that side. Automatically it will be like a small canal."

Kirtanananda joked we could put some crocodiles in it, and along with Prabhupada, everyone laughed.

Bhavananda Maharaja had been on hand through most of the meeting, and he also expressed his feelings. "Srila Prabhupada, I was somewhat disturbed after the incident, but I'm feeling much better now. After that incident, in the jail, I was discouraged. I was feeling, 'Oh, Srila Prabhupada is working so hard to develop this Mayapur, and the people don't appreciate it or... What is the use?' But that's all gone now. So many people are coming, and books are being distributed. Increase."

Jayapataka: "Bhavananda, just the day after he left there, there was a letter addressed to him. One gentleman wrote and said that 'I am fifty years old, and I am a M.A....' He was a professor of something. And then he said that 'Now my children are all grown up, and I'm simply working. I have heard that you are a pure Vaishnava, so I want to take shelter and serve Krishna at your ashram.' So although people are putting in the newspaper so many things, but they are understanding that 'No, he is a Vaishnava.' So, people believe what they want to believe. The devotees are devotees. When we see people, they always say they don't believe that the report is true. Everyone doubts the reports. Only those who are of envious mind believe, because they want to believe that."

It was all good news. And on receiving such reports

Prabhupada becomes noticeably animated. The flow of visitors is increasing, but rather than taking it as an imposition, he draws energy and satisfaction from their presence.

After Jayapataka Maharaja finished his Mayapur update, Prabhupada took a short break to have his face washed. Samples of Prabhupada's urine have been sent to the doctor due to the blood and pus that he passed last night. Prabhupada's sister came in at 7:30 a.m. to see him. They had a very emotional exchange. Bhakti Charu Swami acted as an intermediary, since Prabhupada's voice was so faint she could not hear him properly.

Prabhupada amazingly requested her to cook for him. He said that he cannot drink fruit juice, so he may as well eat something solid. He requested *kicarī*, *begun* (eggplant), and *subji*. The last time Prabhupada took a whole meal of any solid food was in Bombay.

When Prabhupada saw her, he began to shed tears and said, "Ask her to forgive me for my offences. She is not only my sister, but she is my Godsister as well. She is initiated by Srila Prabhupada. She is a Vaishnavi. If I ever have committed any offence, then it is Vaishnava *aparādha*."

Pisima protested, "No, no! He never ever committed any offence."

"Tell her that I cannot eat any fruit juice. Now I want to eat something solid. Can she cook something for me? Ask her to cook some *kicarī*. Let her cook anything that she wants to cook for me." And to Bhakti Charu, "You see to it personally that she gets anything she wants. Today I am going to eat some solid food. It doesn't matter whether it does good to me or bad to me. Nothing can be worse than this. She is a Vaishnavi—it will be good for me.

"Probably I became a little puffed up of my opulence

127

and success. Now God has shattered that pride. If you don't have your body, then what's there to be puffed-up about?"

Bhakti Charu: "Prabhupada, whatever you have done, you have done for Krishna."

Prabhupada: "That may be, but in this world unknowingly you commit offences."

Bhakti Charu: "You cannot ever commit offences, Prabhupada. You are God's very dear one. How can you commit offence?"

Prabhupada: "I am a little temperamental person. Often I used words like 'rascal'. I never compromised. They used to call it *'Kurul nie prachar'*— *kurul* [pickaxe] in one hand and *Bhāgavatam* in the other. That's how I preached. Anyway, make arrangements for her. See that no inconvenience is caused."

A little later Tamal Krishna entered with two telegrams, one from a leading Godbrother of Prabhupada, and one from our Sydney temple.

Tamal Krishna: "Madhava Maharaja sent you a telegram from Chandigarh. It says, 'Extremely anxious for your health. Praying to Srila Prabhupada and Lord Gaura-Krishna for Their blessings unto you.' "

Prabhupada was happy to receive it, more so since last year Madhava Maharaja had actively tried to impede the development of our Mayapur project. Prabhupada had appealed to another Godbrother to

128

speak with him to not oppose ISKCON's development there. But now Prabhupada slipped into the same mood of humility and reconciliation he has displayed to all his Godbrothers during their recent visits. He replied, "Send him back telegram: 'Thank you. Excuse my offenses—all Godbrothers.' "

Then Tamal Krishna Maharaja read out the Sydney telegram. " 'Dearest Srila Prabhupada, please do not leave us, for without your lotus feet we have no shelter. We are trying to distribute more books. Your eternal servants at Sydney Mandir.' "

Prabhupada's answer was brief but along the line of the last few days, increasing our hopes. "Yes, I am willing to stay. After all, it is Krishna's desire."

The reading of the telegrams over, Tamal Krishna asked, "You want kirtan, Srila Prabhupada?"

Prabhupada: "Yes."
Tamal Krishna: "*Jaya* Sri Krishna Chaitanya."
Prabhupada: "*Kīrtanīyaḥ sadā hariḥ [Cc Ādi* 17.31]. Kirtan is our life."

Hridayananda Gosvami has arrived with a new offering to His Divine Grace. He and Tamal Krishna happily presented a new printing of two volumes of *Kṛṣṇa* book trilogies in Portuguese language. They printed 100,000 copies, now being distributed in Brazil.

Prabhupada, with deep satisfaction, exclaimed, "Thank you very much. Printing of books is our real work."

Prabhupada asked to see the books. One featured Sri Radha-Krishna on the front and Srila Prabhupada on the back. He grinned broadly and exclaimed, "Very nice."

Prabhupada asked how they are selling.

Hridayananda: "Very nice. Over a thousand per day."

129

Prabhupada:	"Oh. What is the price?"
Hridayananda:	"Price? They're charging to the public around eighty cents."
Prabhupada:	"So you have got a good collection?"
Tamal Krishna:	"Good collection, Hridayananda?"
Hridayananda:	"Yes."
Prabhupada:	"Print more books."
Hridayananda:	"Yes. In Brazil the *Bhāgavatam* is also very, very popular."

Deeply moved by the efforts of his disciples to print and sell the fruits of what he once called "my very hard labor," Prabhupada declared, "This is life. This material world and the bones... The bones are not our [life]... This is life. We are not concerned with bones and stones. Our real concern is the living force. *Apareyam itas tu viddhi me prakṛtiṁ parām, jīva-bhūtāṁ mahā-bāho yayedaṁ dhāryate jagat* [*Gītā* 7.5]. The living force is sustaining the bones. Bone is not important. It may remain; it may go. It doesn't matter. Real life, what is sustaining the bone, is steady. We have got history that there was a rishi, he had only bones. So there is a science by which you can sustain life—only bones. Hiranyakasipu did it, practically."

Tamal Krishna:	"You are also doing it, Srila Prabhupada."
Prabhupada:	"So take care of the bones as long as possible. Real life is here. Always remember that. And material world means they are simply all protecting bones and flesh together. They have no idea what they are. Bones and flesh. *Bhūmir āpo 'nalo vāyuḥ* [*Gītā* 7.4]. *Apareyam.* It is useless. Not useless—inferior. Real? That *jīva-*

130

bhūta, which is sustaining.
"Thank you very much. Print books, and as I have given in my will, half, again print, and half spent for propaganda as you like. In this way go on. Jayapataka, you are doing that?"

Tamal Krishna: "Jayapataka, are you doing that? Half spending and half for printing?"

Jayapataka: "In Bengal, because the people are so poor, we are giving the books and just taking five or ten percent profit for the small books, for propaganda purpose, so that we can reach many people."

Prabhupada: "Yes. Whatever propaganda require you spend, but print books and distribute. Whatever English book we have got, if we translate into Bengali, we have got enough stock."

Jayapataka: "Yes. We have a treasure house."

Prabhupada: "In this way, in all languages, distribute. Thank you very much. Hare Krishna."

Jayapataka: "*Jaya* Srila Prabhupada."

Prabhupada: "Chant Hare Krishna."

The devotees continued with a soft kirtan as Prabhupada brought the meeting to a close.

About an hour later, Akincana Krishna dasa Babaji came, along with Ashrama Maharaja, a disciple of Gosvami Maharaja. Prabhupada was resting, but we gave them seats at Prabhupada's bedside and they joined in the kirtan until Prabhupada woke. Prabhupada was pleased to see his old friend and hear him sing kirtan. It was another heartfelt, humble exchange. Prabhupada told him, "Please forgive me if I committed any offences."

Akincana Krishna dasa Babaji, who always has the holy names on his lips, responded with deep appreciation, "Hare Krishna, Hare Krishna."

Prabhupada told him, "All over the world there is a beautiful field to preach Krishna consciousness. I didn't care whether I'll be successful or not. All of them are willing to take—they are taking also. If we preach together, then the saying of Chaitanya Mahaprabhu, *pṛthivīte āche yata nagarādi grāma...* We have everything. Spread the holy name and distribute *prasādam*. There is a beautiful field; in Africa, in Russia, everywhere they are accepting."

Godbrothers:	"You have done a lot."
Prabhupada:	"These books have been translated in many languages. Prabhupada repented in Radha-kuṇḍa, saying that 'I wanted to write some books.' Once he said about Baghbazar temple that, 'At times I feel like taking these stones off and sell them and write some books.' I wanted to take a lesson from that and decided, 'It doesn't matter whether I can write or not, I'll give it a try.' "Once I told Vasudeva, 'Prabhupada wanted me to write, but what can I write?' and he said, 'It doesn't matter, just write whatever you can, just scribble on the paper.' You all know that."

Prabhupada arriving back in Vrindavan on October 2, 1977.

Gurukula boys dancing for Srila Prabhupada under the Tamal tree.

Top and bottom left:
On parikrama around Krishna Balarama Mandir.

Prabhupada taking darshan of the
Deities.

Devotees gather around Prabhupada as he takes darshan.

The Bhaktivendanta Institute held its first conference "Life Comes From Life" under Prabhupada's guidance.

MAIN SPEAKERS

Thoudam Damodar Singh. Manipur, India. Ph.D. in physical organic chemistry, University of California. GBC, and Director of Bhaktivedanta Institute.

Michael Marchetti. Boston, U.S.A. Ph.D. in theoretical chemistry, Georgetown University.

Richard Thompson. Boston, U.S.A. Ph.D. in mathematics, Cornell University.

David John Webb. London, England. M.A. in natural sciences, Oxford University.

Robert Cohen. Houston, U.S.A. M.A. in geology, Rutgers University.

HIGHLIGHTS OF THE CONFERENCE

• Molecular Biology
The goal of scientific research is to find the absolute truth or basis of all phenomena, governing both life and matter. According to modern science, the ultimate space is vaguely incorporated into certain physical laws — basically the laws of quantum mechanics. Conceptually, these laws involve only subtle pushes and pulls among particles. Although the theory of evolution asserts that these laws are sufficient in themselves to account for all the marvels of life, honest and intelligent scientists are beginning to realize that the theory is failing to explain many subtle aspects of life — for instance, love, meaning and purpose. How can simple pushes and pulls be responsible for all the wonderful phenomena that we encounter in life?

We would like to show that the recent announcement of Khorana's synthetic gene is not different from the proposal of a synthesis of urea in 1828, so far as our understanding of life is concerned. In other words, a complete molecule or a combination of such molecules will not account for the true nature of life.

We propose that life is non-physical and non-chemical. It possesses consciousness and obeys higher order non-physical laws. They new scientific hypothesis can explain all the observed facts of life more scientifically than any of the previous theories.

• Information Theory
A fundamental proposition of information theory states that information content of a closed mathematical system cannot increase. In modern science, nature is described by means of mathematical models of low information content. The physical structures of living organisms, on the other hand, are of such complexity, and diversity as to indicate a very high information content. From this it follows that these structures could not have arisen by means of the simple natural processes envisioned in the theory of evolution. An additional source of information is required. The implications of this analysis regarding the origin of life are discussed.

• Quantum theory
Modern science has failed to account for consciousness, and in modern physics the existence of consciousness has given rise to special paradoxes and contradictions. The quantum theory is developed with special emphasis on the interpretations of von Neumann and Daniel, Linger, and Poupel. It is concluded that a new theoretical understanding is required concerning relations for consciousness. Such an understanding may be based on the description of the atomic living entity, or atma, given in Bhagavad-gita. This entails definite implications concerning the scientific study of life.

FIRST INTERNATIONAL SCIENTIFIC CONFERENCE

on

LIFE COMES FROM LIFE

Sponsored by:

BHAKTIVEDANTA INSTITUTE

Founder – Acarya

His Divine Grace A. C. Bhaktivedanta Swami Prabhupada

Current scientific theory holds that "life" is a product of molecular interactions, and that all the different activities of life — for example, thinking, feeling and willing — are due to coordinated chemical reactions. However, this approach has failed to explain the subtle aspects of life, such as value, meaning and purpose. A new scientific paradigm is, therefore, needed.

Bhaktivedanta Institute is sponsoring a scientific conference on the theme, "Life Comes From Life," to be held in Vrindavana, India on Friday, October 14 through Sunday, October 16. Scientists will gather from around the world to discuss fundamental questions on the nature and origin of life. The basic theme of the conference is that life cannot be reduced to a com-

The members of the Bhaktivedanta Institute from left to right: Jñana Das, Swarupa Damodara Das, Brahma-Tirtha Das, Madhava Das & Sadaputa Das

Despite his fragile condition, Prabhupada still took his darshan of the Deities.

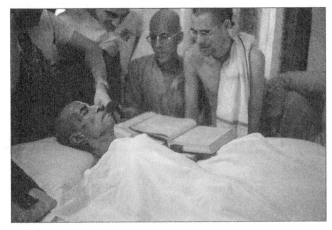

Prabhupada called for his editors, Pradyumna Prabhu and Jayadvaita Das and continued translating the Srimad-Bhagavatam, Canto 10, Chapter 13.

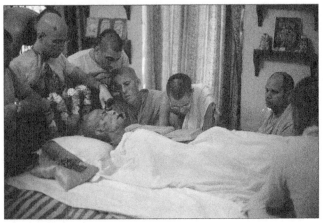

Instead of in private, he now translated in the midst of his loving disciples.

Then Prabhupada indicated us disciples surrounding his bed. "The nice thing about them is that whatever I tell them, they obey it with absolute sincerity. That is why I have the faith *pṛthivīte āche yata.*"

Prabhupada told them that the reputed scholar Dr. Stillson Judah had described him as "charismatic," and how Judah had written books on us. He wanted to show them Judah's book *Hare Krishna and the Counterculture*, but unfortunately the copy we had, and which Prabhupada took with him all around the world, had been left behind in Bombay.

Prabhupada said that he was now bedridden and unable to do anything but that his disciples are doing so much. He called for Kirtanananda Swami and had me show his Godbrothers the photos of New Vrindaban.

Hari-sauri: "This is a palace that they're building in our New Vrindaban farm community. This is built by our own men. It is not complete yet, but it's being built, the dome. Kirtanananda Swami is in charge. These are the devotees. Everything is being made by our men, everything. They learned how to cast concrete, how to make these pillars, archways. This marble-laying is all done by our men. They came here and learned, and they have a marble shop. This is the kirtan hall inside. This is on the walls. Here's the floor. This is onyx and marble together. This is pressed concrete, sculptured.

"This is a support piece, little decorative. This is a guesthouse

that was built by the devotees. This
is another new building they're
building now, and this is the present
installation and silos for storing cow
fodder. This is a part of the farm."

As I turned to each new photo and added in short
descriptions, his Godbrothers gave little exclamations
of appreciation. "Very beautiful."

More Godbrothers arrived, and as they talked,
sometimes in English and sometimes Bengali,
Ramesvara Maharaja entered, laden with a large
portfolio of photos, some from the BBT, others from the
new temple in Fiji, and yet more from the Janmastami
celebrations in Los Angeles.

The latest artwork being produced in the BBT studio
in Los Angeles is exceptional. Ramesvara showed
photos of fourteen new paintings of Krishna *līlā* for the
Tenth Canto, Part Two, of *Śrīmad-Bhāgavatam,* drawing
exclamations of awe and delight, not just from our
visitors but from Srila Prabhupada and his disciples
as well.

Ramesvara: "This is Krishna and Trinavarta
demon, the whirlwind. This is
Krishna releasing the two demigods
from the arjuna trees. This
one is Krishna kicking the cart.
Sakatasura. Krishna and the demon
coming from the cart."

Kirtanananda exclaimed, "They're wonderful, Prabhupada."

Ramesvara: "This one is Krishna and Balarama
in the cowshed of Nanda Maharaja
for the name-giving ceremony.

> And Gargamuni is there. This one
> is Narada Muni cursing the two
> demigods for sporting naked and
> drinking. This is Krishna killing the
> giant witch Putana. Krishna is very
> small on her chest."

The next one was of Krishna stealing butter. Ramesvara informed the small gathering that the painting was now hanging on the wall in the Shah of Iran's palace. Prabhupada, with obvious pride in his disciples' work and preaching, told his Godbrothers about Parivrajakacharya Swami's preaching to the royal family. They were amazed. We could see that Prabhupada's preaching was practically inconceivable to them.

Prabhupada's artists seem to have reached a whole new level of excellence. His eyes teared when he saw their depiction of Mother Yasoda chasing Krishna with a stick for His stealing butter. His Godbrothers were laughing, exclaiming "Oh!" and "Hmm" at each picture.

Ramesvara continued, "This painting is the fruit vendor, aborigine, giving Krishna all the fruits, and He is turning her basket of fruits into jewels. We showed this painting to the princess and told her that if you give something to Krishna, He returns it millions of times. She liked this. This is the cowherd boys sporting in the mouth of Aghasura."

Prabhupada was smiling broadly, "Hmm. Very nice."

Ramesvara: "This is Krishna eating dirt, and
               the boys are telling Mother Yasoda.
               So she is forcing Him to open His
               mouth, and she sees the whole
               universe."

Prabhupada: "Hare Krishna."

135

Ramesvara:	"This painting shows Krishna about to bifurcate the Bakasura demon. This is Krishna's first birthday, Janmastami, and Mother Yasoda and Rohini are bathing Krishna, abhiseka. This painting is Krishna eating butter. These are fourteen new paintings for one book."

Apart from the BBT artwork, Ramesvara Maharaja also brought pictures from the recent opening of the Krishna-Kaliya temple in Fiji. The temple was built by the endeavors of one of the richest families in Fiji, the Punja brothers. The eldest, Deoji, and his two wives and younger brother were initiated by Prabhupada during his visit there last year, Deoji receiving the name Vasudeva dasa. Ramesvara and I and half a dozen devotees from Australia had attended the August opening, along with Yasodanandana Swami, who organized and performed all the necessary pujas. With great pleasure Ramesvara showed Srila Prabhupada the photos. "This is the abhiseka of Krishna-Kaliya."

Hari-sauri:	"This is Gaura-Nitai here, and Krishna-Kaliya is here at the front. This man here is Bhaskaranya Swami, a local man. He came and chanted during the abhiseka. He stayed up until two in the morning with us, and he began chanting *japa* after that."
Ramesvara:	"This was the procession on the opening day. We marched the Radha-Krishna Deities all over the neighborhood, through the center of the town, and hundreds of people

followed. There was a *shenai* band. This was the *agni-hotra* ceremony on the day the temple opened."

Fiji had been suffering a serious drought for many months, but the night before the official opening, as the preliminary installations were conducted by Yasodanandana Maharaja, there was a rain shower, but only in the immediate vicinity of the temple. The next day, immediately after the fire sacrifice, as we opened the curtains for the first darshan of the Deities, there was a huge rainstorm over the entire district. People were openly crying with joy. The whole affair was very successful.

The next photo Ramesvara showed was of the main altar, with Krishna-Kaliya and the Nāga-patnīs. This prompted me to ask about the standard of worship, because this is the only temple we have seen with Krishna-Kaliya as the main Deity. "Should Krishna be dressed very, very opulently like this, Srila Prabhupada?"

Prabhupada: "Oh, yes."

Hari-sauri: "Yes. They had a question in Fiji. They wanted to know whether He should be dressed simply or opulently."

Ramesvara then displayed another batch of photos of the recent Janmastami celebrations in Los Angeles. The devotees there had made an extraordinary birthday cheesecake for the Lord. On Tamal Krishna's prompt, Ramesvara described its special features. The multi-layered edifice weighed 2,000 pounds and stood about fifteen feet high. On different levels were small towers, each of which were made to spin by small motors.

Tamal Krishna: "That is amazing. The guests were eating big handfuls of cake *prasādam.*"

Prabhupada: "Was there enough for everyone?"

Jayadvaita: "Oh, yes."

Ramesvara: "It lasts for one month, the supply."

As everyone laughed with delight, Ramesvara described the elaborate arrangements the devotees had made for the festival. "This is another picture of Janmastami in Los Angeles. The whole street is closed by the city, and we built a stage in front of the temple, and Sudama's men were performing *Rāmāyaṇa* and *Krishna-līlā*, and there were rugs in the street for people to sit on and under the pandal on the grass, and they were watching. About five thousand people came."

Ramesvara next showed photos of the three sets of new clothes they had offered on the day to the Deities of Sri-Sri-Rukmini-Dvarakadhisa, including a set made entirely from flowers. And another set was offered the next day, on Srila Prabhupada's Vyasa-puja, and yet another set for Jhulana-yātrā.

Tamal Krishna Maharaja took his cue to further bolster our prayers that Prabhupada remain with us. "I think you must go there, Srila Prabhupada, again. They are calling you to come."

Deeply satisfied at the display of the many opulences he has made manifest through his and his disciples' hard work, Prabhupada appealed once again to his Godbrothers, as he has done many times in the past, "I have given them the philosophy of 'American money and Indian culture.' Combined together, the face of the world will change.

"Don't keep Indian culture airtight, and don't keep American money for sense gratification. Use it for Krishna. So, they are doing that. And Krishna is giving them intelligence. *Bhakti-yogaṁ dadāmi tam.*"

Ramesvara displayed photos of several other Deities from America. Then he showed a mock-up of all of Prabhupada's books, including *Bhagavad-gītā* in several foreign languages, lined up on a book case. As he did so, Gopal Krishna came in with the newly printed Hindi version of *The Scientific Basis of Krishna consciousness*, written by Svarupa Damodara prabhu. The book has Maha-Vishnu on the cover. Twenty thousand copies have been printed, and Prabhupada was happy to hear that it will be distributed at the upcoming science conference.

We could see from the reactions of his Godbrothers that Prabhupada's preaching was practically beyond their comprehension. He told them that he had made a little attempt and there was great success. At the end they commented, "If you stay for some more time, then it is good for all of us, for the whole world."

Prabhupada replied, "The duration of my life is over. Now I am surviving only on the extra span. I have done whatever I could."

The Godbrothers' visit lasted over one and a half hours, and they left in awe and genuine appreciation.

The BBT Trustees were meeting during the morning, and Ramesvara came in with a couple of questions. "There are many articles in *BTG* which are written by you, or your lectures, and your famous conversations, like Professor Kotovsky, and Dr. Stahl. So, there is a proposal to take all of these different writings that have been published in *BTG* and put them together in one hardbound book, so that they will be preserved."

Prabhupada said it was a good idea, and Ramesvara went on to propose that in the future other lectures could also be composed in the same way.

Prabhupada liked the whole proposal. "Very good idea."

"Then there is unlimited material," Jayapataka

Swami enthused, and Tamal Krishna Goswami, also one of the BBT trustees, glorified Prabhupada once again. "You've not only written more than anybody, but you've spoken more about Krishna than anyone, Srila Prabhupada."

Then Kirtanananda Maharaja brought in a drink for Prabhupada. He has taken charge of Prabhupada's diet with the idea of keeping him to a strict regime so that he can become healthy quickly. As he held the drink up to Prabhupada's lips, he spoke quite strongly, "Drink! This is to be drunk, not spit out! Drink it!"

Prabhupada dutifully drank about half and then pulled away. Kirtanananda pushed the glass back to him, "The whole thing! Please, Prabhupada. How will you ever get well? Come on! You can take a little more. Your body needs more, Prabhupada."

He laughed tentatively, trying to be forceful, yet still conscious about who he was dealing with. "Srila Prabhupada, you know, Mother Yasoda was very fortunate because she could completely forget that Krishna was God, and she would simply tell Krishna, 'You have to do it.' Unfortunately, my love is not that great, because I still remember you're my spiritual master."

Prabhupada smilingly acknowledged his disciple's concern and effort. "I am doing your order."

Kirtanananda, "Thank you very much. One more?"

Prabhupada again took some but couldn't finish. Kirtanananda pushed him a little more sternly, "Your body needs more, Prabhupada." Again he drank, and as we all enjoyed the transcendental exchange, Kirtanananda said, "Thank you very much," satisfied he had done his best.

There was a pause as Prabhupada washed his mouth and Kirtanananda questioned him about taking some solids. His sister was cooking for him in the small kitchen in the back yard of Prabhupada's house. "Prabhupada, you're not really going to try and eat that *kicari,* are you?"

Prabhupada: "Really? Why not?"

Kirtanananda: "Let's just stay on this for a few days to get your body accustomed, and then if you want something else we can try it. You're doing well, Prabhupada, and if we introduce so many different things and if there's a reaction, we won't know what caused it."

"Then Prabhupada will want to stop everything," Brahmananda said in support.

Kirtanananda: "So if we just go a little bit slowly, it'll get us further in the end."

After a short pause, Prabhupada decided to still go ahead. "Hmm, very thin, I can try to take little."

Just before Prabhupada called for his lunch, Kirtanananda Maharaja again discussed with him whether he should eat solid food even though he could not digest anything, and against medical advice. Kirtanananda's idea was to try to follow some medical discipline, which presently excluded taking solids.

Prabhupada had little enthusiasm for it. "From medical point of view," he said, "you cannot give life. The life is finished. Where is medical point? Hmm? According to duration of life, that is finished. You cannot give a dead body life."

Kirtanananda: "But your body is not dead, Prabhupada. Your body is not dead. Your life is very strong."

Prabhupada: "Then again you go to miracle. As soon as you say, 'Your body is not dead.'"

141

Trivikrama and Tamal Krishna both repeated, "Then you go to miracle."

Prabhupada: "That is not medical point [of view]."
Kirtanananda: "I don't... It doesn't appear that..."
Prabhupada: "No. You said 'medical point.' "
Kirtanananda: "Yes."
Prabhupada: "So, medical point does not mean that you can give life to a dead body."
Kirtanananda: "That is fact."
Prabhupada: "So, my body is now dead according to medical point. You cannot give life. So let it be doomed. It is not possible from medical point of view to give life to a dead body. What is this? It is dead body."

Upendra announced that *prasādam* had come, and Srila Prabhupada brought the discussion to a close. "So, you can, for the time being, disperse. Whatever possible, I'll take. Then you come and chant."

Everyone left, and Prabhupada sat up and began to slowly eat. After about five spoonfuls, he turned to me and Tamal Krishna Maharaja with a smile. "Medical science finished!"

After his short repast, he again addressed Kirtanananda's dismay and gave his own clear diagnosis, "If you think I'm taking poison, the body is already finished. So dead body, you take poison or ambrosia, it is the same. Blind man, night or day—the same thing. Rather, if you depend on miracle, pray to Krishna that 'he may survive.' "

Hari-sauri: "We rely on Krishna, not on the medical science."

"Medical science finished", Prabhupada repeated emphatically.

Tamal Krishna Maharaja said he thought that Krishna must have sent Prabhupada's sister. "No one has informed her—she just came by herself."

Prabhupada agreed. "Therefore I am taking!"

Prabhupada took about 8-10 spoonful's of *prasādam*, and then afterwards Kirtanananda gave him some syrup to get rid of the blood and pus in his urine. He informed Srila Prabhupada that Dr. Gopal, who is the physician at the Rama Seva Ashram, had prescribed some tablets and syrup after testing his urine this morning.

Bhagatji told Prabhupada that the doctor may want a blood sample. Prabhupada shook his head. "That is the difficulty."

Hari-sauri: "Yes. No blood. Prabhupada doesn't want a blood test."

Prabhupada did agree to take the tablets, and after a short discussion with Bhakti Charu and Bhagatji, he told us, "Go on, kirtan."

His "meal" finished, Prabhupada then sent everyone out so he could take his bath. As we cleansed his body, he had Bhakti Charu read aloud from the new Hindi *Scientific Basis of Krishna Consciousness*.

Prabhupada had Svarupa Damodara come and give a report on his "Life Comes from Life" conference which begins tomorrow. He is keenly interested to hear about the conference.

Svarupa Damodara and his men have been busy making preparations to receive a host of scholars from various universities and institutes in Delhi and Agra. Prominent persons, such as the ex-president of the executive board of UNESCO, who will give a speech on the opening night, have been invited. Scholars from various disciplines such as chemistry, physics, biology, and mathematics have promised to attend, as well as a group of medical doctors from Agra. The whole thing stands to be a major event.

Svarupa Damodara told Prabhupada, "Everybody was very positive on our approach. In fact, they encouraged us a lot, and they told us that's unique—trying to understand the concept of life from religious point of view connected with modern science. So we have decided that the function will be started with the *Brahma-saṁhitā* prayer with our *gurukula* boys to open the conference, followed by the short speech by the chief guest. Then we'll start our main talk. Our main talk is going to last at least two hours. Each of us will speak. And then I've decided to open about half an hour for questions and answers and general discussion. On Sunday I'm leaving more than an hour for discussion. We'll summarize the whole conference and also make some conclusive remarks about the previous two days' talk that we are making."

Srila Prabhupada was keen to make sure all our guests would be well looked after, with nice *prasādam* and comfortable rooms. He took assurance from Kirtanananda that he and the other GBCs would cooperate to make it a success. The conference is being held in the large hall of our *gurukula*, and fresh curtains and lighting are currently being installed. Tamal Krishna also informed him that the whole guesthouse has been vacated and cleaned.

Satisfied with all the preparations, Srila Prabhupada turned his attention back to himself. He asked us, "According to horoscope, life is finished. Still, I am living. What should be interpreted?"

Kirtanananda: "The astrologers all say that you are transcendental, that if you want you can change your horoscope. And that's what you told us, that Krishna said the choice is up to you."

Prabhupada: "So, what do you think?"

Tamal Krishna: "I think, Srila Prabhupada, that you should continue to try, and that Krishna will help you, because we all want you. The whole world wants you very much, and there's no reason why Krishna cannot do this. If we remain determined, then Krishna will surely fulfil our desires. We're not desiring for any selfish reason that you should live. We're desiring for the benefit of the whole world. There's every reason to continue to try and make the effort to remain."

"So, something to eat," Prabhupada asked. "What shall I eat?"

There was a long pause, punctuated with some discussion whether he should take a liquid or solid meal. It remains a puzzle what is best, since his body is so fragile and reactive.

Prabhupada again asked about the conference, how many men would come.

Svarupa Damodara estimated about one hundred would attend on Sunday, the main day. He told Prabhupada of some important men who are coming. Prabhupada told him to take the opportunity. It will be very prestigious. Svarupa Damodara told Prabhupada they have a TV appearance lined up, and school and university programs as well. Prabhupada was well pleased with his men's efforts.

Svarupa Damodara told Prabhupada of one man from the UN who has spoken against the modern "unscientific" scientists and will speak favorably for us. He has already said that the Krishna consciousness movement is like a UN.

Prabhupada immediately smiled and said, "Yes." Then he told them, "So, this is the beginning, and arrange for such conferences one after another, many. Do something so that before my departure I can see something." After a short pause, he added, "Our only ambition is to establish that God is one, He is a person, and He is Krishna."

"*Jaya!*"

"And we have to follow what Krishna says, then our life is successful."

Prabhupada asked about one of the scientists who is inaugurating our function. Svarupa Damodara said the man was retired but active, and had written an article describing the mind and body relationship, which he had sent to Svarupa Damodara for his comments. In modern science, in the West, they sometimes think that mind is the soul.

Prabhupada: "According to our *shastra*, mind is meant for speculation. It does not give us any definite knowledge. My mind is working in one way, your mind is working in another way. There is no conclusion. This is the result of mental speculation *Manorathenāsati dhāvato bahiḥ* [*SB* 5.18.12] and *Gītā* also says that *manaḥ-ṣaṣṭhānīndriyāṇi prakṛti-sthāni karṣati* [15.7], that the spiritual spark, being bound up by the mind and senses, is struggling hard in this material nature. He is simply struggling. No fixed-up position. Everyone will say, 'I think this is right.' What is right he doesn't know. That is philosopher. Is it not?"

Prabhupada took assurance from Bhavananda that all arrangements for the conference were good, and asked Tamal Krishna if the *prasādam* was good. He remembered that a few days ago we had all said it was a good standard.

Tamal Krishna gave a strong endorsement, "Yes. I personally feel that the *prasādam* here at lunchtime is some of the nicest *prasādam* I have ever eaten. Every day it's consistently very nice, served very nicely, and sufficient quantity.

"So kindly maintain this standard. That is very important item."

The irony of his concern that we should make sure everyone should eat—against our inability to induce him to do so—was not lost, and he added humorously, "I am not eating, but I am hearing and getting the appetite."

Tamal Krishna mentioned how we also eat together. Prabhupada responded with the fourth verse of *Gurvaṣṭaka*: "*Catur-vidha-śrī-bhagavat-prasāda-svādv-anna-tṛptān hari-bhakta-saṅghān kṛtvaiva tṛptiṁ bhajataḥ sadaiva.* This is also *bhajana*. It is satisfying that others are taking first-class *prasādam*."

Svarupa Damodara explained his overall strategy. "Inside we are going to say very strongly about our philosophy and science. And anybody who's going to oppose that, we're going to duel them. Also, we'll show some films, our Hare Krishna films, just after the conference. The evening, I have some entertainment program. That program is for showing our films and our activities, ISKCON activities throughout the world. So I have brought all the slides from Los Angeles that we have from our BBT department, and also I have all the films ready. Also, they can attend *maṅgala-ārati,* and in the evening they can attend the *sandhyā-ārati.* And also, some of them want just to see our temple, Krishna-Balarama. They have heard that the architecture is very nice and it's very nicely decorated. Some of them already have heard about it, so they just want to see how the temple is here. And so, I think, overall, our idea is also to make them devotees."

Prabhupada: "Yes. That is wanted. So go and arrange. That's all."

Immediately thereafter, Prabhupada consulted with Pisima for something to eat, and she gave him puffed rice with a little cream. He took a very small amount.

About 4:30 p.m. Puri Maharaja, Ashrama Maharaja, Ananda Prabhu, Purusottama Brahmachari, and about twenty others, including some ladies, came from the Gaudiya Matha to see Prabhupada. They all filed in and sat around his bedside. It was another sweet exchange. Puri Maharaja led a short kirtan. When he stopped, Prabhupada humbly asked them all to forgive him for his offences.

Ashrama Maharaja told him, "You are the eternal. You will rule over us, guide us, chastise us."

Prabhupada: "Forgive all of my offences. I became proud with my opulence."

Puri Maharaja: "No, you never became proud. When you started preaching, opulence and success followed you. This is the blessing of Sri Chaitanya Mahaprabhu and Sri Krishna. There can't be any question of any offence."

Prabhupada: "According to my horoscope, the duration of my life is over. I don't know why God has kept me here now."

Ashrama Maharaja: "The karmic span of life is over, but now the devotional span of your life has started. In the devotional span, everything is auspicious. You have helped millions of people, by the mercy of Prabhupada, by the mercy of Sri Chaitanya Mahaprabhu. What more is there to achieve in this life?"

Prabhupada: "In the shastra it is said, *duḥkha*, suffering, is a kind of austerity. It has to be welcomed so that one can perform this austerity and become purified. Now you all forgive me."

Prabhupada said he was "*mahā patita.*" But they replied that there were never any offences and that he had saved millions around the world. Therefore he should be called "*mahā patita-pāvana.*"

Puri Maharaja told him, "Your body is divine. You are fully conscious. Tirtha Maharaja was unconscious for eighteen days in the hospital. This is the symptom of your divinity."

Prabhupada asked Puri Maharaja to help develop our Bhubaneswar temple.

Their discussion went on for about one hour. Pointing out Hamsaduta Maharaja, Prabhupada proudly informed his Godbrothers about his preaching in Sri Lanka. He had Tamal Krishna Maharaja read Hamsaduta's letter to Dr. Kavoor.

Tamal Krishna told the visitors that Hamsaduta had captured a very big scientist in Ceylon. "Dr. Kavoor was saying that life comes from chemicals. So Hamsaduta Maharaja challenged him that 'If life comes from chemicals, then I will give you ten lakhs of rupees if you come to this hall and you make chemicals into life.'

"He challenged him to a big thing, and in the newspapers, every day for two or three months, there was discussion between Hamsaduta Maharaja on behalf of the belief that life comes from life, not from chemicals—life comes from Krishna. So, he defeated this man, big scientist."

Puri Maharaja was laughing, "*Ācchā*. Ah, good."

Prabhupada told Tamal Krishna to read out the newspaper article in which Hamsaduta had publicly challenged Kavoor to produce the necessary chemicals and check his own death.

"'Let him make himself deathless,'" Tamal Krishna read out, "and restore his old and worn-out body with youthful luster and beauty. He may find this task too difficult, so perhaps he could just produce a simple form of life like a mosquito or a bedbug. Better still, let him recombine the chemicals of the praying mantis he decapitated, as described in his article, and bring it back to life. Or, is the science of Dr. Kavoor only a one-way road of destruction of life? But it may be that science is not yet ready to produce a finished product of life, so he could make a plastic egg and inject into it the yellow and white chemical substances, incubate such an artificial egg, and thereby produce one chicken, which could then go on laying eggs and producing more and more chickens. Even this task may be a little too difficult for Dr. Kovoor, so perhaps he could simply produce a drop of milk or a grain of rice or an ounce of gold by chemical combination. Then we could begin to take him seriously. However, everyone knows that these are impossible tasks for even the most powerful so-called scientist. Dr. Kovoor will undoubtedly give the reader in his next exposition a long-winded barrage of words to cover up his bluff. The sum and substance of it will be, 'We will do it in the future. We are trying.'

In any language, this is just a bluff."

Puri Maharaja was laughing, especially when Kovoor's declarations were called a bluff.

Puri Maharaja: "Yes. Proper dose you have given. Krishna must bless him."

Tamal Krishna told Puri Maharaja that Hamsaduta had offered first five lakhs of rupees, and then doubled it to ten, if Dr. Kovoor could meet the challenge.

Puri Maharaja: "He cannot be called as 'doctor.' How could he be a doctor?"

Hamsaduta: "Quack. Quack doctor."

Prabhupada started laughing again and told us a joke. "There is a story. A bridegroom was selected. So, the other party, bride's party, inquired how the bridegroom was quite qualified. So they said, 'He's a doctor.' Then they inquired, 'What kind of doctor? Doctor of philosophy, doctor of medicine, or...?' So he said, 'No, no, no. He's not all these nonsense. He's a big doctor.' 'What is that?' 'Con-doctor!' "

We all laughed very much, and Prabhupada so much that his teeth showed.

As they talked, Prabhupada told Bhakti Charu to make sure his guests were given nice *prasādam*. While they were waiting for that, Tamal Krishna showed the guests all the photos brought by Ramesvara Maharaja, including some of the recent Los Angeles Ratha-yātrā.

Jayatirtha informed them that the *rathas* were fifty feet high.

Puri Maharaja: "Ācchā? Jagannatha's *ratha* is only forty-five feet."

Tamal Krishna: "But this is Los Angeles. Everything is big there. You see Jagannatha. You see Him?"

Puri Maharaja was laughing in appreciation. "Yes. Jagannatha, yes. Dark eyes."

Tamal Krishna: "Very good eyes. And such a crowd. Two lakhs people attended. So many people came."

Puri Maharaja translated into Bengali about the festival as Tamal Krishna continued on turning the photos.

Tamal Krishna: "Lord Jagannatha is all-attractive. You cannot keep Him here. He's going out the door. One of the sannyasis was giving a big lecture; we had some elephants, and the children were riding on them. See: 'Free Love Feast'—*prasādam* was distributed. Fifty thousand people took full *prasādam* free of charge. You can see all the people."

Needless to say, all the visitors were impressed to see the scale of Prabhupada's preaching and responded with genuine respect and appreciation. Eventually some puri, *halavā,* and *gulābjāmun* was given to each visitor, and they all took their leave. Prabhupada relaxed and continued to relish the kirtan.

At about 7 p.m., Tamal Krishna came in and discussed with Prabhupada about his eating. Prabhupada complained he had no taste (appetite and digestion). Previously at lunch he had told us that taste was coming gradually.

Prabhupada: "And now... Just now, I have no taste."
Tamal Krishna: "So, I don't think there is any problem. I mean, what you ate today was more than I saw you eat in

three months, Srila Prabhupada. You ate a Love Feast today. So whenever we eat a Love Feast, we never have much appetite in the evening. Usually we simply chant."

Prabhupada: "So, I am trying to drink a little fruit juice."

After a short discussion between the servants, they settled on the juice of the sweet lemons from Iran. Tamal Krishna asked Bhakti Charu to make it and then keep it ready, so that it will immediately be ready whenever Prabhupada wants it.

Immediately Prabhupada objected. "No, no."

Atreya Rishi prabhu told them it should be fresh, and Prabhupada agreed. "Yes. That lemon should be preserved, not otherwise."

It reminded me of an incident in Bombay last year when I cut up a watermelon for Prabhupada. Because it was so large, I gave him a portion of it and then put the rest of it in the refrigerator for later consumption. Prabhupada saw it and stopped me, saying, "Cut fruit should be distributed immediately."

With many of the GBC still here, groups of them have been meeting to discuss and finalize various management issues. Tamal Krishna Maharaja informed Prabhupada about arrangements for funds for finishing the Bombay temple. "In order to finish the Bombay temple, we're sending some money to them for completion. So, we have a committee called the Mayapur-Vrindavan committee. Persons on the committee are Jayapataka Swami, Giriraj, Gopal Krishna, Atreya Rishi, Ramesvara Maharaja, Gurukripa Maharaja, and myself. That committee was formed by the GBC last Mayapur festival. So they decided that they would give a loan. Because the BBT was a little short of money... The BBT sends the money to Bombay, so the BBT wants to loan some money from the Mayapur-Vrindavan account in Los Angeles, and they'll pay it back with the same bank interest. Is that all right? You have given power of attorney, now that the MV Trust has approved it, Giriraj and I can sign on your behalf. See, we'll never sign on our own. We only sign after we get authority from the respective committee or from Your Divine Grace."

Prabhupada was pleased that his men are taking up the responsibility, especially the banking. "That's all right. Very good."

The recent visits by members of the various Gaudiya Mathas have been sweet, and generated good will between Prabhupada's disciples and them. In the beginning of ISKCON's activities in India, since 1970, Prabhupada's Godbrothers were not always co-operative or complimentary, but now the mood has begun to change. Tamal Krishna Maharaja was one of the earliest devotees to come to India, and over the first four or five years he had many dealings with them. He offered a nice realization to Prabhupada:

"To the devotees who came to see you from the Gaudiya Matha, you said you were *mahā-patita*. But they said, *Mahā-patita-pāvana*. We all appreciated that, Srila Prabhupada. Actually, Srila Prabhupada, I don't think that your Godbrothers really have any bad feelings. If, as you describe, because you had to preach amongst such fallen persons as us, the offence is really on our part, not on yours. I think actually they know that. Of course, they're a little sorry that they could not do what you did, but actually the offence is ours. We are not very trained up. It is not your fault. It is just that we are so fallen that we are only now beginning to learn a little etiquette. So sometimes, not purposefully, but because we're very fallen, we sometimes make mistakes and offences. And because we've taken shelter of Your Divine Grace, you are always giving us protection."

Prabhupada smiled and appreciated his devotional comments and sentiments.

Shortly after, Yasodanandana Swami came in and chanted the *Brahma-saṁhitā*. Tomorrow's conference will be inaugurated by Maharaja and some of the *gurukula* boys chanting these prayers. Prabhupada seems especially pleased with him for training them. He told Maharaja, "They will appreciate tomorrow."

Yasodanandana: "Yes. I'm training the boys. There's three boys I'm training especially in the morning—Dvarakadhisa, Ekendra, and Katyayana. I'm training them to chant the *Brahma-saṁhitā* and *Bhagavad-gītā* every day. Tomorrow we have arranged that for the beginning of the conference the boys will chant *namaḥ oṁ viṣṇu-pādāya, namaste narasiṁhāya, namo mahā-vadānyāya, namo brahmaṇya-devāya,* and four verses from *Brahma-saṁhitā,* tomorrow at 10.30 a.m. And every day I'm training some of these boys to chant *Brahma-saṁhitā* and *Bhagavad-gītā*. Is that all right, Prabhupada?"

Throughout the evening, different devotees were coming and going, relishing the opportunity to chant for Prabhupada in his room. Prabhupada listens intently to their kirtan, although he is physically completely incapacitated. He needs to adjust his position on the bed frequently, and he instructed Upendra and the rest of us, "Turn me over occasionally, this way and that way, even I do not say."

Svarupa Damodara gave an update on his coming scientific conference. He had previously mentioned that some big men in Delhi had suggested that we set up a branch of the Bhaktivedanta Institute there, and Prabhupada thought they had offered us a place.

Svarupa Damodara: "No, they didn't offer a place, but they wanted to help to establish a center for the Bhaktivedanta Institute."

Prabhupada: "How to help?"

Svarupa Damodara: "Various ways—money and supporting us. They said it's very essential."

Prabhupada asked what sort of support were they offering.

Svarupa Damodara: "Actually, he was speaking in general terms. This Professor Malsanda, he's the head of the Physiology Department in the All-India Institute of Medical Sciences. He's a very religious man. He's also a very well-known scholar. He's a medical doctor by profession. He belongs to many different scientific worldwide organizations, and he feels very strongly that we should have a center in Delhi for the Bhaktivedanta Institute."

Prabhupada: "So, money is required?"

Svarupa Damodara: "He didn't say anything specifically, but he said he would be very happy to help us in establishing a center there. He's very favorable to our philosophy, and he invited me to his own home, and we discussed at great length about the philosophy that we are trying to present in the scientific community, and he feels that it's very genuine and they should help us to push forward."

Always pragmatic, Prabhupada complimented him but added a word of caution. "With this cooperation, this institution will be very prestigious. So if it is possible, organize. But don't overburden."

Tamal Krishna: "What is that overburden?"
Prabhupada: "Other business may not suffer."
Tamal Krishna: "Publishing books should not suffer, and lecturing, like that."
Prabhupada: "We already have place in Bombay."
Svarupa Damodara: "Yes."
Prabhupada: "So if Bombay is sufficient, don't bother in Delhi."
Svarupa Damodara: "Yes. I will do it slowly, first of all to make sure that whatever we have done is going on nicely; then we can expand later on. But in India it is true that everybody I met is very respectful to Srila Prabhupada's movement and to what we are trying to do."
Prabhupada: "Yes. That much we want to keep. The people may not think of it as bogus."
Svarupa Damodara: "Our chief guest for tomorrow

has already arrived. And he's
very impressed. He brought
also an architect. He's a retired
engineer. Also, we already have a
mathematician from Delhi University
for tomorrow. So I took three of
them on a tour of our temple and
gave them nice *prasādam*. They
were very impressed."

Tamal Krishna: "This has never happened before,
Srila Prabhupada. You are the real
acharya for this age. You perfectly
know how to spread Krishna
consciousness. You're making people
who would ordinarily never take
interest in Krishna consciousness
become devotees."

Prabhupada chuckled at the news of such
esteemed guests coming to Vrindavan for a science
conference. It reminded him of an exchange he had
with a businessman when he first moved there. "In the
beginning, when I was selling *Back to Godhead* alone,
one practical businessman, Mr. Bande I think, he said,
'Swamijī, why you have made Vrindavan headquarter?
It is not a place for culture."

Svarupa Damodara confirmed Prabhupada's choice
to begin their program in the holy *dhāma* by citing the
reactions he has had from his invited guests. "They
said the selection is ideal. They said this type of
conference should start from Vrindavan. They feel that
way, many of them. Yesterday Dr. Mishra, the head of
the Biophysics Department in the All-India Institute of
Medical Sciences, called me to his home, and I went,
and we had about half an hour discussion. He told me
that he wanted to do this by himself for a long time

several years ago. Then somehow, when he saw our flyer, his wife told him that 'You've been trying to do like this for so many years, but somebody has started doing it.' So she told him, 'You must join them.' Actually, he wanted to come from tomorrow, but some people are coming from Germany, because he has a big grant. He's actually an internationally well-known scientist. But he's coming on Sunday, and he's also going to speak about half an hour."

Tamal Krishna asked if the Bhaktivedanta Institute would be eligible for grants, and Svarupa Damodara said, "Yes. Once we get incorporated in Bombay, we can also get grants from the government; also in the United States when we get it properly established."

Svarupa Damodara told Prabhupada that the name Bhaktivedanta was becoming well-known and respected. "When they hear 'Bhaktivedanta,' they immediately know that this is Prabhupada. Many of them told me that 'Oh, I have heard Swamiji's lecture in Delhi. It's very nice and very impressive and very convincing.' Many of them told me like that."

Tamal Krishna confirmed it, recalling the pandals Prabhupada has held in Delhi over the last few years. "Your lectures in Delhi drew the most intelligent class of people, Srila Prabhupada. The other swamis, when they would lecture, they would get just the typical pious Indian people, but yours also drew a very intelligent group of people, sophisticated people."

Prabhupada laughed, "They danced—with coat-pant, I have seen."

By this time it was 9.30 p.m., and Prabhupada brought the discussion to a close. He requested two spoonfuls of warm Glucose, and in keeping with Kirtanananda's new role as his medical supervisor, he had Maharaja administer it.

Tamal Krishna told Kirtanananda, "Preserve the sweet lemons. Prabhupada sometimes wants sweet lemons for drinking, so you should preserve."

And Prabhupada requested the most important medicine, "And chant Hare Krishna."

Kirtanananda: "Hare Krishna."

Tamal Krishna: "Should we have some chanting now, Srila Prabhupada?"

Prabhupada: "Yes, chanting twenty-four hours."

OCTOBER 14, 1977

Early in the morning, around 8 a.m., Tamal Krishna informed Prabhupada that according to the log book in which we are keeping a detailed record of his ingestion and passing, he had not passed water for nearly ten hours, so Prabhupada took a small amount of sweet lemon juice. He also told Bhakti Charu to have Pisima make *dal* and *roti* for him.

Prabhupada requested Pisima to recite a *nṛsimha-mantra* over him, which she did while he received his massage. She chanted the mantra while lightly rubbing her hand on his chest. As she turned to return to her cooking, Prabhupada said, "She is a Vaishnavi, and God has sent her at the right time to cure me."

He has shown no discomfort from taking solid food, but he complained that he had no taste. So we decided to give him sweet-lemon juice from Tehran, which he found palatable.

Atreya Rishi and Parivrajakacharya Swami left for Tehran this morning after chanting many hours. Atreya told Prabhupada he will return every weekend with a fresh supply of sweet lemons.

Prabhupada: "The sweet-lemon juice is nectarine. It is very nice. Such sweetness in your country is the great mercy of

Bhagavan, and you are trying to
spread Krishna consciousness nicely.
Krishna will bless you."

Prabhupada is taking sips of Yamuna *jala* every
fifteen minutes or so. He keeps pictures of Krishna-
Balarama and Radha-Syamasundara next to him and
often looks for a long time at Them.

This is the first day of the science conference. Tamal
Krishna gave Prabhupada an enthusiastic description.
"All arrangements have been made. First I saw where
they are taking *prasādam*: first-class, all long tables
in a big room, long tables, tablecloths, and proper
plates, knives, forks, spoons. Perfect for them. Nice
fans, very gorgeous-looking curtains. Everything real
high-class. And serving *kacaurīs*, hot *jalebīs*, all nice
preparations. And our men, oh, they look very, very
scientific. [Laughter] They're wearing shirt, coat, and
pants. Svarupa Damodara looks like a scientist now.
He has transformed himself. All of them, Madhava,
Sadaputa, and Jnana dasa, they all look very..."

Prabhupada:	"Elegant."
Tamal Krishna:	"Very elegant. All the scientists who are attending are dressed a little informally, but our men are very formal. They have ties on. Everybody has a badge. All the people who are attending have a special badge mentioning the scientific conference's name and the individual person's name. That's in one place. Then in another room is the conference room. It was the room where we were going to have

161

the bank—a really big room with a fancy backdrop. Some decorator has come and made a very fancy backdrop. There's a long table and podium with microphones and very nice seats. In the dining hall, all the seats have special white linen cloths over all the chairs. Very fresh-looking and clean. And in the other room it's very cool. There are curtains so that the sun can't come in, and now there's a big *yajña* going on. Yasodanandana Maharaja and the *gurukula* boys are inaugurating the conference by chanting Sanskrit mantras, and some of the scientists are... Actually, they were amazed to see how our men could chant like that. The whole building is first-class for this purpose. When we build this Bhaktivedanta Institute Hall. . . It's the most wonderful idea to have this conference here, Srila Prabhupada. These scientists, they're going to be converted to Krishna consciousness. I was certain of it by seeing these arrangements. They never could have... They're being tricked."

Prabhupada: (grinning) "Yes."

Tamal Krishna: "It's wonderful."

Prabhupada: "How many scientists have come?"

Tamal Krishna: "I don't know. There must be somewhere between fifty and a

hundred. But they're expecting...
Today is a working day. It's Friday.
Tomorrow and Sunday everyone is
going to come. Everyone wants to
come. They consider it prestigious to
come here, because the whole thing
is being done on an international
level."

Prabhupada: "Svarupa Damodara..."

Tamal Krishna: (laughing) "He's your top preacher.
I could see that in the future this
man... He's the most important
preacher, because people are basing
everything on these rascal scientists.
I think this is only one of your many
plans, Srila Prabhupada. There's no
doubt that you have to make every
effort to get back to health. This
is only one plan, and I'm seeing...
It's really inconceivable how these
scientists... I never thought to see
such people walking into Vrindavan.
Who would have ever expected
it? They all look like Darwin's
representatives. But our men look
even more scientific than they
do. That's the best part of it. And
although they are dressed in shirt...
Even though Svarupa Damodara is
in shirt, coat, and pants, he has a
big tilak on, and *mālikā* [beads]."

Prabhupada: "That is wanted."

Tamal Krishna: "Very good. And then our sannyasis
look so nice. There's Aksayananda

163

Maharaja and Bhakti-prema Swami. They were both there, very nicely dressed, with *daṇḍas*. The whole thing is complete. The participants get to stay in a nice guesthouse. Then there will be building of Bhaktivedanta Institute Hall. All of these things are a complete arrangement. I think these men are surprised to see that how such a thing has sprung up, as they had not been aware of it before. And when they see these books, Srila Prabhupada, that the scientists have written, I think that will floor these men. They will be completely amazed to see it. Normally, if anyone else dared to do such a thing as this, to prove by science that life comes from life, it would be a very immature attempt by some religious person, and it would not have very much weight. But here they are coming face-to-face with people who are actually scientists, and they will not be able to deny our arguments. I think that your Guru Maharaja is very pleased with this program, Srila Prabhupada."

Prabhupada: "I have given the ideas. Now you give the shape."

Tamal Krishna: "We want some more ideas also. You have to give enough ideas for at least ten thousand years. [Prabhupada chuckles softly.] This is a great idea, Srila Prabhupada. It really is. It's wonderful. I think that each year if we hold at least one conference in Vrindavan, it gradually will become one of the main events of the scientific community of northern India. No doubt about it. In fact, I'm certain that people will be begging to be able to come. There'll be big competition for who is able to be given the permission to come and the reservation in the guesthouse. I think we'll have to build many guesthouses here."

Prabhupada: "Yes. We shall do."

Tamal Krishna: "And also I took darshan of Krishna-Balarama, and Lord Balarama's club looks like it will destroy anyone who dares to interfere with Krishna's plan. [Prabhupada chuckles.] He has a very big club, all silver. And many people were coming, many pilgrims. You were just asking me whether as many were coming as when we were previously here. There are as many. The temple was very much crowded with people having darshan. I could tell that some of the people were *pāṇḍās*, guides. They have to bring everyone to this temple, because the people want to see Krishna-Balarama Mandir. People were making a lot of expressions of joy to see Krishna and Balarama. They were very surprised to see how beautiful They were appearing. And also Radha-Syamasundara is a very big attraction, because that boy [head pujari, Omkara dasa] dresses Them very beautifully. All the Deities look very nice today. They look especially happy about this science conference, I think. If we do this in Bombay also, Srila Prabhupada, it will be tremendous success."

Prabhupada told us that respectable gentlemen don't like to come to Vrindavan because there are so many gundas. "*Paṇḍas* are gundas!"

Later Prabhupada inquired about the science program again. Not many are attending, but this is the first day.

Bhagatji is holding a feast program for all the local Vaishnavas and our GBC and sannyasis. Prabhupada was a little disturbed that this should go on during the conference, but Tamal Krishna explained that after the conference many men would have left so Bhagatji was keen to feed them before they go.

Prabhupada took *prasādam* again today but ate very little. He has no taste for it. He took a little *roti* and *dal*.

Later Prabhupada was looking at Bhavananda and said, "Just now I am forgetting your name. This is the position." When asked if he would like to hear *Bhāgavatam,* Prabhupada said *kirtan* is better. *Bhāgavatam* is a little straining.

A telegram arrived describing how in France,

25,000 hardbound *Gītās* had been distributed in one week. One boy, Bhakta Richard, did over 1,500 himself. Prabhupada was very happy and said, "Yes. We do not want liberation. We want to serve the purpose of the Gosvamis, in association with pure devotees. To stop birth and death is not our purpose."

Svarupa Damodara came and gave a brief report on the conference. Later on, after I came in and gave a report on the conference, Prabhupada said, "If the preaching goes on, then I can remain in any condition."

Hari-sauri: "The preaching will always go on, Prabhupada. [Prabhupada smiled at this.] If you are here, we can go on increasing."

Prabhupada: "Yes, increase book distribution."

I said that if he remained with us, we could all go out and achieve anything.

Prabhupada asked if he should take the risk of milk, but I advised not for a few more days, because it causes much mucus. Prabhupada agreed.

Hari-sauri: "Is there any difficulty from the solid food?"

Prabhupada: "No taste."

Hari-sauri: "No taste. But at least it may give some strength back."

Prabhupada: "How can it? If it cannot enter into the system?"

Hari-sauri: "It's not being digested? [Prabhupada shook his head.] If you were to take something like soup, that would be more easily digested; just the liquids, that would have much of the goodness."

167

Prabhupada: "I cannot take, no taste."

Hari-sauri: (after a pause) "At least with the chanting that gives a higher taste."

Prabhupada: "Hmm."

Then he asked for the time—5:40 p.m. He is waiting for the conference to finish at 6 p.m. Then the scientists will come to see him.

When they came in, they were all dressed up in shirts, ties, and suit-pants. Prabhupada insisted they be given chairs to sit on. He treated them very respectfully. "You have got coat-pants, you sit down on the chair."

Prabhupada asked if there was any reaction from the other side. Svarupa Damodara said there was none. They had a press conference; *The Times of India* and four others were there, and All India Radio came. Svarupa Damodara mentioned that Prabhupada's Godbrother O.B.L. Kapoor had spoken for five minutes and that it was all *māyāvādī*. Dr. Kapoor said that molecules are actually invisible, and because everything is made of molecules then everything is invisible and therefore nothing exists. Material energy does not exist. Svarupa Damodara pointed out to him that actually material energy is a fact but it is inferior, and spiritual energy is also a fact but it is superior.

Later Prabhupada told Bhakti Charu that the *kavirāja* may be told of his condition and if he wishes to come he can do so.

About 9 p.m., Prabhupada asked again what are the critical days. Tamal Krishna brought the astrologer's report, and Pradyumna was able to read it with much more clarity.

Prabhupada: "So, the final inauspicious date, when does that come?"

Tamal Krishna:	"The final inauspicious date?"
Prabhupada:	"Yes, death. The fatal day."
Tamal Krishna:	"What is this Prabhupada? Ketu Mahādaśā?"
Prabhupada:	"That is the most inauspicious date."
Tamal Krishna:	"It says you are currently undergoing the fag end of Ketu Mahādaśā and that will last until thirteenth of January 1978."

It said Prabhupada's life is up to 81 years, four months approximately. Mercury is *ṣaṣṭheśa* (disease). Moon, Jupiter, and Mars in the eighth house is very bad. The patient may not recover. Eighth house is house of death. There is negative effect throughout September, October, and November, and Saturn becomes more malefic and almost stationary. In February-March, it becomes stagnant on Jupiter and Ketu and the last week of February, and goes through the same degrees again in reverse. Many other things were mentioned.

The astrologer recommended *mahā mṛtyum japa*, as Shiva is Lord of Sani, this will give prolonged life. He repeated the life is 81 years, 4 months approximately.

Prabhupada:	"So, *japa* is *mahā-mantra japa*, and *Bhāgavata*. So either read *Bhāgavata* or chant Hare Krishna. And let me lie down like this, that's all—as it is going on. Huh? Can you make this program?"
Tamal Krishna:	"This program is already going on."
Prabhupada:	"Let it go on, that's all."
Tamal Krishna:	"And you should try to drink whenever you have desire."
Prabhupada:	"Yes."
Tamal Krishna:	"You shouldn't try to fast until death."

Prabhupada:	"No, that is useless. Do you recommend that?"
Tamal Krishna:	"No, definitely not! I recommend that somehow or another you go on lying there and we'll go on chanting and we'll pass until March–April 1978, then we'll take you to Mayapur for the festival and then we'll do a world tour."

Prabhupada smiled. "That is very nice program." Prabhupada asked Pradyumna, "You can read *Bhāgavata* from the point where I have stopped. Is it possible?"

Pradyumna:	"Yes, Prabhupada."
Prabhupada:	"And when he's tired, kirtan. Huh, Kirtanananda? This is *mahā yajña, mahā japa.* And as far as possible let me lie down like this. What can be done? Is that conclusion all right?"
Upendra:	"Yes, Prabhupada."
Tamal Krishna:	"I also say that Pisima is here, so whenever she cooks something, you take, and take Yamuna *jala* and sweet-lemon juice. Take things also, as you are doing. You shouldn't artificially fast or stop eating."
Prabhupada:	"No, that is suicide. So, when you are beginning? Do it. Upendra, you keep honey ready, and whenever I shall require... As soon as he stops, then begin kirtan. Someone may take note."
Tamal Krishna:	"Jayadvaita is here. Arundhati, Pradyumna."

Prabhupada:	"The whole staff is here. In this way it can go on. It will require expert editing, and at the same time there will be discussion of *Bhāgavatam.* What do the editors say?"
All:	"Yes!"
Prabhupada:	"Read each word very distinctly. Doesn't matter if it takes time. You all think, and I'll hear and do the needful. Anyway, it will be discussion of *Bhāgavatam.* Let us try—*sv-alpam api asya dharmasya.* So read, one after another, slowly but surely."

So, the amazing happened: In the midst of his worst physical crisis with no hope for increase in health, Prabhupada incredibly began his translation work again. Everyone was in ecstasy. We all thought of how Krishnadasa Kaviraja had worked, and now here again Prabhupada was repeating history.

Pradyumna began reading, first the verses, then the *ṭīkās* as Prabhupada asked for them. Prabhupada asked him to translate sometimes, and he corrected him sometimes. Sometimes he had Jayadvaita read his commentaries from *Kṛṣṇa,* and in this way he spoke his purport. They began from Tenth Canto, Chapter 13, Verse 33, and Prabhupada did about seven verses before finishing for the night.

OCTOBER 15, 1977

Very early in the morning, Prabhupada listened to a report from Svarupa Damodara about the scientists who are here for the conference, how they are appreciating Prabhupada's efforts here, as well as the temple architecture and the *gurukula*. Prabhupada was pleased.

He then asked for a massage with oil made from smashed mustard seed and camphor and heated on a charcoal fire. Rupanuga, Abhirama, Bhagavat, and others applied the oil all over Prabhupada's body. He appreciated it and said that the body should be kept fit so that it will be able to work. He said this oil will warm him and stimulate as well. When Bhagatji arrived, he called for a professional masseur, as Prabhupada wants at least four hours of massage each day with this oil.

Bhagavat asked Prabhupada about the dal and roti he took. Prabhupada replied, "Simply touch."

Bhagavat: "How was it tasting?"

Prabhupada: "It was very tasteful, but my tongue has no taste. Maybe gradually, by stimulating the body."

Svarupa Damodara told Prabhupada how a professor from Agra had requested another conference in Vrindavan next year.

Prabhupada: "Let them make advance in scientific research, but they cannot capture the real thing. Just like, I have heard it, when Socrates was condemned to death, the judges inquired, 'How Mr. Socrates wants to be entombed?' When the judges inquired Socrates, 'How you want to be entombed?' Socrates said, 'First of all capture me, then there is question of entombing!' "

Abhirama: "Yes, it is historical fact."

Prabhupada: "Yes. What is wording?"

172

Abhirama: "He said, 'First of all you will have to capture me.' "

After a pause, Prabhupada commented about the conference that "somehow or another it has become successful."

Bhagatji went off in the morning and brought a man named Nathuram from Mathura, a professional masseur. As he began, Prabhupada told him, "You are like my son. Now you have to cure me." He replied, "We are all your sons. We will pray to Radharani." He massaged Prabhupada for over ninety minutes with oil mixed with opium. When he did the stomach, he said that Prabhupada's intestines had a knot in them and therefore there was no hunger. He applied hot water bottles and rind leaves smeared with oil to keep the heat in. Prabhupada liked his massage a lot and commented that none of our men could do it; this man knows the art. The man doesn't smoke or drink or eat meat and is a devotee. Afterwards, I saw him attend *sandhyā-ārati.*

Vanamali, the *kavirāja*, came in the morning. He said that Prabhupada was simply very, very weak although there was nothing wrong with the body. However, he was surprised to see the discoloration of his urine and took it with him to examine. Later, he told Bhakti Charu Swami that Prabhupada had a form of gonorrhea, which is very dangerous if not treated. He said that much fluid should be taken in to flush out his system. The cloudiness, he said, was semen which has not been able to be used by the body, so if this disease continues, this will form hard particles and block up the urinary passage.

Bhavananda is going to stay rather than return to Mayapur, to help take personal care of Prabhupada.

In the afternoon, Prabhupada asked what it was

that he was taking which caused the blood to come in his urine. I suggested it was the orange juice which is very strong for the kidney. I advised Prabhupada to take pomegranate juice. I asked if the sweet lemon was giving strength.

Prabhupada: "I don't think so."
Hari-sauri: "But it gives taste, though?"

Prabhupada agreed. He said he liked the pomegranate juice.

Later, Prabhupada talked to Tamal Krishna and Giriraj about the bank transfers. The head man from Delhi was "disgusted" with the PNB organization here. They will remove the present manager, and they are very apologetic toward us. Prabhupada was pleased with the way Tamal Krishna and Giriraj have dealt with the affair.

When they came later, after their meetings had finished, Prabhupada told them, "What is that *phish-phish?*" (They were whispering together.) "Deal very carefully, and as far as possible don't keep money in the bank; invest in books. That is my request. If you keep money, there will be so much trouble."

Then there was a little discussion about how the bank is too attached to rules.

Tamal Krishna: "Jayapataka has complained there is no stock of books."
Giriraj: "It may be because we are dealing with only one printer."
Prabhupada: "Then analyze many printers. Never mind the price—keep huge stock of books. Why unnecessarily keep in bank. I think that in the BBT there is 5-6 lakhs. Why not transfer into books? Hindi can be distributed all

over the world—Gujarati; English
to Australia. Why money should be
kept in the bank?" Prabhupada said
Jayapataka can print in Calcutta.

Giriraj presented to Prabhupada a coat that had
been worn by the Deity Srinathji, which the Maharaja
of Udaipur had sent for Prabhupada. Then he read
to Prabhupada a beautiful prayer he had written to
Lord Krishna for Prabhupada's recovery. Prabhupada
listened carefully to each and every word, taking
great delight in the expression of love and gratitude
expressed by his disciple.

Giriraj: "My dear Lord Krishna, You are
known as Yogeshvara, the master
of all mystic powers. So it is
very easy for You to perform the
impossible, as You have done
many times in the past. By Your
merciful glance You restored life
to the boys and cows who had
died by drinking the water of the
Yamuna River which was poisoned
by Kaliya. And You swallowed the
devastating forest fire to protect
the inhabitants of Vrindavan. In the
rāsa dance You expanded Yourself
to be simultaneously present by
the side of each *gopī*. And as *guru-
dakṣiṇā,* You recovered the dead
son of Your teacher. When the
hunchback maidservant of Kamsa
smeared You with sandalwood
pulp, You made her straight and

175

beautiful. And as a householder in Dvaraka, You expanded Yourself into sixteen thousand Krishnas and simultaneously satisfied all of Your sixteen thousand wives. When Sudama Brahmana offered You chipped rice, You transformed his poor cottage into a beautiful palace suitable for the king of heaven. And to satisfy Mother Devaki, You returned her six dead sons from the kingdom of Bali. To appease the Dvaraka *brahmaṇa,* You also reclaimed his dead sons from Maha-Vishnu. When Srila Prabhupada sat with seven dollars under a tree in Tompkins Square Park, You transformed that tree into so many royal palaces, and You expanded that seven dollars into millions of dollars. And when Srila Prabhupada spoke Your message, You turned the *mlecchas* and *caṇḍālas* into Your devotees. And when Srila Prabhupada went all by himself to sell his *Srimad-Bhāgavatam* volumes, You expanded him into ten thousand loving salesmen who are working day and night without asking any salary, and You expanded his suitcase of books into fifty-five million pieces of literature in twenty-three different languages. And when Hare Krishna Land was

lost to the demons, You returned
it to His Divine Grace. So from
these examples we can understand
that for You, the impossible is
not difficult, but rather, You have
performed so many impossible feats
for Your devotees. Therefore, if You
desire, please give Srila Prabhupada
a new body."

Prabhupada was deeply moved and transcendentally enlivened. "Excellent. Print in *Back to Godhead*. I am getting little glimpse—He may agree to your prayer, yes."

Prabhupada whispered to Bhagatji, "Visvambhara, everywhere they want me; you also."

Bhagatji:	"I wish that I may go early."
Prabhupada:	"No. Why you should go?"
Bhagatji:	"I wish you finish the *Bhāgavatam*."
Prabhupada:	"That is my desire."
Bhagatji:	"Krishna will not fulfil your desire?"
Prabhupada:	"Krishna is independent."
Prabhupada:	(to Giriraj) "Now I am getting little glimpse. He may agree to your prayer."

After a short pause he told Jayapataka, "Now stock books immediately. Print. He'll pay [Tamal Krishna]. There is no question of becoming miserly. You print as many books as you like. All money will be paid if you have no money."

Jayapataka informed him that three Bengali books—*Bhakti-kata, Jñāna-kata, Bhagawaner-kata*—are now being printed. "One of our parties did 12,000 books, went to Bombay and had to come here. There was no stock. Vrindavan gave 2,000."

177

Prabhupada was a little disturbed. "Why stock is lacking? Why this mismanagement? There is no question of shortage of stock. I give you open order: print more than necessary. If you don't print, what can I do?"

Bhakti Charu asked if they should print in Calcutta.

Prabhupada: "I do not know, but get it printed in huge stock!"

Bhakti Charu informed him that Bhubaneswar had money for construction purposes. Prabhupada told him that construction wasn't as important as printing.

Prabhupada translated in the morning again, about four more verses. The masseur also came and massaged Prabhupada for about two hours.

In the evening, Nava Yogendra Swami arrived from Africa, and Pancha Dravida Swami from South America. Nava Yogendra brought lots of fruits on silver plates, and dried fruits and nuts.

OCTOBER 16, 1977

Prabhupada had a very bad morning, coughing up large amounts of very thick, jelly-like mucus. He had drunk some milk yesterday evening. We gave him Benedryl, but it didn't have much effect. He also translated during the night. Tamal Krishna asked him to drink more and asked Prabhupada why he wasn't drinking much. Prabhupada said, "I cannot." Prabhupada did, though, drink some pomegranate juice with his golden straw.

In the afternoon, Dr. Ghosh from Allahabad came. Prabhupada was very grateful. He had left immediately from Darjeeling and came via Calcutta as soon as he heard Prabhupada was sick. After he went out, Prabhupada pointed out to us how much a friend he was that he had immediately come. He requested us to give him the best room and look to all of his needs. Prabhupada told us that he is the only one remaining. All his contemporary friends are now gone. Dinanath Misra has also gone. Prabhupada said that Krishna has made Dr. Ghosh happy in all respects, from monetary point of view, family life, position. "He is the biggest medical practitioner in Allahabad. Everyone knows, even in the street, Dr. Ghosh. Take care of him very carefully."

Prabhupada took a mix of papaya and coconut milk, avocado and pepper, and a little *subji* for lunch. He is actually very weak and talks in a very low voice. The main difference now is that he is making a fight for survival, whereas when he first came it seemed he was ready to leave. Only by his great compassion for his fallen disciples has he decided to stay and struggle in this way. He is drinking, but not much—only 250–300 cubic centimeters per day. Therefore, he is very weak.

Dr. Ghosh came later and advised he take some *channa* and sugar. He gave Prabhupada a massage, which Prabhupada liked. The masseur also came and massaged Prabhupada for about two hours.

We had a GBC meeting in the morning, and everyone gave a time when they could next visit Prabhupada, and a schedule will be arranged around that. Ramesvara and Satsvarupa Swamis have already gone, and Kirtanananda Swami will leave today.

In the evening, Baradraj came and explained to Prabhupada his masterplan for a proposed new doll exhibit that Ambarisa dasa will help to pay for. It begins with an explanation of what the soul is, how he is put into nature, and gradually how he can be elevated until he achieves perfection by going home, back to Godhead. He explained how one exhibit shows a man and then chemically analyses to show life doesn't come from chemicals. Then from the molecular level they will show how gradually the fetus develops. Therefore there is life right from the beginning.

At this point, Prabhupada said, "Life begins from water."

Baradraj asked, "How is that, Prabhupada?"

Prabhupada briefly outlined the gradual evolution of the soul through different species. "Just like the sea. Sea, and from within the sea an exhibition of life begins in the form of sea animals or fish or similar. Then life develops, evolves. Life... Sea does not generate life, but in this material world, life begins from water—*te tam bhuktvā svarga-lokaṁ viśālaṁ kṣīṇe puṇye martyalokaṁ viśanti.* From higher planets they fall down with water and then again like bubbles, begin from water. Then life. As the water dries up, then vegetables, then *jalajā nava-lakṣāṇi sthāvarā lakṣa-viṁśatiḥ...* moving animals, ants... In this way, birds, beasts, then four-legged animals, uncivilized man, then civilized man, Vedic knowledge, then God realization. This is the process."

Baradraj explained how in the second part they want to show how everything originates from the Lord's glance.

Prabhupada: "Yes, everything originates from His energy. He is original cause of two energies, material and spiritual. Therefore He is the original cause."

Baradraj told him, "In the second part we also want to show how the Lord out of His infinite kindness and mercy has created the material world so that the living entities can be corrected."

"We also have a diorama here of Isaac Newton showing the model of the universe to his friend, and his friend says, 'Oh, such a brilliant thing, such a wonderful model. Who has made this?' And he says, 'Nobody. It just appeared here.' And he makes his point that if such a small thing has taken so much intelligence and skill, then what to speak of the great universe that we see before us? How could it have come from nothing?"

Prabhupada told him, "Yes. It is a chance to come to understanding. The ideas are there and, if properly exhibited, it will be wonderful."

Baradraj told Prabhupada how one exhibit shows animals and men and how animals are superior in sense perception, i.e. elephants eat more, dogs' smelling is better, etc. Prabhupada suggested the vulture for seeing better. Baradraj continued that human beings will be shown as being superior and have some responsibility. Human life is for advancing and upgrading. Then they will show that the world is in chaos due to giving up responsibility.

Prabhupada: "That is explained by Bhaktivinoda Thakura: *māyār bośe, jāccho bese.* This song, those that have eyes to see, will see that all of them are being washed away by the waves of maya."

Baradraj said that the solution will be shown by the speaking of the *Bhāgavatam* on the banks of the Yamuna.

Prabhupada: "Very good. The second chapter, find out the verses: *yaṁ pravrajantam anupetam apeta-kṛtyaṁ* [*SB* 1.2.2]."

Giriraj read the whole verse, which describes

181

Sukadeva leaving home, and Prabhupada asked him to read the next verse.

Prabhupada: "This is the one: sasāriṇaṁ karuṇayāha purāṇa-guhyaṁ" [SB 1.2.3]. Prabhupada had him read the translation and next verse: nārāyaṇaṁ namaskṛtya naraṁ caiva narottamam / devīṁ sarasvatīṁ vyāsaṁ tato jayam udīrayet [SB 1.2.4].

Prabhupada: "These things can be indicated. So, you have made the outline first-class. Now if it is done carefully, at least in the West it will be very, very wonderful."

Baradraj: "We're just trying to fulfil your desires, Prabhupada."

Prabhupada: "Do it. Krishna will fulfil."

Baradraj asked where Prabhupada would like the next exhibit. He mentioned Prabhupada had previously wanted one in London. Prabhupada said, "Yes, London has many tourists." Then Baradraj asked if London was better than Washington.

Prabhupada said, "No, Washington is also... London many hundreds of tourists come daily."

Jayatirtha said there was a plot available near Madame Tussauds. Prabhupada used to stay in that area when he first went there. He thought that was a nice place.

Then Prabhupada covered himself up, and kirtan began again. He translated a little in the night also, and had a fairly restful repose.

182

OCTOBER 17, 1977

In the morning, Prabhupada called Acyutananda Swami and asked him what his plans were. He told Prabhupada that he was returning to the West. Prabhupada was satisfied.

Dr. Ghosh said too many people were crowding in the room and using up oxygen and spreading germs, so the chanting party moved to another room.

Around noon, Govardhana, the Detroit temple president, arrived, and Prabhupada asked for a report. Govardhana was a little overcome. Tears flooded his eyes, and he couldn't speak for a few minutes due to being upset on seeing Prabhupada's present condition. After regaining his composure Prabhupada asked whether the men in the ghetto district were giving any trouble. Govardhana gave a favorable report, and Prabhupada was pleased.

Prabhupada was hardly audible and didn't move at all. Sometimes he appears very, very weak, and although he has agreed to stay, actually, at times he talks of leaving us; thus constant encouragement is needed.

In the afternoon, Tamal Krishna went to bathe in the Yamuna, and Upendra was not attending because of a cold. Prabhupada complained about "feeling alone" after he asked for Tamal Krishna twice and Upendra once and neither were available.

Dr. Ghosh has stressed the drinking of lots of fluids to clear out the kidneys and says that his stomach and liver are all right.

For lunch, Prabhupada had fried portal, eggplant, three puris, a whip of coconut milk, avocado, and papaya, and another whip of soaked figs, raisins, and apricots.

Dr. Ghosh brought Dr. Gopal, a young doctor from

the Ramakrishna Hospital, who seems very competent. He diagnosed a severe infection of the kidneys which could be fatal if not treated. He gave some medicines for it and stressed increase of liquid intake. Prabhupada's pulse was ninety-six, but the doctor said it skips a beat every eighteen. His blood pressure was normal at one hundred thirty.

After the doctors had gone, Prabhupada asked Giriraj about Bombay. He told Prabhupada that they want to gold-plate the chakras on top of the domes to protect them from the deleterious effects of the sea breezes. Then they discussed about the opening date. Prabhupada said it should be as early as possible. Different dates were discussed. January 8, 1978, was suggested because Yasodanandana Swami will be in Japan until then. Prabhupada still thought it should be as early as possible. Then Tamal Krishna asked Prabhupada if it was necessary to hire the South Indian brahmans, because in Bombay people have asked our men to open a temple; they don't really care whether local brahmans do it or not. They are not so fussy as in Vrindavan. We all felt Yasodanandana Swami could do it.

Prabhupada smiled. "Western brahmans! That was my prediction. As they are importing ghee, milk, similarly brahmans—go-brāhmaṇa-hitāya ca! That's nice. That is good proposal."

Tamal Krishna suggested opening on Srila Bhaktisiddhanta's disappearance day on December 29. Prabhupada said that would be nice. "We have no such difference, disappearance or appearance."

Giriraj:	"Except in your case, we don't want disappearance."
Prabhupada:	(laughed) *"Jivo va marova!* Because we are going to accept eternity, so appearance and disappearance of

this body is not a very important
thing. *Nitya-līlā.* Eternal life, that
is our Krishna consciousness. So
the earliest possible date. As far as
possible, our men. We can keep some
assistants, local men. If we keep one
or two South Indians, they may take
it we are doing with co-operation, so
one or two may be kept, South Indian
or local men.
"Perform the *yajña* little gorgeously,
that's nice. If you distribute to
local brahmans, some silken cloth,
grains, they'll come. Let them cook
themselves and distribute *prasādam.*"

Then Prabhupada called for a report on the doctor's
diagnosis from Bhavananda. He told Prabhupada about
the infection and the prescribed medicines, which
Prabhupada agreed to take. The infection is called
renal damage and this could change into uremia. They
advised Prabhupada should take high protein foods
and however much urine is passed, the next day an
extra 400 cc of fluid should be taken in. He stopped the
hydrogen peroxide mouthwash advised by Dr. Ghosh,
as it could be dangerous.

One reason Dr. Ghosh came is to establish a clinic
here. He explained his scheme to Prabhupada, and
Prabhupada listened to it. Then Prabhupada explained
that first of all Dr. Ghosh should become a devotee. He
had Tamal Krishna Maharaja try to explain this, but
Dr. Ghosh is very difficult to get through to. He is fully
absorbed in working for others. That is his service to
Krishna, he says—to work for others. Simply to attend
our program of *ārati* and chanting, etc., is not enough.
He wants to work. Tamal Krishna was trying to explain

185

that once he is absorbed a little in devotional practice, then we can begin on his scheme, but it was a task to make him understand.

Prabhupada spoke to him directly, "You have to practice how to live in Vrindavan. How I shall be detached from *viṣayī*. We are attached to this body, children, wife, and house. So long we have got the desire that this body, wife, children will give me pleasure, we cannot live in Vrindavan."

Due to Dr. Ghosh's obvious attachments, Prabhupada kindly suggested he come and live with his wife and practice vanaprastha, gradual detachment, and after some time we can take up his purpose.

After the doctor left the room, Prabhupada commented, "As it is natural for people to be attached to wife and family, Dr. Ghosh is attached. He has to practice *vanaprastha*. Just like Dr. Sharma [our *gurukula* principal]. He has made up his mind. The method is mentioned in the shastra. Otherwise such schemes will be waste of time."

I mentioned that Dr. Ghosh is not very good at hearing.

Prabhupada replied, "He has got *śraddhā*, some faith. After *śraddhā*, *sādhu-saṅga*; you are all Vaishnavas, gradually he'll understand."

OCTOBER 18, 1977

Jayatirtha, Harikesa, Balavanta, Gurukripa, Acyutananda, and Yasodanandana all left today.

In the morning, Prabhupada was very weak. He called in Tamal Krishna and complained that he didn't want to take the medicine because it disturbed his sleep. However, his urine is considerably clearer today, and it seems to be having some good effect. We were lightly massaging Prabhupada, but his body is quite cold all over, especially his feet. He is so weak we could hardly hear his voice, and we were trying to encourage him to carry on with the medicine and also increase the amount he drinks to clear out the kidney infection. As Tamal Krishna gave so many reasons for drinking, saying that the lack of sleep is offset by the good effects, Prabhupada protested, saying that he cannot drink. "I cannot drink, drink, drink. Drinking is a botheration. How can I take constantly?"

Tamal Krishna told him that he should drink three or four times, but he has to do more because he only takes a little at a time.

Prabhupada said, "I cannot take so much. What can I do?"

Bhavananda explained to Prabhupada that one effect of the disease is that one doesn't feel like eating and drinking. He told him that it requires one to force oneself to drink in order to get better. At the mention of force, Prabhupada became concerned, thinking that if he gets too ill, then maybe we will force him to take medicine.

Prabhupada: "Then if problem comes, they will
                    forcibly..."

Tamal Krishna told Prabhupada that he should not expect that a natural urge will be there for eating; just as a person who is not Krishna conscious has to follow rules and regulations in the conditioned state, a person who is diseased has to force himself to take medicine before getting the cure.

Prabhupada explained, "That condition is finished [the disease]. I have no stamina to force."

In this way it went on, back and forth, with Prabhupada very negative to every suggestion, and Tamal Krishna Maharaja continuing to try to encourage and persuade. He was practically begging Prabhupada that he must please try to get well.

Bhavananda:	"Prabhupada, your presence on this planet is the only thing which is keeping the onslaught of Kali-yuga from really taking effect. We have no idea what will happen if you should leave."
Prabhupada:	"It is not in my hands—Krishna and Balarama."
Tamal Krishna:	"I think that Krishna and Balarama want you to fight, Prabhupada."
Prabhupada:	"Now I am falling..."

We had to ask Prabhupada three times to understand what he said. He sounded distant, like he was sinking when he said "falling."

Prabhupada:	"I am falling down. Try for urine."
Tamal Krishna:	"Your urine is darker, Prabhupada. In ten and a quarter hours you've only taken one hundred fifty cc. Try to take more, then your urine will become clear. You'll get more determination if you try to drink more, and the disease will go. I'm in favor of increasing drinking and eating. I know it may be a little difficult, but it's the proper way to get better."

He went on to guarantee Prabhupada that we will never allow him to be taken to a hospital, as he has given clear instruction about that. He told him that the lack of sleep could be counteracted by taking some medicine for that purpose.

Bhavananda cited the *Gītā*, saying that if a person has jaundice then in the beginning the cure is bitter,

188

so then also this medicine may be bitter but he should continue and it will work.

They both presented more arguments for Prabhupada to stay with us and not give up, and we continued to lightly rub his arms and legs.

Prabhupada: "This light massage is good. Dr. Ghosh says no massage, and the other doctor says there's no harm."

Tamal Krishna explained that Dr. Ghosh is a little old-fashioned, but Dr. Gopal knows more modern, milder medicines. For example, Dr. Ghosh says Prabhupada should gargle with hydrogen peroxide, but Dr. Gopal said it is too strong and could be dangerous, and prescribed something milder.

Prabhupada: "So they disagree. Which is correct?"

They felt Dr. Gopal was better, and Bhavananda said that Dr. Gopal had explained that the inability to eat and drink is due to the infected kidney. They discussed more about Prabhupada taking more liquid and suggested Complan.

Prabhupada: "So what you want me to do now? Give me a little Complan."

We were relieved to hear him say that, but he carried on in a negative vein.

Tamal Krishna: "Every one of us, all your disciples, are in agreement that you require to force yourself to eat and drink more. What can we do if you don't?"
Prabhupada: "When I don't take anything, then I feel more comfortable."
Tamal Krishna: "But you don't get better. That is the

189

policy of death."

Prabhupada: "So let me die peacefully."

Tamal Krishna: "But we already explained to you we don't want you to die."

Prabhupada: "If I become discomfortable, naturally..."

Tamal Krishna: "But that is only temporary discomfort till one gets better. Medicine is only required till one gets better; then you can throw out the medicine."

Prabhupada: (yawned loudly) *"Jaya* Krishna and Balarama! Now I am feeling comfort."

Bhavananda: "But your urine is cloudy again."

Prabhupada: "Whatever it may be, if you leave me to my fate, then I feel comfortable."

Hari-sauri: "But the other day you said that to fast like this means suicide."

Prabhupada: "Hmm?"

Tamal Krishna: "I asked you the other day if you should fast, that you shouldn't fast till death, and you said 'No, no, that is suicide.' "

After a short pause, Prabhupada said, "Now I am puzzled!"

Tamal Krishna: "We are not able to let you go, Prabhupada. We are not strong enough, and we want you to be with us. We need you longer."

Prabhupada: "Anyway, what can be done? You can give me that preparation?"

Then Prabhupada inquired where Giriraj was. "I wanted to speak to you all. Therefore I was asking for Giriraj. If by Krishna's desire I do not exist during the Bombay opening ceremony, then the ceremony should be very gorgeously performed, and everyone should be given sumptuous *prasādam*—whoever comes. Of course, the ceremony should be performed as early as possible."

Giriraj came in at this point, and Prabhupada had Tamal Krishna repeat it to him.

Prabhupada: "And one thing: don't try to make all the preparation in the temple. Order the foodstuffs from confectioners. Have good stock and distribute— sweets. There are many nice sweet suppliers in Bombay. Order from them. How do you like this idea?"

Giriraj: "It's a very good idea, except that we feel you should be personally present."

Prabhupada: "Hmm, therefore I say it is up to Krishna's desire. You are trying. I am also trying. Now it is up to Krishna and Balarama's desire."

Bhagavan: "You are the jewel that will make it all gorgeous, Prabhupada."

Prabhupada: "So, I am giving the idea."

Tamal Krishna: "The Complan is here Prabhupada."

Prabhupada: "So, what should I do?"

Tamal Krishna: "Sit up and drink."

Prabhupada agreed and drank the whole glass.

We were all happy that Prabhupada was making the effort to please us. Then he lay down again, and we sat around his bed, lightly massaging him.

Prabhupada: "You are all pure Vaishnavas. You have sacrificed everything, material comforts, for Krishna's sake. That is Vaishnava. *Anyābilāṣitā-śūnyaṁ.* You have no other desires. You European and Americans, you were born amongst material desires, and then you became free from material desires. Therefore you are Vaishnavas, *anyābilāṣitā.* So you are so merciful."

Jayapataka: "Because you are *paramahamsa,* Prabhupada, you are seeing everyone else as being surrendered to Krishna. But only by your mercy, you are forcing us to serve Krishna."

Prabhupada turned his attention to the arrival of a Bengali gentleman who has come from New York to ask for initiation from Prabhupada.

Tamal Krishna: "Yes, Prabhupada, Mr. Sukumar Roy Choudhuri."

Prabhupada referred to his letter sent out on July 9, naming eleven disciples to act on his behalf as initiators, "So, I have deputed some of you to initiate?"

Tamal Krishna: "Yes."

Prabhupada: "So I think Jayapataka Swami can do that, if you like. I have already deputed. Tell him. So deputies— Jayapataka Swami's name was there? So I depute him to do this at Mayapur, and he may go with him. I have stopped for the time being. Is

	that all right?"
Tamal Krishna:	"Stopped what, Srila Prabhupada?"
Prabhupada:	"This initiation. I have deputed my disciples. Is it clear or not?"
Devotees:	"It's clear."
Prabhupada:	"You have got list of names? And if by Krishna's grace I recover from this condition, then I shall begin again; or I may not. But in this condition, to initiate is not good."

After a short pause Prabhupada turned his attention back to Dr. Ghosh. "Dr. Ghosh has a scheme, but actually the scheme is given there in the *Bhagavad-gītā* and *Srimad-Bhāgavatam*. We want to introduce in our *gurukula*. We haven't got to manufacture such scheme. Is that correct? Let them rise early in the morning and cleanse. That is the first scheme. This will keep health nice. *Cātur-varṇyaṁ mayā sṛṣṭaṁ*—unless in the human society the *varnashrama* system is introduced, no scheme for social order or any order will be successful."

Then Prabhupada asked about our proposed scheme for developing Panihati, and Jayapataka Swami explained that a change in government had slowed things down.

Prabhupada:	"So do it very cautiously. Who is present here?"

Tamal Krishna listed those present: "Giriraj prabhu, Jayapataka Swami, Bhavananda Maharaja, Hari-sauri prabhu, Bhagavan prabhu, and myself."

Prabhupada:	"So, if you want you can give me little fruit juice! You are satisfied?"

We were all ecstatic. Tamal Krishna asked Bhavananda, "Prabhupada said are you satisfied if he takes a little fruit juice?"

Bhavananda: "Oh, yes. And if you could just take a little of the medicine."

In this way, Prabhupada again began to drink, simply on account of his love for his disciples. He is tolerating such difficult conditions of existence on our plea, although he has the power to leave at will and enter a much better stage of existence.

Then after that, we began to give him a gentle massage.

Tamal Krishna: "The professional masseur does with oil, and we are doing with love."
Prabhupada: "That oil creates some ants."
Tamal Krishna: "Yes, the oil attracts by its sweetness, but we are only trying to attract you by the sweetness of our massage. No ants will come." Prabhupada smiled.

Later, Dr. Ghosh was in, and Tamal Krishna showed Prabhupada a painting done by Pandu dasa. It showed Krishna on Govardhana Hill with two small cowherd boys in the background. Prabhupada commented, "Oh, Krishna alone?" Then Prabhupada gave the painting to Dr. Ghosh and explained that it was so that he could increase his attachment to Krishna, *yena tena prakāreṇa*.

Prabhupada again talked with Svarupa Damodara, who presented a complete plan for his future activities. His headquarters will be in Atlanta, where he wants to stay and write for a few years. He wants some more rooms in Bombay, and then he requires a hall in

194

Vrindavan to be built. Tamal Krishna explained that there was no need for this hall, since the scientists did not come to this first conference in great numbers. But Svarupa Damodara gave convincing arguments in favor, saying that the *gurukula* needed an auditorium, and that actually the scientists were very impressed and said they would bring more people along, since now they could see how nice was the facility already existing.

Then Laksmi Nrisimha dasa, the president of the Puerto Rico farm, came and gave a report of a new property that they have purchased there. He invited Prabhupada to go there if he gets well.

Today also was a record for Prabhupada, as far as drinking goes. When informed that he had drunk more liquid, over 1000 cc, and had passed more urine, 495 cc, than on any other day on record, thus setting a "new world record," Prabhupada laughed very much.

Prabhupada did not translate either yesterday or today.

OCTOBER 19, 1977

Although Prabhupada drank more yesterday, he does not show any real signs of improvement. He is still just as weak as ever. He lies very silently and cannot move at all without help. It says in the shastra that no one can understand the activities of a pure devotee of Lord Krishna, and we can see this practically as Prabhupada's position is completely unknown to us. We are all slightly puzzled as to what to do and how to act. Although his pulse is strong and he is taking a lot of liquid and passing stool and urine, there is still hardly any external manifestation of life. Bhavananda and Tamal Krishna have to coax Prabhupada all day to drink and take medicine. Tamal Krishna also spends a good deal of time giving convincing arguments for why Prabhupada must live and stay with us. Upendra and Satadhanya Maharaja are rendering very efficient bodily services, as are Bhakti Charu, who does the cooking, and dispenses the medicines along with Abhiram. Prabhupada's condition is always critical, and whenever he becomes a little discouraged and speaks about leaving us, one thing that does encourage him a lot is to be surrounded by his senior disciples.

Prabhupada spent another restless night, which he blames on the allopathic medicine. Also, he is passing stool very frequently now, and by the days' end, three times, so these symptoms are distressing.

Giriraj and Bhavananda Maharaja both have some minor ailments and have been to see Vanamali *kavirāja* for medicine. Prabhupada inquired, "Why for everyone and not for me?"

We had been thinking that the allopathic medicine would probably be better than the medicine given by the *kavirāja*, because generally his medicine has not proved to be very effective. However, Prabhupada has been inquiring today about why the *kavirāja* is not coming. We have been calling Dr. Gopal, who examined Prabhupada and said he will be visibly stronger within a few days. He appears very expert at dealing with Prabhupada and seems to understand his transcendental position. He said that the passing of stool was not a bad sign but indicates the clearing away of poisons, and said it was natural for one who is taking only liquid. He recommended that Prabhupada should take some solids also.

When Prabhupada conversed with Bhakti Charu, he told him, "What is the use of eating when it only comes out as stool and urine; how will it give nourishment if it just goes in and out?"

In other words, he was saying that simply in and out does not mean nourishment, and practically we see that Prabhupada is not visibly stronger by increasing his intake of juices. When Bhakti Charu began to feed Prabhupada mashed potato and custard, it caused him to vomit after having only a mouthful. So much mucus and saliva immediately came out. This has happened two days in a row now when he tries to eat anything solid, and he has become completely averse to it.

Despite this, there are some matters which Prabhupada is still having to deal with. Ten years ago, Prabhupada bought some postal receipts for his family members, which are coming due next month. So, after some discussion, he instructed Tamal Krishna that these may be given to Vrindavan Chandra De, his former son, instead of a one lakh rupee loan that he is negotiating to borrow from Prabhupada.

Then later on, Prabhupada changed his mind and said that the flat in Calcutta that Vrindavan is staying in may be given to him, and the Society can keep the postal receipts instead.

Mahamsa Maharaja arrived and gave a report on the farm in Hyderabad. Prabhupada especially inquired about the *prasādam* distribution there.

Prabhupada requested Baradraj to lead kirtan. While doing so, Baradraj accompanied himself on the harmonium. Prabhupada was hearing with very great ecstasy. His head was moving back and forth as he lay in bed. He was so ecstatic that he lifted his arms and hands during another kirtan led by Hamsaduta Maharaja and said, "*Jaya!* Everyone join together and chant Hare Krishna!" The kirtan is actually Prabhupada's only solace, and he listens very intently throughout the day. And if there is a mistake made in the singing, he immediately corrects it. He especially enjoys hearing Baradraj and Hamsaduta Swami.

OCTOBER 20, 1977

Prabhupada could not sleep, and in the morning we tried to feed him, but he vomited again. When Dr. Gopal came to examine him, he said, "Can you take anything besides *miśri jala*?"

"Yes," Prabhupada answered, "the best thing is *hari-nāma*. Let me hear *hari-nāma* and peacefully pass away."

Then the doctor fed some cold custard to Prabhupada, and he took about four spoonfuls and said that he felt a little better after eating. But then he continued, "Constant medicine is disgusting. Constant medicine gives brain trouble." The doctor decided to reduce his medicine by half this morning. Nevertheless, early on in the morning, Prabhupada had been translating.

Later, Prabhupada called in Tamal Krishna Maharaja and discussed with him the flat in Calcutta which is being occupied by his former family. Prabhupada told him that he wanted the flat to be given to them so that Vrindavan Chandra De could work for the BBT. Therefore, he had given them a place to stay and they can live a lifetime, all of them. But they cannot have the right to mortgage or to sell. They can have the right simply to live. He said, "If we give them the right to proprietorship, then this rascal [his eldest son, Mathura Mohan De] may sell. That I cannot allow."

Then a little later, I came in and I informed Prabhupada that all the Indian-printed *Gītās* were sold out in Australia. So Prabhupada immediately called in Tamal Krishna and told him to tell Gopal Krishna to hire more printers, two or three. He told him, "Money, there is no scarcity."

OCTOBER 21, 1977

In the morning, Dr. Ghosh took his leave. He was

feeling that Prabhupada was in good hands, and under the care of Dr. Gopal. When he asked permission to go, Prabhupada asked him, "You are not going to open dispensary?" Dr. Ghosh replied, "Yes, I want to, but they must come forward." Prabhupada said, "Doctor and all say to eat, but I cannot. Even kings do not get this service." Prabhupada was referring to the loving treatment being given to him by all his devotees. Then he told Dr. Ghosh, "Come immediately. Your life is successful. All sons grown up. My family life was [not]. We started life together." In this way, he was telling Dr. Ghosh to come back. Prabhupada laughed. "I have done big, big business, but Krishna wanted to bring me to do this work."

He commented on his present situation, "In the morning there is sleep. In the night, not." Then he had us turn him on his side and asked Bhavananda Maharaja to scratch his back for him, and he continued, "Yes, when I sleep, do not disturb."

Tamal Krishna said, "Is there any request for any special kirtan? Baradraj is here. He can sing whatever you like."

Prabhupada said, "He is the best artist." Because Prabhupada had sung a few bars of *haraye namah Krishna*, Tamal Krishna suggested that song, and Prabhupada nodded. Baradraj began to sing, accompanying himself on the harmonium. Prabhupada saw Nava Yogendra Maharaja in the room, and told him, "You have brought many valuable presentations. Sell them and engage the money in Mombasa. Sometimes presentations are sold for high prices by bid."

Brahmananda and Tamal Krishna Maharajas have decided between them not to administer any medicine to Prabhupada today, because of the disturbing side effects. Already we can see the difference. Prabhupada was noticeably more alert and relaxed. Over the past couple of days Prabhupada has been taking a little custard and, at times, even some ice cream. Today they suggested that he could pick his favorite preparation. They all gave various suggestions which Prabhupada rejected. But when Upendra mentioned *laddu*, Prabhupada said, "Yes, bring me *laddu*." Tamal Krishna made a comment that there must be a feast, so in this way the conversation was going on in a very light mood, an almost joking mood. When Prabhupada lay down, however, he became a little serious and said, "Before the spiritual master, do not cause any laughing by any talk. Laughing means taking things lightly, and this is the etiquette—gravity must be maintained. This is your teaching. You are simple, so understand me rightly or not."

Prabhupada quoted from the *Brahma Saṁhitā: rāmādi-mūrtiṣu kalā-niyamena tiṣṭhan* [5.39] and one other song, and said, "These two mantras should always be repeated. That will be great benefit to me. Then Hare Krishna and Sri Krishna Chaitanya. Kirtan must always go on with mantras, so you and I can hear them, and then physically massage with mustard oil on the head.

Then he asked, "So, translation, whatever I have done at this stage is going on all right?"

"Yes, Srila Prabhupada," Jayadvaita assured him. Then again they suggested Prabhupada could translate, and he agreed.

Tamal Krishna asked whether or not Yadubara could come in and film. Prabhupada said, "Yes, he is very good devotee. Yadubara has freedom to do anything he wants." Tamal Krishna mentioned that his wife, Visakha, was also very qualified. Prabhupada said, "Yadubara is now first before his wife."

Prabhupada did some translation work in the morning while all the devotees sat tightly around— Pradyumna reading from the Sanskrit book, Jayadvaita Maharaja holding the microphone to Prabhupada's mouth as he spoke the purport, and Yadubara and his wife filming the whole scene.

A little while after the end of the translation work, Tamal Krishna and Bhavananda Maharajas discussed with Prabhupada whether he would take medicine or not. Prabhupada had asked whether Dr. Gopal was coming today. They thought trying to persuade Prabhupada to take medicines all the time was not the position that they should adopt, due to Prabhupada's transcendental situation. Bhavananda Maharaja told Prabhupada, "We wish to obey your command." Prabhupada said, "You say you will obey my command. I am patient. How can I command?"—meaning a patient cannot command the doctor.

Tamal Krishna:	"Placing yourself under our care."
Prabhupada:	"Yes." And then after a pause, "The doctor says 'when you call, I will come.' That means he is not taking responsibility. If required, you can consult the *kavirāja*. But if you say 'whatever you command', that means hopeless."

Tamal Krishna said, "Our plan is for you to survive, but your plan and Krishna's plan must also be that for our plan to be successful. We do not want to impose our plan upon you."

Prabhupada then said, "If you are puzzled and I am patient?"

Tamal Krishna assured him, "We are not puzzled for treatment. It is a spiritual consideration."

Prabhupada agreed, "Treatment is material."

Tamal Krishna said, "Yes, and the treatment is with some success because you are remaining alive."

Prabhupada replied, "Yes, so go on with the treatment."

Bhavananda said, "So we will go on with the medicine and kirtan. Kirtan is most important."

Tamal Krishna added, "And you go on with the *Bhāgavatam* translation."

Prabhupada said, "Yes, time may come when I will discuss. They [Pradyumna and Jayadvaita] may now come." He also told them, "Send one letter to Dr. Ghosh. 'There are two rooms for you; one for dispensary and one for living accommodation, according to your choice. You are welcome. Just open a small dispensary for giving medicine for common ailments for all the inhabitants here.' We have already talked like this; he may not feel shy. Give him all facility."

Some devotees came from Bengal and reported that now fourteen Mohammedans have been arrested and taken into custody by the police. After being released on bail, they came and fell down at the devotees' feet and begged them not to be too strict.

Prabhupada commented, "Yes, actually they are culprits."

Jayapataka Swami is getting ready to return to Mayapur. He said, "I want to print a book and bring it back." Prabhupada encouraged him, "Yes, print books—there is no scarcity of money. Bengal village to village, town to town. We have got enough place to live in Mayapur."

Then Prabhupada had Jayadvaita read the edited copy of his recent translation work. "You all hear and comment."

Prabhupada's translation work is completely different from before. Whereas previously he would have had the doors locked, to work without being disturbed, now he asks who is present, and even calls for specific individuals. His translation work is simultaneously an opportunity to preach to the devotees present, as well as to write the book. He frequently asks, "Is it clear?"

When hearing the edited work, he sometimes gives further comments, and sometimes while translating, he will begin lecturing to everybody. Today while listening to Jayadvaita read the book *Kṛṣṇa*, Prabhupada fell asleep. So we performed kirtan instead, and there was no translating.

At around 1 p.m., the feast was brought before Prabhupada. He first tried the *laḍḍu* and immediately spat it out, not liking it at all. One preparation after another he rejected, not being able to taste any of them nicely.

Then again in the evening, Prabhupada called for Pradyumna and Jayadvaita prabhus and amazingly, he translated for well over an hour. He then proceeded to lecture strongly for well over another hour. He was having his ears cleansed, so he began to lecture on the senses. "We are restricting the tongue. If we take Krishna *prasādam*, we restrict the tongue, and all other senses become controlled. And spiritual life means sense control. We are not going to kill the senses. The yogi wants to stop artificially, but that is not possible. The senses are there. Life means senses. So the senses are there, but designated. We have to free the senses from the material designations. When the designations are washed away, with our senses purified, one can engage in the service of Krishna. This is called *bhakti*. Is that clear? Discuss *Bhāgavatam* daily as much as possible, and everything will be clarified."

In this way, Prabhupada preached to us all as we sat by his bed and absorbed the nectar coming from his lotus mouth.

Dayananda prabhu arrived in the late evening, having come from Tehran with a few crates of fresh fruit, and he gave a report of his activities there. After they spoke, Dayananda said with firm conviction, "Prabhupada, we have never met anyone with such transcendental qualities as you."

Prabhupada said, "It has to be developed. Transcendental qualities are already there. Only when we are designating on the material platform is it not manifest. We are covered, but when we become prone to give service to Krishna, it becomes revealed. Now print books and distribute."

OCTOBER 22, 1977

Early in the morning Tamal Krishna was attending Prabhupada, and when His Divine Grace woke up, he related a dream that he had just had. "Just now I dreamed that a Vaishnava *kavirāja* with big tilak marks was preparing *makara-dvaja*," he told us. "This *kavirāja* was preparing it."

Makara-dvaja is a medicine which is made from pure musk, gold, pearls, and other preparations. It is a very powerful medicine, and it generally is used in Ayurvedic treatment when everything else fails. Prabhupada had this dream that a Vaishnava was preparing it and he decided that this was a sign from Krishna, so why not try it?

Later on, Prabhupada called Tamal Krishna and asked about his horoscope again. He said his horoscope had "dragged life through so many catastrophes," but ultimately, he asked, "how long the life is?" Tamal Krishna answered that five or six years had been given, but others say up to one hundred years. Prabhupada concluded that there was no standard.

Because Prabhupada was apparently stronger yesterday without taking the help of medicine, we decided not to give him any medicine again today. But then, as Prabhupada was asking for Dr. Gopal to come, it was decided to give him his medicine after all. After asking about the astrologer, Prabhupada said, "Anyway, do things very carefully. I am already dead, but still I

204

am giving you instructions as far as I can. This is not life, a bundle of bones."

Tamal Krishna said, "You are the inspiration," and Prabhupada responded, "Yes, that I shall do until the last breathing."

When Dr. Gopal came, he examined Prabhupada. He had expected increased strength, but really there has been no change. Prabhupada told him regarding food that, "Soon as I hear the name, I become afraid." It was clear that Dr. Gopal was stumped. He listened to Prabhupada's breathing and suggested perhaps there was a lung infection. He requested that x-rays be taken. Prabhupada said he had no objection provided that the machine could be brought to his room.

When Dr. Gopal left we all came into Prabhupada's room and discussed with him, concluding that Dr. Gopal was now simply speculating. Prabhupada said, "I think this doctor's treatment, failure. He simply guesses. Now let us leave everything to Krishna. Doctor's treatment is finished. They will simply guess and make things complicated."

Then Prabhupada asked what the doctor had prescribed, and Svarupa Damodara Prabhu said he had prescribed some heavy kind of drugs.

Prabhupada said, "Then they will say, 'now you move to hospital.' Then who will take care of me?"

Bhavananda Maharaja reassured him, "While we will never allow it, Srila Prabhupada, they [the doctors] will gradually do it." Once again Prabhupada admonished us, "Do not remove me to hospital. Better kill me here. If you are disgusted, then that is another thing."

Bhavananda expressed our core concern, "Our fear is that you will be disgusted."

Prabhupada: "No, I am not disgusted. I will treat myself. Let the *kavirāja* come. One

	after another, the doctors will make things complicated. What is your opinion?"
Bhavananda:	"You have perfect knowledge, spiritual and material. Therefore we have taken you as our spiritual master."
Prabhupada:	"All of you agree?"
Everybody:	"Yes."
Prabhupada:	"Then I will give direction. I want to know about this *makara-dvaja*, consulting both the *kavirāja*." Then after a pause, he said, "If you remove me from here, I will immediately die. I cannot live without your company."
Tamal Krishna:	"And we cannot live without you."
Svarupa Damodara:	"You stay forever, and we will stay with you."
Prabhupada:	"Do that, and stop all this medicine."

Prabhupada, as a former pharmacist, fortified his conviction that there should be no hospitalization in his treatment by giving some practical examples of people he knew who had been incorrectly treated.

Svarupa Damodara, along with others, cited their own recent experiences. "I have many medical friends. They frankly admit that oftentimes they kill the patients in the name of treating."

Prabhupada told us that just recently, Hitsaran Sharma, the secretary of one of the richest families in India, was wrongly diagnosed.

Prabhupada:	"In pathology his prescription was replaced by another. He had some trouble. So his case was transferred

	to another."
Tamal Krishna:	"His diagnosis was given to someone else. They made a mistake, and then they treated the other person."
Prabhupada:	"And he was being treated as tuberculosis."

Adi-kesava also added that sometimes the surgeon accidently leaves instruments inside the patient and has to cut them open again to remove them.

Prabhupada went on. "I have got many experiences in my family life. One servant, Kashiram, was howling, howling. So we took him to the hospital, and so many student doctors surrounded. They diagnosed something, strangulation or something like that. Then they were prepared to surgical operation. Then another experienced doctor came. He said, 'Let us wait today.' So he was kept in the hospital, and we came back. That Kashiram was a friend of another servant of the neighborhood, and so he said, 'Babaji, he has drunk a little.' And next morning he came back and said, 'The doctor said, 'You are all right. You can go.' "

Tamal Krishna laughed along with the rest of us at Prabhupada's recollection. "He was just drunk from liquor."

Svarupa Damodara said he had a similar experience. "It is my own personal experience. In 1974 I came here in India. I got malaria in the United States in summer 1975. Then temperature was very high. I went to the Baptist Hospital in Atlanta. They thought it was a viral infection. They couldn't diagnose. Then they gave some medicine, and then I went. But it started again the following day, then I went to another doctor. He could not diagnose. So they gave me glucose injection, a big bottle, thinking that was a strange viral infection. So about six, seven doctors, they couldn't diagnose for three-four days. Then one day there was a doctor who came from Vietnam, and he had some experience in tropical disease. He thought it might be malarial fever. Then, after that, I was surrounded by many doctors thinking that it was a strange disease. But it was not right. They did all the wrong medicine, thinking it was a viral infection. This is in America, just two years ago."

To add to our justification for avoiding the prospect of hospitalization, Tamal Krishna narrated his own family trauma. "I told you the story of my father recently, Srila Prabhupada, how he had the arthritis in the hip, so they gave him a new hip. Then it moved to the other hip, and they replaced the other hip. So after eight weeks he was in the bed in the hospital, and then they said, 'Now you can try to walk.' So they gave him crutches, and they stood him up, and after eight weeks of all these operations, as soon as he stood up he had a heart attack and died right on the spot. They were very sure. 'Now you're all right,' they told him."

And finally, Pancha Dravida Maharaja related his own tale: "My great-uncle had tonsillitis, so he went to a friend who was a doctor, and the friend said, 'That's all right, we'll operate, and I will not charge you anything.' So he went into the hospital, and in the operation the doctor dropped a scalpel, and after that... He was very big, and he became very small, never could eat again."

After these narratives, Prabhupada gave his conclusion regarding medical treatment: "No protection."

Bhavananda said, and all of us agreed, that outside of the holy names, there is no protection. Prabhupada told us, "Let us take a little *Bhāgavata* treatment. Everything will die. Let me die peacefully. Life is diminishing. But at least while *Bhāgavatam* is being discussed, our life is not diminished."

Then he asked, "Can you think of transferring me to Mayapur?" Tamal Krishna immediately responded, "Yes, we will like to carry you Prabhupada, Mayapur."

Prabhupada went on, "You can keep me in my

quarters [in Mayapur] and take a little care, that's all. Here in one room, always closed, [not so good]; there, I can take fresh boiled vegetables and a little of whatever vegetables are grown there. You boil them, and I can take whatever vegetables there are growing." Bhavananda named several vegetables which are growing, and Prabhupada was prospective.

Prabhupada asked, "Brahmananda, what do you think?"

Brahmananda replied, "Yes, you should go, Prabhupada."

Prabhupada said, "*Gauḍa-maṇḍala-bhūmi, jebā jāne cintāmaṇi, tāra hoy braja-bhūmi bās.* We have got such a nice, open, palatial building. So that is my proposal. Now you think of it seriously and arrange for it."

Tamal Krishna: "Now you shall go and shower your mercy on the Vaishnavas of Bengal."

Prabhupada: "All right, I shall go to take the dust of their lotus feet. So, Bhakti Prema Swami, you are also coming?"

Bhakti Prema: "Yes, Prabhupada."

He asked who was in the room. Baradraj was leading a soft kirtan, and Tamal Krishna Maharaja listed off the others: Dhrstadyumna Maharaja, Svarupa Damodara, Tripurari Maharaja, Nayanabhirama, Bhavananda Maharaja, Upendra, Trivikrama Maharaja, Pancha Dravida Maharaja, Brahmananda Maharaja.

Prabhupada: "So let us go in a team. Enough place, you can have two rooms and either you remain in Mayapur or Vrindavan, it is the same. There is no difference. And (humorously) if there is any danger, Bhavananda has a gun."

Prabhupada was laughing like this. Then he said, "Bhavananda, I am thinking what preparations to make. Simply fresh vegetables, mung *dal* also. So let us go in a team."

Thus Prabhupada began to make plans to go to Mayapur. At the same time men were deputed to try to find this Vaishnava *kavirāja* who was making the *makara-dvaja* which Prabhupada had seen in his dream.

OCTOBER 23, 1977

I spent the day in Delhi purchasing my ticket back to Australia, plus various paraphernalia for the *yatras* there. I also paid a visit to Ashu Tosh Ojah, the astrologer, for clarification of some specific points in Prabhupada's chart.

OCTOBER 24, 1977

Further serious discussion about transferring Prabhupada to Mayapur led us to believe that it was the best option, but there are pros and cons as to which method of transport is best. It's getting cold here in Vrindavan, and train travel can be difficult.

Tamal Krishna pointed out that the climate is not completely predictable in this Kali-yuga. "It's getting very cold in the mornings. Now, if suddenly it gets much colder, to travel on the train would be very difficult, because these trains are hard. You can't keep them warm. They don't have heat in them. So we don't feel it's very safe to wait unduly. Our opinion was that so far as your health or strength goes, it's not going to increase significantly in one or two weeks. Even when you take this *makara-dhvaja*, it will take time to gradually get back your strength. So waiting is not so much for the purpose of gaining back strength. The climate is working against us if we wait, because it's getting colder. One of the main reasons to go that Your Divine Grace had, was to get into a nice climate, fresh air, open-air atmosphere."

Another pressing consideration is the hunt for a good *kavirāja*. In Sri Rangam, the head priest there is very friendly with our Society. Both Acyutananda and Yasodanandana Swamis have stayed with him at his house. He might prove to be very useful in procuring the medicine. It seemed a promising option, and after discussion, Prabhupada agreed that an experienced British brahmachari, Smarahari prabhu, could go there immediately, along with a Hindi-speaking Indian devotee.

Tamal Krishna thought it a good idea for Bhakti Charu Maharaja to be the other man. "That's also one advantage, that there should be one Western devotee, one Indian devotee, just in case he has to speak Hindi or something. And besides that, Bhakti Charu Maharaja has got experience with you with all of these different *kavirājas*. He knows your history, so he can explain it properly to the *kavirāja*."

Prabhupada wasn't happy that Bhakti Charu be the other man. He is too useful to Prabhupada for him to be away for any length of time. "No, there is no explanation. He must be sincere, the *kavirāja*, and must know how to do it. That's all."

Tamal Krishna: "Yes, that can be done. So, Srila Prabhupada, here is Smarahari, and he's going to be leaving today for South India. We've given him the instructions, and he's the proper person. He knows that chief priest in Sri Rangam temple, and first thing is he's going to find out what are the ingredients of this *makara-*

dhvaja. Then he's going to purchase the ingredients himself, and then he's going to go to the Ramanuja *kavirāja* and have him make it right in front of him. He will supply the ingredients so that he knows the ingredients are bona fide, first-class. And he'll see that they make it in front of him."

Prabhupada: "According to the direction of the Ramanuja..."

Tamal Krishna: "Yes. Well, he'll have the Ramanuja man make it. First he'll ask, 'What are the ingredients?' Then he'll go and get those ingredients, and he'll bring it to the Ramanuja man. And the Ramanuja man will make it."

Prabhupada: "The man must be sincere and experienced."

Tamal Krishna: "Then, after that, he'll come directly to Mayapur. The whole thing—how long will it take? About two days to get there? A day or two... Maybe within a week's time he'll be in Mayapur, Srila Prabhupada, if they make it quickly."

Prabhupada: "It will take time [to make the medicine], as he said."

Tamal Krishna: "That man said it would take time—a week. Of course, we don't know if that's a fact or not, but it'll take about a week's time if it only takes a day or two. If it takes a week, then it may take a total of two weeks'

time until he reaches Mayapur.
When Gopal and Satadhanya were
in Delhi, they went to see one man
who was a very important Marwari
kavirāja. They asked him about the
ingredients of *makara-dhvaja*."

Bhavananda: "They asked that question about what
medicine the poor man would take."

Tamal Krishna: "What medicine the poor man would
take. So he said, 'Poor man or rich
man, it doesn't matter. The price
of it is about forty-eight rupees per
tola, because the gold that is given,
it's given back at the end.' It's just
passed through, the gold. It's not
utilized itself. So forty-eight rupees
a tola. This is what he said, very big
Marwari *kavirāja*."

Prabhupada: "Yes, that I have heard."

Tamal Krishna: "So, this Ramanuji *kavirāja* was
charging five hundred rupees a tola.
And Vanamali, when we gave him
gold, he never returned any gold. So,
this is the position—cheaters."

Prabhupada: "Vanamali was also."

Tamal Krishna: "Something. Anyway, before we leave
I'm going to speak with Bhagatji.
Bhagatji is the one who gave the gold
and pearls to Vanamali. So I think
Bhagatji will be able to recover it.
We'll leave this medicine with Bhagatji,
and he can give the medicine to
Vanamali and take the money.
"So, Smarahari will be leaving

today, just now. And we've already
spoken with Delhi, and they're
going to purchase the airline tickets.
Today is Monday. Either we will
leave Wednesday or we will leave
Friday. We're not going to travel
on Thursday. And they've already
informed Calcutta and Mayapur."

Prabhupada: "Who will go with me?"

Tamal Krishna: "Your Divine Grace, Bhavananda
Maharaja, myself, Bhakti Charu
Maharaja, Satadhanya Maharaja,
Upendra Prabhu, Svarupa
Damodara, Baradraj. That'll be
on the plane. Then in the train,
Pradyumna, Arundhati, and some
other devotees. So eight of us will be
going on the plane with you, seven
plus Your Divine Grace, and you will
have three seats. Altogether, we're
purchasing ten seats. So I don't
think there will be any difficulty.
We're going in full team. Scientist
is with us. In case of any special
knowledge, Svarupa Damodara will
be there. Bhavananda with his gun.
[Laughter] Full team. I think it will
be a nice journey, Srila Prabhupada."

Over the last few days Srila Prabhupada has
expressed his desire to help reunite or at least co-
operate with his godbrothers. He is forming a new trust
called Bhaktivedanta Swami Charity Trust. It will have
one or two godbrothers like Madhusudan Maharaja
and Madhava Maharaja on the trust board, along with

214

a majority of ISKCON members. It will hold a corpus in the bank in fixed deposits and only the interest per annum may be spent. The funds will be used to help other temples that are struggling financially. He cited two examples: his old friend Srila B.R. Sridhara Swami, who is trying to complete the *nātha-mandira* at his temple in Navadvipa; and the *yoga-pīṭha* run by Bhaktivilasa Tirtha Maharaja's successors, where they have not been able to construct a *nātha-mandira*, or assembly hall, for many years. In this way Prabhupada is seeking to extend his good will and encourage co-operation among his Godbrothers.

After his mid-morning bath, Prabhupada heard a truly inspiring report from Tulasi dasa about the opening of a new temple in South Africa. He was invigorated to hear about the success of the festivities and the support of the large Indian community, who for the first time were drawn in thousands to an ISKCON festival, not merely as onlookers but as enthusiastic participants. Prabhupada declared, "Movement will go on with or without this body."

Tamal Krishna Maharaja read out Tulasi dasa's report as well as some of the news articles that accompanied the many photos. "'By Krishna's grace the most wonderful Janmastami celebration was held at the Cato Ridge Farm ashram in South Africa. The celebration included the opening of a new temple and *prasādam* facility.' "

"He sent a lot of pictures, Srila Prabhupada. Amazing pictures. Here's a news clipping from the *Leader*. It's a newspaper. It says, 'Hare Krishna festivity. All roads led to the Hare Krishna farm ashram at Cato Ridge last Sunday where thousands of well-wishers and devotees celebrated Krishna Janmastami. His Holiness Sriman Jayatirtha dasa Prabhu came out especially from the United States for the occasion and to officiate at the

215

opening of the new temple of the International Society for Krishna Consciousness.'

"One picture shows the devotees; it says, 'Members of the International Society for Krishna Consciousness and followers of A. C. Bhaktivedanta Swami Prabhupada lead the crowd in the singing of Hare Krishna kirtan. In the foreground is the havana-kuṇḍa on which the sacrificial prayer was performed prior to the opening of the new temple.'"

Tamal Krishna read out some of the captions on the many photos: "'A view of the large gathering...' it shows thousands of people, Srila Prabhupada, '. . . at the Hare Krishna farm ashram at Cato Ridge at the weekend when the new temple was officially opened. The function was held in conjunction with Lord Krishna's birth anniversary celebrations.'

"Here's the temple. 'Head of the group, Tulasi dasa, seen with other devotees in front of their new temple.'"

Adi-kesava: "It's a very beautiful temple with pillars and arches. I don't know how they built it so soon. [Laughs] It's a big temple they built there."

"It says, 'The International Society for Krishna Consciousness, more widely known as the Hare Krishna movement, opened its temple to coincide with the celebration of the birth of Lord Krishna.' Here's another article; pictures of devotees opening the temple; another article. Sriman Jayatirtha dasa Prabhu, one of the top officials...'"

Prabhupada's pride in his disciples shone brightly through his countenance. "Still, they criticize us.

216

Hmm? Affirmations, good character, good health..."

Tamal Krishna read out another article. "'Procession draws hundreds. The hundreds lined the streets of Durban on Sunday to watch young and old Hindus taking part in the colorful procession which was held as part of Lord Krishna's birthday celebration...' It tells all about a celebration in the city of Durban organized by our Society."

Prabhupada, ever the preacher, declared, "It will be good for propaganda."

Tamal Krishna read snippets and showed the photos from the many accompanying materials "'Krishna-aṣṭamī. Lord Krishna's celebration." Full center page. 'A voyage of discovery.' 'A Christian tribute to Krishna consciousness,' it says. There's a picture of Your Divine Grace here. It's an article reprinted from *Back to Godhead*. It says, 'All material in this special feature taken from *Back to Godhead,* the official magazine of the International Society for Krishna Consciousness.'

"The same thing they did in Fiji, they have done there in South Africa. Because many of the articles... This is also all about our Society. All of these pages. 'Hare Krishna puzzle is unraveled.' 'Jagannatha car festival is one of the oldest in history.' Then it tells about the program, how to get to the farm. Then he sent photographs. It's a very beautiful temple, Srila Prabhupada. I don't know if you can see it. This is the temple. You see the white structure here? You can see it has arched domes? Not domes, but arches."

Prabhupada:	"Very good."
Tamal Krishna:	"Can you see it? Look at the pandal they had."
Prabhupada:	"They have got a new barrack."
Tamal Krishna:	"Festivity. Here's Tulasi dasa doing the fire *yajña.* Should I read you his

letter now?"

Prabhupada: "Very good news. Now we can see. This material body may remain or not remain, this movement will push on. That is wanted. Where is such thing throughout the whole world?"

Tamal Krishna: "There aren't, except in our temples. He says, 'By Krishna's grace the most wonderful Janmastami celebration was held at the big farm ashram in South Africa. The celebration included the opening of a new temple and *prasādam* facility, two new Life Membership cottages, and three overnight guest rooms, initiation of four new devotees, and two brahman initiations, a play, a massive *prasādam* distribution, *go-pūjā,* a transcendental treasure hunt for the children, ecstatic chanting by all, and distribution of books, records, posters, and tapes. We enclose pictures of the various events, as well as newspaper articles. The newspapers were all one-hundred-percent favorable, and one even had a four-page article on ISKCON.'

'The Gujarati ladies from Durban and Pietermaritzburg all came early to help cook *Puris* and *halavā.* They cooked about one quarter ton of *halavā* [Prabhupada chuckles] and over eight thousand puris, all

of which were distributed. At least
fifteen thousand people attended the
two-day festival, and all of the most
important big Indian businessmen
and millionaires attended. Two days
before the event, a large marquee,
able to hold twenty-five hundred
people, was erected, and the
initiations and the play were held
inside. The play especially was most
successful, as the top Indian stage
and lighting men in South Africa
were giving us technical assistance.
It was so nice that even some of
the ladies were in tears during the
performance.'
'The *go-pūjā* was also a massively
popular event, as none of the local
people had ever seen such a thing
before. In fact, many people came
up to the devotees and were saying
things like 'I left India thirty years
ago, and I never saw anything like
this before.' "

It is another victory in Prabhupada's selfless and
incessant attempt to fulfil the desires of his spiritual
master and Sri Chaitanya Mahaprabhu.

Later in the day some excellent news came
regarding the search for a Ramanuja *kaviraja* and the
makara-dhvaja. Bhavananda reported that Adi-kesava
Maharaja had contacted an influential friend in Delhi
named Chandra Swami, who had previously been very
helpful in winning our court case in New York.

Bhavananda said, "He has quite a bit of money, and so Adi-kesava called him up, and he had a *kavirāja* in the Ramanuja-sampradāya. And Chandra Swami went to see his *kavirāja*, and his *kavirāja* had just gotten finished mixing *makara-dhvaja* medicine. He'd been preparing it for the past ten days. And Satadhanya Maharaja and Adi-kesava were just now going over to see this *kavirāja*. That Chandra Swami has purchased seven tolas of the medicine for Your Divine Grace as a gift. They are going over to pick it up."

Prabhupada was moved to tears. "Just see!" he jubilantly declared. "Krishna arranges. Just see!"

Trivikrama Maharaja said, "Krishna's so kind."

Prabhupada, his voice cracking with joyful emotion, said, "Very good. No, I saw somebody, Ramanuja, he is preparing for me. This is all Krishna's plan. It is being prepared in Delhi, and He is giving information and doing. So very good news."

Tamal Krishna asked if he wanted more chanting. Prabhupada responded, "Chanting is our life."

Tamal Krishna: "So there's no need to send anyone to South India."

Prabhupada: "No. I have got it already."

Bhavananda: "And that *kavirāja* in Delhi said that no, the gold is absorbed in the medicine."

Tamal Krishna: "Phew! These events are all like a dramatical play, Srila Prabhupada, great drama. It's simply like reading the *Caitanya-caritāmṛta*."

Prabhupada: "*Ebe jaśa ghuṣuk tribhuvana* [*Sri-guru-vandanā* 4]. He has contributed seven tolas? Hmm?»

Tamal Krishna: "Yes. So now you will get both things—the *makara-dhvaja* and

Mayapur. Krishna was showing you while he was making it, Srila Prabhupada. Prabhupada was watching him make it, and Krishna gave him the vision to see.»

Prabhupada: "No, Krishna, God, He gave me information."

Trivikrama: "Just like Sanjaya."

Tamal Krishna: "These activities are all as wonderful, Srila Prabhupada, as the books you have written. We are seeing that you are one of those personalities, as great as the personalities that you've written about."

Prabhupada: "So dose, everything, take detail."

Tamal Krishna: "We have to take detail of the dosage and everything about it."

Bhavananda: "Yes. They're going to get all of that tonight."

At this news everyone's hearts were uplifted, and kirtan recommenced, led by Hamsaduta on the harmonium.

OCTOBER 25, 1977

In the early morning Prabhupada was feeling a little forlorn. He could detect there was a decrease in the number of men doing his kirtan. He asked, "So, everyone has left?"

Upendra replied, "Most of the GBC."

Prabhupada became melancholy. "I feel very unhappy when no one is here. They are avoiding me. They don't want to come."

Upendra told him, "Baradraj and Hamsaduta are here. Would you like them to have kirtan?"

"At least *japa*," Prabhupada told him. "When I look around I see the room is empty and I feel very unhappy. When I see no one around me, I feel lonely."

Baradraj tried to reassure him. "We'll get some others, and Hamsaduta and I will begin kirtan."

But it did little to cheer him. "Why not all of you?" Prabhupada asked. "You cannot all do kirtan? Why not others?"

A little later Prabhupada was talking with Tamal Krishna. Referring to the *makara-dhvaja* he told him, "I am feeling all right, but there is some difficulty."

Tamal Krishna: "This *makara-dhvaja* is meant to be taken when all energy is finished."

Prabhupada: "Yes, *dull* and *anupama;* two Hindi words."

Tamal Krishna: "Yes. I told Bhavananda to tell them to bring that information. *Anupama* means how often and what ingredients to be taken with."

Prabhupada: "*Makara-dhvaja* is different from *anupama*, gives different physical reactions." Then after a pause he asked, "The *kavirāja* was already preparing and almost on the finishing point?"

Tamal Krishna: "Yes. It may have been he that you were seeing in your dream."

Prabhupada: "Yes." After a short pause he repeated, "Please don't leave me here. Keep me surrounded. That will encourage me. Surround me and chant Hare Krishna."

Prabhupada's main concern is that the kirtan go on. Now almost all of the senior devotees have left, save for a few. Also, he decided to cancel any arrangements for travelling to Mayapur. Despite the previous optimism, his illness is too severe for any kind of travel.

Then Atreya Rishi prabhu came in. Prabhupada told us, "There is very little hope for my life. Let me drink little fruit juice. You chant Hare Krishna softly, all together. But do not leave. And if there is sunshine, you can put me in the sunshine upstairs. But do not put me in the hospital. If I actually get some strength, then I shall think of going to Mayapur. At this stage, it is cent percent risky. Unnecessarily too much risk should not be taken. Boldness is good, but unnecessary boldness is not good."

Prabhupada later asked again about the astrologically-predicted crisis days—yesterday and today. And he asked again about Mayapur, saying, "In this condition, how is it possible?"

Tamal Krishna: "To carry you? Well, I think that for you, anything is possible. But you were right. It was a little extraordinary to attempt, and we are little safer to wait. Still, I was quite confident that we could do it."

In the afternoon, Prabhupada took some vegetable broth which had been made by Atreya Rishi. After resting all afternoon, in the evening Satadhanya Maharaja brought from Delhi the *makara-dhvaja* that he had obtained for free from Chandra Swami's *kavirāja*. The doctor has given forty-eight doses—two a day for twenty-four days. This is a very powerful medicine which is to be taken with honey. Satadhanya reported in more detail about the help that he received from Chandra Swami. Apparently he is close to Indira Gandhi's inner circle and very favorable to ISKCON.

In the late evening when everything was very quiet,

Prabhupada called me over to his bedside, and in almost a whisper said, "So, I want to go on *parikramā*."

I asked him, "Do you feel strong enough?"

"Strong or weak, it doesn't matter. You carry me at least three times around [our temple] and darshan also. By *parikramā*, even if I die, that is good luck. Do you follow?"

I replied affirmatively, and he said, "Instead of dying on road, jerking of train or airplane, why not here?"

I said, "Vrindavan is the best place."

"So arrange like that. It does not matter. At least three times with kirtan, and I may die or live. It doesn't matter."

"For us it matters," I said.

But Prabhupada said, "But what can be done? It is up to Krishna's desire."

At mid-evening Tamal Krishna and I entered Srila Prabhupada's room with a telegram informing us that Samjata dasa, an Australian devotee, had just died in the hospital in Bhubaneswar. He had joined the Melbourne temple at age 51, after leaving his family life. Being an architect, he had come to India to work with Surabhi Swami on designs for a temple in Haridaspur, and had recently been working under Gour Govinda Maharaja in Bhubaneswar. He had contracted a virulent brain virus, his health had deteriorated rapidly, and he had left his body the same day. Since Bhubaneswar is part of Jagannatha Puri-dhāma, I asked Prabhupada about Samjata's destination after death. "Is that a guarantee for going home, if someone leaves their body in the *dhāma*?"

"At least," Prabhupada answered, "he gets high standard of life for many years. That is stated in the *Bhagavad-gītā*." He asked me to find the relevant verses and read them out, which I did, including the Sanskrit:

224

prāpya puṇya-kṛtāṁ lokān / uṣitvā śāśvatīḥ samāḥ
śucīnāṁ śrimatāṁ gehe / yoga-bhraṣṭo 'bhijāyate

"The unsuccessful *yogī*, after many, many years of enjoyment on the planets of the pious living entities, is born into a family of righteous people or into a family of rich aristocracy."

atha vā yoginām eva/ kule bhavati dhīmatām
etad dhi durlabhataraṁ/ loke janma yad īdṛśam

"Or he takes his birth in a family of transcendentalists who are surely great in wisdom. Verily, such a birth is rare in this world."

tatra taṁ buddhi-saṁyogaṁ / labhate paurva-dehikam
yatate ca tato bhūyaḥ / saṁsiddhau kuru-nandana

"Taking such a birth, he again revives the divine consciousness of his previous life, and he tries to make further progress in order to achieve complete success, O son of Kuru." [*Gītā* 6.41–43]

Thus Srila Prabhupada confirmed Samjata prabhu's auspicious future.

Shortly afterwards, Prabhupada called Hamsaduta Swami over and told him about his plan for *parikramā*. "How do you like this idea?"

Hamsaduta said, "Yes, very good."

Prabhupada told us, "Instead of dying train-jerking or airplane-jerking, why not *parikramā*? Die or live, it doesn't matter."

Hamsaduta was enthusiastic at the prospect. "*Parikramā* is noble."

Prabhupada said, "Oh, yes. Either in palanquin or make a stretcher, but have *parikramā*. Do you like this idea?"

"Yes, I think it's a good idea.", Hamsaduta said.

"So with all leading members," Prabhupada said, "let me have *parikramā*. If I live, that's all right; if I die, that's all right. Both ways." And then again he called Baradraj over and said, "You've heard what I said?"

Baradraj:	"Yes, Prabhupada."
Prabhupada:	"Do you like this idea? What is the harm?"
Baradraj:	"All the devotees will love to see you."
Prabhupada:	"Hmm, yes."

In this way, late at night, Prabhupada decided that he would now go out on *parikramā*.

OCTOBER 26, 1977

In the early morning, despite the continuous presence of a small kirtan party, Prabhupada again began to lament, "Now I have become poisonous. Everyone is avoiding me. What is to be done? Things are deteriorating. What is to be done now? What is the use? Everything is frustrated."

Tamal Krishna:	"What do you mean 'what is the use?' "
Prabhupada:	"I am passing stool."
Tamal Krishna:	"Everyone passes stool, Prabhupada."
Prabhupada:	"Everyone eats. Passing stool without eating means whatever strength is there is lost."
Bhavananda:	"Our hope is not in medicine but prayer placed at the lotus feet of Krishna."
Prabhupada:	"That is my only hope."

Bhavananda said that if all hope is frustrated it will not harm to take medicine one more day.

226

Prabhupada said that he had hoped the medicine would give him strength but by passing stool what strength was there is gone.

So in the morning, Prabhupada complained to Tamal Krishna that the *makara-dhvaja* was not acting. He said that things are deteriorating, and he could feel weakness.

Bhavananda pointed out that he had been sat up in bed for forty-five minutes, which was a record time, so they thought that Prabhupada was actually looking stronger.

Discussion again turned to the idea of doing *parikramā*, so they suggested that if he was feeling a little deteriorated, then he should not do the *parikramā*. But Prabhupada said that the *parikramā* must go on.

Then he said, "I am already puzzled."

Tamal Krishna asked, "You said you are puzzled, Srila Prabhupada?"

Prabhupada said, "Atreya Rishi, I am puzzled."

Tamal Krishna said, "If you continue to desire to live, then Krishna will fulfil your desire."

Prabhupada replied, "In this condition, I do not wish to live."

Pancha Dravida Swami said, "The purpose of this medicine, Prabhupada, is to cure this condition, and to bring you back to good health. It's not that you will continue in this bad condition. It is our hope that you will regain your strength. There is an English saying that the night is darkest just before the dawn. So now you are feeling this way, but we are hoping very soon that medicine will take some effect, and you will feel stronger."

Tamal Krishna: "I was thinking yesterday that you had wanted to go all over the world once again to strengthen our society. I was thinking that since

227

you are not going, all the devotees
are coming here to be with you, and
simply being with you, everyone
is becoming stronger—simply by
contacting you, taking care of you,
they are all advancing in Krishna
consciousness. And I think that
anyone who has your association,
Prabhupada, will never fall away
from Krishna consciousness. And
you are also instructing and
translating every day. For the first
time the devotees are allowed to be
near you when you are translating.
They are allowed to hear you
speak, and I do not think that your
existence has no value. It has so
much value even now."

Pancha Dravida: "If the devotees are staying away, it
is not because you are poisonous, it
is because we are poisonous. I know
due to my sinful habits, I am now
poisonous; that when I am in your
presence, I feel so contaminated and
unworthy."

Bhavananda: "It is true, Prabhupada. If you lose
your desire to remain, no medicine
will be effective. But if you desire
to remain, then the medicine can
become effective."

Prabhupada: "In this way, to remain, not desirable.
Every day a crisis."

Bhavananda: "We have to think that if Your Divine
Grace leaves, what will be the result

	to ISKCON society, to your disciples individually, and to the entire planet?"
Prabhupada:	"That I am thinking, that such a big society, the aims and objects may be dismantled. I am thinking from that vision."
Tamal Krishna:	"Last May when everyone assembled here in Vrindavan, that Atul Krishna Maharaja came and after he left we were discussing to the effect that there is a movement, and if you should leave, then they will take the Society from us, the properties. You told us at that time, 'You are all children. None of you have any intelligence.' So that was only five months back. We have not grown that much in the five months. We are still children. You have always practically directed us in all of our activities, and when we have followed your instructions, then we have been successful."

Then Prabhupada asked what time it was; it was 8 a.m. So, then he asked, "Now let us go on *parikramā*."

Tamal Krishna:	"If you continue to try to survive, then Krishna will definitely fulfil your desire."
Prabhupada:	"In this condition, how I can desire to survive?"
Tamal Krishna:	"There should be some improvement. Then desiring becomes easier."

229

Then Atreya Rishi told Prabhupada that some fruit had been sent by the royal family of Iran, who were asking about Prabhupada's health. Prabhupada said, "Hmm. Preaching outside is going on. But I am not."

Then we got Prabhupada ready and sat him in his palanquin. We carried him out on *parikramā* around the temple. All the devotees came out and chanted and danced as Prabhupada was taken in procession three times around the temple, and then in for darshan to see the Deities. After staying for a few minutes in front of the Deity, he again came back into his room. Afterwards he said, "I am not tired. I was quite comfortable."

One of the devotees said, "We are also feeling refreshed." Tamal Krishna told him, "So this *parikramā* can be gradually increased, Prabhupada. If you like, we can take you around every day, and if you like we can sometimes take you around Vrindavan."

Prabhupada: "Yes."
Hari-sauri: "Today is Rasa-purnima."
Pancha Dravida: "And tomorrow begins Kartik."
Tamal Krishna: "And Kartik is the proper time to begin *parikramā*."

Prabhupada responded positively, "Yes, daily. So, my suggestion for *parikramā* last night?"

Svarupa Damodara: "Is successful."
Prabhupada: (laughing) "Yes. So when there is sunshine, if you take me up on the roof, I will remain in the sunshine. Then there is no need of lying down in one place."
Pancha Dravida: "Your disciples are very excited."
Prabhupada: "I am also excited. *Jaya*. I had no difficulty. We could circumambulate more. I was quite comfortable."

Prabhupada was helped on to his bed, and before he lay down, he took a little orange juice.

OCTOBER 27 1977

Srila Prabhupada called for his editors in the morning, and in a short half-hour session he completed the final three verses of the Tenth Canto, chapter thirteen. Verses sixty-two through sixty-four describe the submission of Lord Brahma to Krishna. Translating from the book of commentaries, Pradyumna prabhu described the special features of Brahma's surrender. "Then it says that Lord Brahma very hastily got down from his *vāhana, tvareṇa, tvareyā, nija-dho...* and fell down with his body on the earth. So, there's that rule that the *devas* never touch the ground when they go. It says, *iti niyamola...* This regulation, he went down, he touched the earth because it was Krishna."

The last verse we read was about how Brahma saw Krishna was there, the Supreme Brahman, and then he got down from his carrier, his swan carrier, and he did obeisances, *daṇḍavat*, and he touched the lotus feet of Krishna. And he was crying, and so his tears were washing the feet of Krishna.

"Abhiseka," Prabhupada interjected. And to further questioning from Pradyumna, he said, "[He is the] cause of everything. There's a child loitering in Vrindavan, there's morsels of food. That's extraordinary."

As Pradyumna worked steadily through the Sanskrit, Prabhupada added, "The presence of the Supreme Personality of Godhead just like a human child—that made him astounded."

He quoted from *Caitanya-caritāmṛta:* "*aham ihasi nandaṁ vande yasyālinde paraṁ brahma* [*Cc Madhya-līlā* 19.96]. There is a verse. You know it?"

Pradyumna:	"Yes. It is in the *Sri Caitanya-caritāmṛta.*"
Prabhupada:	"Yes: *śrutim apare smṛtim itare bhāratam anye bhava-bhītāḥ / aham ihasi nandaṁ vande yasyālinde paraṁ brahma:* Let others study Vedas, *smṛti, Bhārata, Mahābhārata, Bhagavad-gītā,* and praise all material existence, but I am going to worship Nanda Maharaja, in whose courtyard is crawling the Supreme Brahman. Nanda Maharaja is so great that the Parabrahman is crawling there. So I'll worship."

Prabhupada summed up the import of the *līlā,* emphasizing that only the devotees of the Lord can understand the dealings of the Lord and His devotees. The mental speculators cannot.

"The speculative process is futile. *Sri Īśopaniṣad* also—anyone who is favored by Krishna, only he can understand. Brahma tried to show his limited opulence. Now he came to the understanding that it is not possible. While offering prayer he tried to rectify the mistake. It says in *Bhagavad-gītā,* what is mercy of Krishna, they think is imagination. So Brahma verified, the eternity of writing transcendental words and the flickering nature of material world. *Janma karma me divya yo jānāti tattvataḥ.* He can be liberated; otherwise not. That liberation can be attained only by devotional service. *Bhaktyā mām abhijānāti yāvān yaś cāsmi tattvataḥ* [*Gītā* 18.55]: 'One can understand the Supreme Personality as He is only by devotional service. And when one is in full consciousness of the Supreme Lord by such devotion, he can enter into the kingdom of God.' Otherwise it is not possible. Actually,

232

the speculative process is not sufficient; it is different from self-realization. The *Māyāvādīs* think this is all imagination, so they give up the real path of progress and remain on this... That is the sign of their ignorance. Simply to understand the science, *tesam*, for them, that labor is [their] only gain and nothing more. Only by Krishna's mercy—nobody can understand the Absolute Truth.

"So Brahma desired, and he thought of living entities in Vrindavan, considering their fortune. The ordinary inhabitants of Vrindavan are better than the *jñānīs* and *yogīs*. Even ordinary householders are liberated. *Jaya, jaya vṛndāvana-vāsīs*. Where there is no devotional service of Krishna, that is the prison house of material world."

Pradyumna began the next chapter, fourteen, by reading some of the summary: "After offering himself to the feet of Krishna, praising Him, Brahma circumambulated the Supreme Lord and then went away. Then Krishna brought back all the calves and boys that had been taken by Brahma back to the sandy bank of the Yamuna."

Prabhupada was happy with the session: "Nice." But he was feeling tired and brought it to a close.

Pancha Dravida Swami and several other devotees were reading aloud from *Kṛṣṇa* and Prabhupada derived great pleasure from their recitations. "It will be *bhavauṣadhi*. There is no other. I shall ask, whenever I require it, fruit juice. That is my food, and this kirtan is my medicine. And *parikramā*. Settle up this."

Satadhanya: "Fruit juice, kirtan, and *parikramā*."
Prabhupada: "Believe in Krishna. I am hearing
                kirtan, how very nice here. It is
                stated in the *shastra, nivṛtta-tarṣair
                upagīyamānād bhavauṣadhāc chrotra*

	(*SB* 10.1.4). This is the medicine, panacea, for material disease. So kindly let me hear kirtan as far as possible, long as I live. That is all right?
Devotees:	"*Jaya*, Prabhupada. Yes, Prabhupada."

Hari Prasad Badruka, whose family have placed in a joint Trust with ISKCON five hundred and sixty acres of land in Medchal, near Hyderabad, came to give a report. Last December Prabhupada spent nearly two weeks at the farm, named 'New Naimisaranya'. He had high hopes of developing what he had called 'a new phase of this movement'— *varnashrama-dharma*.

Unfortunately, despite putting three of his senior disciples—Mahamsa Swami, Hamsaduta Swami, and Tejiyas prabhu—in charge, the project has somewhat floundered. Prabhupada had inaugurated a nightly pandal of kirtan and *prasādam* to attract the inhabitants of the surrounding villages, and about one hundred were attending each evening. However, it lasted only a couple of weeks and then stopped. If they distribute *prasādam* at all, it is only on weekends.

Still, Hari Prasad gave a largely upbeat report. On Prabhupada's query, Hari Prasad told him, "Everything is all right."

Prabhupada asked, "It is improving?" Hari Prasad reassured him. "Yes, it is."

Pancha Dravida Swami, who has recently become involved in the project, told of a new financial structure. "We have an arrangement now that Spanish BBT is sending funds every month to Hyderabad temple to finish the construction, and then, to pay back the loan that you gave, we're also sending in contributions to pay back that loan. The city center temple is attracting large numbers of visitors and is now the third-most popular temple in Hyderabad. After the Venkatesvara and Birla temples, anybody who comes, they visit our temple."

Prabhupada:	"And *sevā-pūjā* is nice?"
Hari Prasad:	"Yes, everything is very, very much regulated now."

Inevitably, the topic of *prasādam* came up. Prabhupada told us, "Here it was vacant, my lot [Vrindavan]. Now, by Krishna's grace, so many people are coming. *Prasādam* distribution is going there?"

Hari Prasad:	"When you were there at Hyderabad, at the farm, for one or two weeks the *prasādam* distribution was there."
Prabhupada:	"Why they are not distributing now?"
Hari Prasad:	"They have stopped it."

Tamal Krishna Maharaja speculated, "Probably they're not getting the funds from the Food Relief program. Just now the temples have started to send in money for Food Relief, so Jayapataka must be sending them money."

Hari Prasad:	"I do not know. Till I left, three days back, there was no distribution of *prasādam.*"
Tamal Krishna:	"In the past there hasn't been on some days?"
Hari Prasad:	"When Prabhupada was there, they had after you left for a week or two continuously."
Tamal Krishna:	"Mahamsa reported that there was *prasādam* distribution."
Hari Prasad:	"For a week or two. No, once in a

	while they were doing it."
Tamal Krishna:	"Mahamsa reports that on the weekends they do it."
Hari Prasad:	"But not daily."
Tamal Krishna:	"No, not daily. He said that on the weekends he does. In Mayapur they do on the weekends."
Hari Prasad:	"But *prasādam* distribution had a real good effect in that time when it was started. Many people had started coming then."
Prabhupada:	"You must see that *prasādam* distribution goes on."
Hari Prasad:	"The weather at Hyderabad is now very pleasant. Paddy is good this year. They have grown. There was drought. For one month there had been no rains when there should have been, in September. Whole of September was dry. Otherwise, entire twenty acres of paddy they had, and six acres which is fed from irrigation from tanks is very good. Paddy, maize also."
Prabhupada:	"Things are improving."
Hari Prasad:	"Yes, they are. There is no worry as far as this management of the temple and farm is concerned."
Tamal Krishna:	"Mahamsa is doing nicely."
Hari Prasad:	"Both are very much dedicated and devoted."
Tamal Krishna:	"Kirtan is doing nice?"
Hari Prasad:	"Tejiyas, his movements are too many. That is a problem."

Tamala Krishna: "He says Tejiyas moves around too much."

Hari Prasad: "He's not fully fixed up on the farm. But as far as temple manage, very much regulated now, after Sridhar Swami has come. It has been all perfectly streamlined."

Tamal Krishna: "Sridhar Swami is doing nicely."

Hari Prasad: "Yes, prabhu."

Pancha Dravida asked about the construction. Hari Prasad affirmed it was progressing, albeit slowly, and he estimated it would be completed in about a month's time.

One thing Hari Prasad requested, though, was regular discourses. He said that when Acyutananda was there, he was attracting crowds of up to one thousand.

Tamal Krishna: "Sridhar doesn't discourse?"

Hari Prasad: "But that type, just reading from *Bhāgavatam* or *Srimad-Bhāgavata*, doesn't..."

Tamal Krishna: "Acyutananda was giving good discourse."

Hari Prasad: "Yes, he was every time, I think. When he was there, three, four hundred minimum crowd used to be there, and they used to take interest in question-answers. And it had become a lively, interesting..."

Tamal Krishna: "Good speaker has to be there."

Hari Prasad: "Yes, good speaker. Or on this Chaitanya philosophy daily, if some lectures are arranged and discourse is arranged. If you can permit, Prabhupada, there's *Bhāgavatam* discourse in the daytime, and all of this who know Hindi fluently on Chaitanya philosophy. Yesterday I saw this *rāsa-līlā* also. If suppose some *rāsa* arrangement also is made."

Prabhupada: "Who?"

Tamal Krishna: "He says that there should be good speaker in Hindi. But Acyutananda could not speak Hindi."

Hari Prasad: "No, no, his was a different thing. Whether Hindi or English, He was attracting very big crowd."

Tamal Krishna: "It has to be good speaker."

Hari Prasad: "His *bhajanas* and all that."

Tamal Krishna: "There has to be something besides the *ārati*, he says. There should be some lecture."

Hari Prasad: "It has become more or less a pilgrim center. Anybody who comes to Hyderabad must visit."

Tamal Krishna: "That temple is finished now? Birla's temple?"

Hari Prasad: "Yes."

Tamal Krishna said it was a successful temple attracting two thousand people at the evening *ārati*.

Hari Prasad: "No, but they can come for this discourse or education on our philosophy and all that. If that starts [at our temple], it would be a wonderful thing."

Tamal Krishna: "That's a fact. Such a nice facility."

Hari Prasad: "It would be a really wonderful thing then. In South India, people are interested in such type of philosophy. And they discuss, they argue, they get convinced or they convince you, and they don't feel offended."

Tamal Krishna: "Yes, I remember they like to discuss philosophy."

Pancha Draviḍa: "So many were coming for hearing Srila Prabhupada when he was there. Has Lokanath Swami ever visited there?"

Tamal Krishna: "So you want him to stay there all the time?"

Pancha Draviḍa: "No, to visit. See how he would do."

Tamal Krishna: "But the thing is someone has to always be there. There has to always be programs."

On the whole Hari Prasad was very pleased. "No, management side of both the farm and the temple is good. It's really, I should say, remarkable achievement."

There is regular discussion about medicines, diet, *parikrama*, departure to Mayapur, and doctors. While Prabhupada is open to various suggestions, ultimately it all boils down to hearing and chanting the holy names, at whose lotus feet His Divine Grace is firmly fixed.

Srila Prabhupada's physical health continues to fluctuate. He passed stool five times during the night and again during the day, with hardly any ingestion of liquids or solids. He also slept for longer than usual.

He said too much sleeping means weakness.

Tamal Krishna: "Yes. Bhavananda felt it was due

239

to not sleeping at night that you were sleeping during the day. But you slept an awful lot today. When I asked you, 'Are you feeling more vitality?' you said, 'I think so.' In what way are you feeling like that?"

Prabhupada: "So, tonight don't give me."

Tamal Krishna: "No, that's all right. But what about that question I asked, Srila Prabhupada? When I asked you, 'Are you feeling more vitality?' you said, 'I think so.' In what sense are you feeling more vitality?"

Prabhupada: "Anyway, tonight don't try to give me."

Bhakti Charu: "Srila Prabhupada, I cooked some boiled rice, boiled it for a long time, and some plantain."

Tamal Krishna: "That's good for stopping diarrhea. I think you should take some, Srila Prabhupada. Instead of taking the medicine, take a little of this *prasādam*. Is that all right?"

Prabhupada: "All right, I'll try to take."

Tamal Krishna: "One thing I've seen is that although you're passing stool more, you're not passing out too much in the sense of total amount. Urine is less now. You're passing less urine. Stool is coming more, but urine is less."

Prabhupada: "No, that is natural. If you pass stool, there will be less urine."

Svarupa Damodara: "Actually, natural passing of stool is good instead of taking by enema. It is good sign, actually."

Bhakti Charu: "Yes, it means that the bowel is moving."

Svarupa Damodara: "Yes. The organs are functioning properly."

Prabhupada: "Just see."

Bhakti Charu: "Miśri?"

Tamal Krishna: "No. 'Just see,' I think Prabhupada said. The urine is finished now."

Svarupa Damodara: "Quite a bit. Looks clear."

Tamala Krishna: "There's more than that even."

Bhakti Charu: "Can I see it in the light, please?"

Tamal Krishna: "One hundred cc's, Srila Prabhupada, and clear. So urine is normal amount. Try to take a little bit to eat tonight, Srila Prabhupada."

Prabhupada: "I'll try."

Tamal Krishna: "Okay. And we won't give any medicine tonight. Tomorrow morning we're giving it. Okay?"

Bhakti Charu noted also that the swelling in his body is also down.

Gopal Krishna prabhu has been working hard, back and forth between here and Delhi and Bombay. Prabhupada has been pushing him continually on two important goals—getting the Government to give residency visas to ISKCON devotees, and the other, to get his books translated into Hindi and other Indian languages.

As far as visas go, we are getting favorable feedback from the government despite agitation from mainly communist elements in the political scene, who accuse us of being CIA agents. We have been promised three-year visas, which will save a large amount of funds. Currently we only get three-month visas, and devotees have to return to their country of origin, get a new visa, and return. It is disruptive and expensive.

Prabhupada said, "Unless one is a rogue, who would not like? [Laughs] Krishna consciousness:

> *yasyāsti bhaktir bhagavaty akiñcanā*
> *sarvair guṇais tatra samāsate surāḥ*
> *harāv abhaktasya kuto mahad-guṇā*
> *mano-rathenāsati dhāvato bahiḥ*

["All the demigods and their exalted qualities, such as religion, knowledge and renunciation, become manifest in the body of one who has developed unalloyed devotion for the Supreme Personality of Godhead, Vāsudeva. On the other hand, a person devoid of devotional service and engaged in material activities has no good qualities. Even if he is adept at the practice of mystic *yoga* or the honest endeavor of maintaining his family and relatives, he must be driven by his own mental speculations and must engage in the service of the Lord's external energy. How can there be any good qualities in such a man?" (*SB* 5.18.12)]

"These are the shastra. *Mano-rathena*, those who are on the speculative platform, they cannot have their spiritual qualities. To the modern world it is a novel idea. It is not idea; this is original qualification. Part and parcel of God, it must be godlike. Gold is gold, may be a small particle. Similarly, living entity, part and parcel of God, so he is God undoubtedly—in a small particle. But that is sufficient for his perfection. They are being misled other ways, in the wrong side. So who will not like it, unless he's a rogue. Huh?"

Gopal Krishna: "Actually, they would even give us permanent residency, but they are scared that if they give it to us they

	will have to give it to everybody else. So therefore they're not giving it to us."
Prabhupada:	"Never mind. We have got big establishment, and our European and American young boys have been trained up. Otherwise, how could I manage? We have nothing to do with politics. Rather, we are giving social service. What we'll do, politics? It is not our business. There are so many people. So the government should give us chance to organize a society for the highest benefit of human beings. And they can see from our books what is our idea."
Gopal Krishna:	"We are printing books and exporting these books, and this way we're earning so much foreign exchange for the Indian economy. They liked it."
Prabhupada:	"Did you show them the invoice of what book already we have got?"
Gopal Krishna:	"I told him the amount. I told him this year we have orders for Rs. 25 lakhs, and I said, 'This is just the first year, and worldwide we print over eight *crores*. So this is just the beginning.' They liked it. I also gave him the Hindi *Bhāgavatam*, as you had told me.

"This man who is handling our case is a Marwari, Mr. Pandy. Marwaris are very pious; they're better than these others. So, he liked the Hindi *Bhāgavatam*

243

very much. I gave him the Hindi *Bhāgavatam,* and the English."

Gopal Krishna further informed Prabhupada that he and Mahamsa Maharaja, along with two Hyderabad Life Members, Mr. Pannalal Pittie and Mr. G. Pulla Reddy (who donated our land in Hyderabad), know the President of India very well. "So I asked to go with Pulla Reddy to the President to see if he will come to Bombay to inaugurate our temple. Also, we are thinking of inviting some foreign ministers of countries like Nepal, which is a Hindu kingdom, and Mauritius. Because if these foreign ministers or some minister from these countries come, it will lend more credit, and we'll get better coverage."

Prabhupada:	"You can show our South African success."
Gopal Krishna:	"Yes. If the President of India comes, then it will get front-page coverage."
Prabhupada:	"Who is the President?"
Gopal Krishna:	"N. Sanjiva Reddy. He's more religious than the previous one."
Prabhupada:	"Sanjiva, he was Home Minister? No?"
Gopal Krishna:	"No, that was Brahmananda Reddy, who you met. We had a program at his house once."
Tamal Krishna:	"When was that?"
Gopal Krishna:	"Two years ago."
Tamal Krishna:	"Where was it?"
Gopal Krishna:	"In Delhi. And Prabhupada met him and asked him for the same thing, for visas."
Tamal Krishna:	"Hmm. You've been asking this for quite a few years, Srila Prabhupada."
Gopal Krishna:	"I think if Indira Gandhi would have

been in power, we wouldn't have got it. But Janata Party is better for us. Brahmananda Reddy would always say he'll give it—I saw him several times—but do nothing."

Tamal Krishna: "What will they give? Will they give you a letter officially or something?"

Gopal Krishna: "Yes. Plus they're writing a letter to the Indian embassies abroad that if any ISKCON devotee applies, he should be given a three-year visa straight."

Prabhupada: "That will be nice."

Gopal Krishna: "Yes. But I was just speaking to Tamal Krishna Maharaja that the GBCs should devise a policy so that this advantage is not misused. Because sometimes devotees just come over here, stay here for some time, do some nonsense, and go back."

Tamal Krishna: "Then they may take away this permission."

Prabhupada: "Yes."

Tamal Krishna: "We should be very careful to choose the right people to come."

Prabhupada: "Yes."

Tamal Krishna: "Not just that anybody goes to an embassy and they immediately get three years and come here, move around India, and in two weeks or two months they leave and go back. Then the government will not like it."

Gopal Krishna: "Yes. And if some Americans find out

245

	that ISKCON had this special status, then someone can also pose as an ISKCON devotee and get this visa."
Atreya Rishi:	"So we should require that they have GBC authorization."
Prabhupada:	"Our GBC should select."
Gopal Krishna:	"Or the GBC will communicate with India, and then India will send a letter."

In pursuance of Prabhupada's desire, Gopal Krishna has set up an Indian BBT in Bombay and now has twenty-two books in various stages of production and printing. Needless to say, Prabhupada is extremely pleased with his efforts. He has been pushing him in earnest to get book production and distribution manifest in India, and after a lot of cajoling Gopal Krishna has responded magnificently. He told Gopal, "Now you must have good godown. Otherwise books will be stolen and then sold on the open market."

Gopal Krishna:	"I also got the loan for the godown. In November we are starting construction of the BBT godown in Bombay."
Tamal Krishna:	"That four lakhs, two lakhs was for the godown and two lakhs for book printing."
Prabhupada:	"Money you'll get. There is no scarcity. Atreya Rishi will give you."
Gopal Krishna:	"Yes, he is very rich."
Prabhupada:	"Their country is very rich now."
Gopal Krishna:	"We used to send devotees to collect from these Middle East countries."
Prabhupada:	"Richest country now, Middle East. Everywhere we can make Vaikuntha

	by Krishna consciousness. Let people understand gradually."
Gopal Krishna:	"When they see your books, that's when they really appreciate our movement."
Prabhupada:	"Who has got such substantial books? Nowhere in the world."
Tamal Krishna:	"That's a fact, Srila Prabhupada."
Gopal Krishna:	"Srila Prabhupada, I also spoke to the Chinese Embassy in Delhi yesterday. I said I'd like to go to China, and I wanted to find out what the possibilities were. They said that since I have Canadian citizenship I should write to the Chinese Embassy in Ottawa. I told them I'm from a publishing house that publishes books on ancient Indian culture. I found out that they do not teach any Sanskrit in China, but they have Hindi and Urdu departments. Peking University has a department on Asian studies that teaches Hindi and Urdu."
Prabhupada:	"Let us introduce in Hindi."

After a while Svarupa Damodara prabhu brought a news article from *The Statesman* about the BI conference that was held here in Vrindavan.

Tamal Krishna asked Prabhupada, "You want to hear it?"

Prabhupada was keen. "Yes."

Tamal Krishna:	"Okay. The heading, Srila Prabhupada, says, 'The nonphysical

view on the origin of species.' Nonphysical view. 'Materialists and men of faith continue to disagree over the origins of life. According to the first group, life is derived from atoms and molecules. The Russian scientist Dr. A. L. Oparin has been propagating this view since 1957. But the challengers demand 'really solid examples of life arising from matter.'

"At a three-day international conference on 'Life Comes from Life' at Vrindavan last week at the Bhaktivedanta Institute, it was stressed...' Srila Prabhupada, do you want it 'Bhaktivedanta Institute' or 'Bhaktivedanta Swami'?

Prabhupada: "Oh, that's all right."

Tamal Krishna: "It doesn't matter. '. . . Bhaktivedanta Institute, it was stressed that life was independent of matter and dependent on higher principles lying beyond the present limitations of physics and chemistry. The assumption that life itself was non-physical was the keynote. The conference was opened by Dr. Prem Kripal, former president of the executive board of UNESCO. Three lectures were delivered by Dr. Thoudam D. Singh, director of the Institute; Mr. Robert Cohen, a geologist from USA; and Dr. Michael

Marchetti, a theoretical chemist
and student of the philosophy of
science, on the fundamental nature
of life and matter, new findings in
paleontology and their effect on the
theory of evolution, and the social
consequences of the materialistic
view of life. The philosophical
foundations of life was the theme
of discourse by Dr. S. R. Bhatt,
Associate Professor of Philosophy
at Delhi University. Dr. Richard
Thompson, a mathematician from
Cornell University, and Mr. David
Webb, from England, dealt with
the application of information
theory to the theory of evolution,
thermodynamics, and the origin
of life. The limitations of science
were discussed by Dr. A. Ramaya,
Professor of Biochemistry of the All-
India Institute of Medical Science.'
"'Dr. Singh opposed the theory that
life could be understood solely in
terms of chemical combinations.
There were intricate features of
life, ranging from the structures
of molecules and living cells to the
subtle ones of human personality.
The simple push-pull laws of
chemistry and physics cannot
account for these phenomena, and
life and matter are understood as
two distinct kinds of energy.'

"'Mr. Cohen said that the proof of
Darwinian theory of evolution must
depend in the end on the fossil
record. Darwin's theory required
that all the different species of
life were gradually transformed,
one into another, through many
small changes, or mutations. 'Yet
prominent paleontologists such
as Eldridge and Gould are now
maintaining that the fossil record
only supports the view that species
remain static in form and that
changes between them, if they do
really occur at all, can only occur
by abrupt leaps. An examination of
possible causes for such leaps shows
that they could only be accounted
for by the action of a higher
intelligence,' he said.'

"'Dr. Thompson dealt with the
mathematical analysis of the laws of
nature studied in modern chemistry
and physics. 'In the light of the
modern theory of information, these
laws can be shown to be unable
to account for the highly complex
and unique structures of living
organisms. It can also be shown that
the quantum-mechanical laws suffer
from serious shortcomings, because
they cannot account for the nature
of any conscious observer. Both of
these lines of evidence supporting

the view that the living being is
a nonphysical entity and that the
behavior of matter when in the
presence of life proves that there
must be further higher-order laws
and principles as yet unknown to
modern science.'

"'All of these conclusions were
in agreement with the observed
phenomena of life, and they
also corroborate the systematic
description of the nature of life
given in the *Bhagavad-gītā*. There
was a general agreement among
the participants of the conference
that this approach to understanding
the nature of life provided a viable
alternative to the materialistic view
of modern science.' "

Prabhupada: "Hmm. A good article."

Tamal Krishna: "Yes. I think they gave a very full
coverage."

Prabhupada: "And very scientifically presented.
And Bhaktivedanta Institute is
advertised."

Tamal Krishna: "Free of charge."

Svarupa Damodara: "Yes."

Prabhupada: "It is a good article."

Svarupa Damodara: "*Jaya*—Prabhupada's mercy."

Prabhupada: "Now it will give thought that life
is a different thing. It cannot be
produced by material molecules. It
is not possible. And *Bhagavad-gītā*
they referred. And Bhaktivedanta

251

Institute we have organized."
Svarupa Damodara: "Yes."
Prabhupada: "So it is good article."
Svarupa Damodara: "When we say *bhaktivedanta*,
they only know Srila Prabhupada,
because there's only one *bhakti-
vedāntī,* so everybody knows."

Tamal Krishna Maharaja informed Srila Prabhupada that he had received a letter sent to him by Haridasa, one of our devotees in Bombay. Prabhupada was happy to hear the contents.

"He found out that the Bombay temple owed the BBT 70,000 rupees. So he says when he heard that you had decided that you wanted to live and not leave us, he got very encouraged and inspired. So he decided on his own that he wanted to pay back this money to the BBT for you. He says, 'I have been encouraging all the preachers here at ISKCON Bombay to go out and collect the money to pay off this debt to the BBT. Srila Prabhupada has made all this arrangement very easy because of his encouragement to us. Even devotees who have engagements where they are not likely to make a Life Member are making Life Members very easily and are collecting money. And even persons not expected to become members are now becoming members. This is all due to the desire in the hearts of the preachers in Bombay to serve Srila Prabhupada. And by his grace, everything is coming very smoothly. This is confirmed in our hearts that without Srila Prabhupada, we cannot do any single work in this movement. Srila Prabhupada gives us encouragement just by kindly agreeing to stay with us. So yesterday, on Dasara day, we collected over 21,000 rupees and made ten members.' "
Prabhupada laughed and said, "Very good."

Tamal Krishna went on reading. "He says, 'We

cannot express in English what we are feeling in our hearts, but we are all very encouraged to go out and collect for Srila Prabhupada and expand his Life Membership program, and we are all very thankful that he has been merciful.' "

Trivikrama Maharaja concurred with Haridasa's feelings. He told Prabhupada, "Everything is happening by your mercy."

Prabhupada humbly gave the credit to his predecessors. "No. *Yasyāsti bhaktir bhagavati.*

["All the demigods and their exalted qualities, such as religion, knowledge, and renunciation, become manifest in the body of one who has developed unalloyed devotion for the Supreme Personality of Godhead, Vāsudeva..." [*SB* 5.18.12]

"Any devotee can become," Prabhupada said, and he cited another favorable message, a telegram, received from the ex-Mayor of Bombay:

"Pray God, Krishna, to give you long life to spread Indian culture in every nook and corner of the universe. Signed Rajiv K. Ganatra, ex-mayor of Bombay."

"He's very convinced, Srila Prabhupada, about Your Divine Grace and this Movement," Tamal Krishna said, "because he travelled around the world and stayed as a guest at our temples, and he was amazed to see how this Indian culture had actually been transplanted and taken root in all of these countries all over the world. He could not believe it. He was so amazed and impressed. He said that he's seen genuinely that this Indian culture has been taken up in true spirit."

Prabhupada said that Mr. Ganatra's statement carries weight. "Yes. And *The Statesman* report is very, very..."

"Very encouraging." Tamal Krishna rejoined, and added, "This Haridasa is transformed. You said that it

253

was due to the mercy of a Vaishnava, Giriraj."

Prabhupada agreed. "Yes."

Haridasa was formerly a thief. When the devotees were beginning in Juhu, he had seen a picture of Srila Prabhupada and noted that he was wearing a gold watch. He decided to meet Srila Prabhupada and steal it. However, when he actually met him, Prabhupada's saintly qualities stole his heart and he confessed his nefarious intentions and asked to join the temple.

"Remember how you said that?" Tamal Krishna said. "Giriraj gave him his association."

Prabhupada quoted *Prema-bhakti-candrikā*. "Vaishnava. *Chāḍiyā vaiṣṇava sevā, nistār pāyeche.* ["Without serving a Vaishnava, one cannot be delivered from the material condition of life."] Vaishnava's *kṛpā*. Vaishnava is already merciful. Vaishnava means merciful. *Kṛpā-sindhu*, ocean of mercy. That is Vaishnava."

Svarupa Damodara recalled that last night, Dr. Pathak, the Dean of the College of Veterinary, said Srila Prabhupada is a touchstone who can transform everybody.

Pancha Dravida declared, "This change with Haridasa is a miracle."

Prabhupada agreed. "Hmm. Bombay is the richest city in India. And now they are willing to help us. So there will be no scarcity of money. Wherever you'll go, you'll get it."

Tamal Krishna: "That project, is so nice, you don't have to go anywhere. They come to you and give money."

Svarupa Damodara: "Yes. (Laughs) That's Prabhupada's mercy."

Tamal Krishna: "You want to know when the godown is beginning to be built?"

Prabhupada: "Hmm."

Tamal Krishna: "November, this coming month."

Pancha Dravida: "It is a long way from this grass hut
we used to live in, Srila Prabhupada."
(Laughter)

Prabhupada: "Gradually the whole world will
be sympathetic. Everyone will
recognize that we are doing real
service."

After Prabhupada took his bed-bath there was
further discussion about medicine, diet, and doctors.
The initial ingestion of *makara-dhvaja* had an adverse
effect, so Prabhupada suggested taking a day's break
and taking only fruit juice. But he did not want to
abandon the *makara-dhvaja* fully.

Bhavananda reminded him, "You said that Krishna
directed you through that dream to take that *makara-
dhvaja* medicine. So, there are six different types of
makara-dhvaja."

"But Krishna directed Ramanuja Vaishnava,"
Prabhupada said.

Tamal Krishna informed Prabhupada that according
to Gopal Krishna, Jayapataka said that he has arranged
one Rāmānujī *kavirāja* in Calcutta. The only drawback
is that the doctors cannot usually travel because all
their medicines are where their practice is, and they
have many patients they are treating. But Prabhupada
said either the doctor could come, or he could go to
Calcutta.

Tamal Krishna: "Well, Svarupa Damodara, you could
call direct to Calcutta and talk with
Adri-dharana, who has contacted
him, and let him discuss and see if
he can bring him here. First of all,
he should ask whether the man is

willing. We can fly him here to Delhi
and bring him here. I'm sure he'll
agree to that. But he should be here."

Svarupa Damodara:　　"I can call from Delhi."

Tamal Krishna:　　"You could call Adri-dharana. He's
the one who found the man."

* * *

It is time for me to leave. I have been waiting as
long as I can, but now my one month as Prabhupada's
visiting GBC secretary is almost up, and the volume
of service Prabhupada has given me in Australia is
too much to put off any longer, especially since we are
attempting to buy a new property in Sydney.

So now I have another dilemma regarding his
personal service:

In February this year, when Prabhupada returned to
Mayapur, I felt the need to take up a new service, but it
wasn't clear to me what that should be. I had discussed
it with Tamal Krishna Maharaja. He suggested that I
ask Prabhupada what I should do. When I told him I
didn't want to disturb His Divine Grace, he told me,
"If you decide on your own what to do, you will always
have some doubt whether your choice was a good one
or not; but if you receive an instruction directly from
Prabhupada, then you don't need to speculate: your
heart will be clear and you can go ahead knowing that
what you are doing is pleasing and what Prabhupada
wants." It was sage advice. I acted on it and that resulted
ultimately in my being appointed by Prabhupada as the
GBC of the South Seas.

Now again I am leaving his personal service, and
again I have a dilemma. I am clear what he wants from
me in terms of my service. Just after arriving back here

I had asked him whether I should remain to help care for him, and his reply settled my heart: "No, for now I want you there [Australia]. Later we shall see." But now my dilemma was how long would Prabhupada be with us. If I go back to Australia and Prabhupada leaves us, that will be heart-breaking. I cannot contemplate such a thing; none of us can. But if I stay here, it is possible that His Divine Grace could remain for many months and gradually recover, as we all hope he will. In which case it would be irresponsible of me to remain here.

Consulting with Tamal Krishna Maharaja again gave me a solution. Atreya Rishi prabhu and Satsvarupa Maharaja have both decided to visit for one month, and then return to their zones for a month—in this way, back and forth, so they can do their GBC zonal service and still maintain their personal vigilance at Prabhupada's side. It was a good resolution to my quandary.

Thus, on this evening of October 27, I went into Prabhupada's room at seven o'clock to bid farewell to my lord and master, His Divine Grace Srila Prabhupada. In the subdued light, with a small kirtan party chanting softly in the background, I went in with Tamal Krishna Maharaja, me on one side of the bed and he on the other. I knelt by his bedside for a couple of minutes. Then I reached forward and gently stroked Prabhupada's arm with my right hand, and took hold of his left hand with mine. I told him, "Srila Prabhupada, now I have to go back to Australia."

Prabhupada raised his right arm slightly and imparted his final instruction to me. In a soft whisper he told me, "Wherever you remain, chant Hare Krishna."

Then after a short pause, I said, "I will come back again in January for the opening of the Bombay temple, and I will see you there."

Prabhupada replied, "I hope so." And again he fell silent. After another half a minute, I touched my forehead to his arm, and with his slight acknowledgement and tip of his head, I left him in Vrindavan for the last time.

NOVEMBER 14, 1977

Our beloved spiritual master, friend, father, and total shelter bade us farewell on November 14, 1977, at 7:25 p.m. in the holiest place of all holy places, Sri Vrindavan-*dhāma*.

$\mathscr{E}$pilogue

OCTOBER 28–NOVEMBER 14, 1977

The flight back to Australia found me with tremendously mixed feelings: bearing unreasonable hope, in defiance of reality, that somehow, by Krishna's special grace, Srila Prabhupada would remain for at least some years yet, to guide us and nurture our delicate and fragile bhakti creepers.

It is a daunting thought to dwell on, that somehow at the age of twenty-seven, with only five short years trying to be a devotee and only seven months as a GBC, I have been given the responsibility for overseeing the spread of Krishna consciousness to millions in the South Seas zone. Somehow Srila Prabhupada and Lord Krishna have given me (all of us!) this chance to serve Them—and serve we must. Service to the Lord and the Vaishnavas is our life, and we are bound by Prabhupada's love and instruction to carry his movement forward to the lost souls of Kali-yuga. Will I be fit to carry this heavy load? I pray so.

I immediately called a meeting of the Australian leaders to Melbourne. I brought them up to date on the events in Vrindavan, and I urged them to make a rotation so that they could visit Vrindavan for a few weeks at a time and still maintain the operations of their temples.

As a matter of great urgency, I also contacted

Rameswara Maharaja in Los Angeles and described
some of the events of the last few days, with a request
that he immediately inform all the Society's leaders of
the dire physical condition of His Divine Grace, with a
plea to send as many devotees as possible to be with
him.

Rameswara Maharaja immediately sent out a
circular dated October 30 to all ISKCON centers. He
quoted from different transcribed conversations that
I had read to him, and presented a three-point plan
how, from all corners of the world, at least one or two
devotees from every temple should be immediately
sent to Vrindavan to encourage Prabhupada by doing
kirtan, massage, and other services for him. At the
same time, the book distribution, Deity worship, and
temple services could be maintained:

TO ALL ISKCON CENTERS
URGENT! URGENT!
PLEASE READ AT ONCE!

Dear Prabhus,

Please accept my most humble obeisances in the
dust of your feet. All glories to Srila Prabhupada! It
is my unhappy duty to notify you of a most disturbing
situation that has developed regarding Srila
Prabhupada's condition. Below are excerpts from the
diary of Srila Prabhupada's personal secretary as read
to me by phone by Hari-sauri Prabhu. They refer to
conversations in Vrindavan on October 25, 1977.

Scene: Prabhupada's room. His Divine
        Grace is resting; Baradraj and
        Hamsaduta Swami are sitting
        silently as he awakens.

Prabhupada:	(To Upendra) "So, everyone has left?"
Upendra:	"Yes."
Prabhupada:	"I feel very unhappy when no one is here. They are avoiding me. They do not want to come."
Upendra:	"Baradraj and Hamsaduta Swami are here. Do you want kirtan?"
Prabhupada:	"At least *japa* while I sleep. When I look around I see the room is empty and I feel very unhappy. When I see no one around me, then I feel lonely."
Baradraj:	"We'll get some others, and Hamsaduta Swami and I will do kirtan."
Prabhupada:	"Why not all of you? You cannot all do kirtan? Why not others?"
Scene:	Prabhupada's room, sometime later. Prabhupada has stopped eating all solid foods and is not even taking medicines. It is evident that His Divine Grace is discouraged. Atreya Rishi arrives from Tehran.
Prabhupada:	"Please don't leave me here. Keep me surrounded. That will encourage me. You keep me surrounded and chant Hare Krishna. There is very little hope for my life. Chant Hare Krishna softly, all together. Do not leave. Now I have become poisonous. Everyone is avoiding me. Things are deteriorating. What is to be done? What is the use? Everything is frustrated."
Scene:	Prabhupada's room. His Divine

	Grace was planning to go to Mayapur, but the trip is cancelled because His Divine Grace feels it would be too risky and he doesn't have sufficient strength. Instead, he decides to be taken out to see the Deities of Krishna-Balarama.
Prabhupada:	"I want to go on parikrama. By parikrama, even if I die, that is good luck. Arrange like that, with kirtan, I may die or live, it doesn't matter. Better than dying by jerking of an airplane."
Hari-sauri:	"For us it matters."
Prabhupada:	"What can be done?"

From the above excerpts we can all appreciate the situation in Vrindavan very clearly. The only medicine Prabhupada is taking is kirtan and being surrounded by his loving disciples. There is no other way to encourage Prabhupada to stay in this world and continue leading us personally.

After discussions with most of the GBC representatives in America, South America, and Europe, I would like to urge all temples to act immediately as follows:

From every corner of the world, temples should send four men (at least one or two) immediately to Vrindavan for the month of November. In December send replacements if the first men cannot stay longer than one month. These men will have the unique privilege of being with Prabhupada six to eight hours daily, chanting, massaging, hearing His Divine Grace translate, carrying His Divine Grace on *parikrama*, etc. They will have the great responsibility of encouraging Srila Prabhupada by serving him personally in this way with devotion and love.

Every temple should increase their kirtan program to 24-hour kirtan if possible. Prabhupada is personally present in each temple and can receive the encouragement and love of His disciples who surround his *vyasasana* in the temples around the world to petition the Lord for his health to be returned. Special *sankirtana* marathons should be planned and all devotees should participate for petitioning the Lord to please cure His pure devotee (remember: *sankirtana* is the best process for petitioning the Lord in this age).

Immediately after the Christmas distribution the devotees who were scheduled to go to India for pilgrimage this year can be sent in shifts (January–April) so that there is a continuous flood of loving devotees surrounding Prabhupada and chanting for him. This year's pilgrimage should be centered around His Divine Grace.

Finally, I would humbly remind all temples that there shouldn't be one moment's hesitation or delay in sending men immediately for November and December. How can we forget that all the money in ISKCON is Srila Prabhupada's money and all the time is meant for serving him, that he is in need of personal service right at his bedside and we must hasten to his call! If each center sends only one or two men for November and December, which are the critical months, there will be dozens of senior devotees attending to His Divine Grace. There is no question of not doing this for Srila Prabhupada. Please, act at once!

Jaya, Prabhus. I hope this finds you well and immediately making arrangements to send men to Vrindavan for this urgent service. Haribol!

Your unworthy servant,

Ramesvara dasa Swami
GBC representative.

P.S. One senior GBC man commented that if we don't send senior men to be with Prabhupada at this time, it is practically demoniac.

* * *

I received the news of Srila Prabhupada's departure two days after celebrating the first Govardhana-puja at our newly-purchased property in Australia, New Govardhana. I immediately flew back to India, back to Vrindavan-*dhāma* and arrived just in time for the *mahā-utsava* held in glorification of Srila Prabhupada as per His Divine Grace's request. Afterwards I travelled with a group of my Godbrothers and Godsisters to Sridham Mayapur, where, on the site formerly proposed for building a house for Srila Prabhupada, we performed the ground-breaking ceremony for His Divine Grace's *puṣpa-samādhi*.

That done, we returned to our respective temples and zones, faced with the most daunting task yet given to us by our beloved Guru Maharaja: maintaining and developing his institution, ISKCON, without his physical presence.

ABOUT THE AUTHOR

Hari-Sauri dasa was born in England on November 17th, 1950. In May 1971 he emigrated to Australia where, on the second day of arrival, he met the members of the newly-emerging Krishna consciousness movement. He was duly accepted as an initiated disciple by His Divine Grace A. C. Bhaktivedanta Swami Prabhupada on April 9th, 1972 in Sydney.

In August of 1975 he moved to the newly-opened ISKCON Krishna-Balaram temple in Vrindavana, India, where he served as temple commander. In November of the same year, he joined Srila Prabhupada's personal entourage, remaining as His Divine Grace's servant for sixteen months.

In March of 1977 Srila Prabhupada appointed him ISKCON's Governing Body Commissioner for Australia, New Zealand and Indonesia, a service he performed for over seven years. During that period he oversaw the growth of the ISKCON society in the South Seas from four temples and asramas, to seventeen, including four farming communities, two schools and several restaurants. He was also instrumental in establishing branches of the Bhaktivedanta Book Trust in Australia and Indonesia.

In 1986 he began the work of transforming the diary he kept while traveling with Srila Prabhupada into a multi-volume set entitled Transcendental Diary.

In 1990 he moved to America and worked as publisher for *Back to Godhead* magazine, the Krishna consciousness movement's spiritual periodical, for a year.

In 1996 he became a resident of ISKCON's world headquarters at Mayapur, WB India, with his wife Sitala dasi and daughter Rasarani, where he continues to reside to the present day (2021).

He is a Co-founder and Trustee of the Bhaktivedanta Research Centre in Kolkata (BRC); a member of the Exhibits development committee for the Mayapur Temple of the Vedic Planetarium (TOVPE); and a Trustee of the Mayapur-Vrindavan Trust (MVT) since 2004.

A Transcendental DIARY

Travels With His Divine Grace
A.C. Bhaktivedanta Swami
PRABHUPĀDA

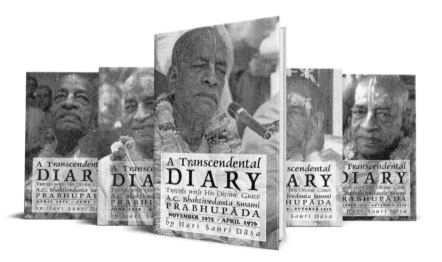

A Transcendental Diary, Travels with His Divine Grace A.C. Bhaktivedanta Swami Prabhupada is a series about the period of 16 months, from late November, 1975, to the end of March, 1977, that Hari Sauri Dasa had the great fortune to travel with His Divine Grace A. C. Bhaktivedanta Swami Prabhupada as his personal servant.

These books represent an expanded form of his personal written diary, coupled with snippets and segments of the recorded lectures and conversations during that time. Added to this are selections of His Divine Grace's correspondence. This is one small attempt to bring to the attention of the world the greatness of Srila Prabhupada, his person, and his message.

A Transcendental Diary series can be purchased through Hari Sauri Dasa's website www.lotusimprints.com and any queries can be sent to harisauri@gmail.com.

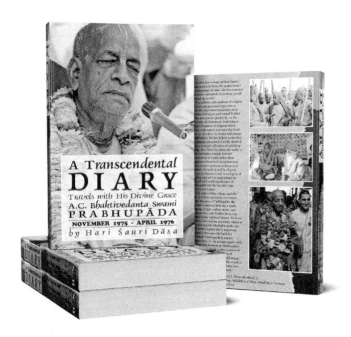

A Transcendental Diary — Volume 1

Covers November 1975 to April 1976

"In this volume we travel with Prabhupada throughout India between November, 1975, and April, 1976. One comes away from this book with a personal connection to Prabhupada, appreciating his love for Krishna as well as his many disciples."

Extract from the forward by
Professor E. Burke Rochford, Jr.
Middlebury College, Vermont.

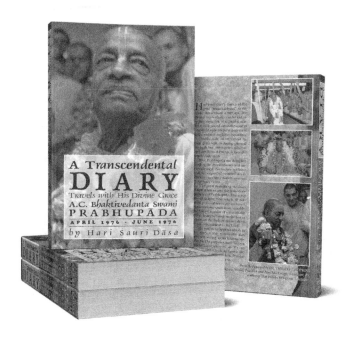

A Transcendental Diary — Volume 2
Covers April 1976 – June 1976

"Hari Sauri Dasa's choice of the term "Transcendental" to describe this account is very apt. The Diary is a remarkably candid and inspiring depiction of a spiritual master at work interacting with his disciples and the public and trying to implant devotion to Krishna in the minds and hearts of often all too human followers. ...Prabhupada is clearly the focus of this diary, and he is brought wonderfully to life in Hari Sauri Dasa's careful transmission of his speech and his style of discourse. Those who knew Prabhupada can hear his voice behind the printed words of the diary."

Extract from the forward by
Dr. Thomas J. Hopkins
Professor Emeritus
Franklin and Marshall College

A Transcendental Diary — Volume 3
Covers June 1976 – August 1976

"On the pages of this volume one finds Swami Prabhupada teaching, conversing, and arguing with gentle but forceful persuasions. Thanks to Hari Sauri Dasa, Swami Prabhupada's magic never seems to wear off. Every encounter, every answer, and every gesture brings out the inner conviction of the great Swami. ...The book is written with a style of personal force, a humble learning, a steady insight into the thought processes of the great Swami."

Extract from the forward by
Dr. Shaligram Shukla
Georgetown University

A Transcendental Diary — Volume 4
Covers August 1976 – October 1976

"Srila Prabhupada attracted thousands of disciples and unknown numbers of lay practitioners. This required strong, firm, and expert leadership of an extraordinary magnitude. A Transcendental Diary allows us to better understand the meaning of personal charisma by providing us with a full and detailed account of Prabhupada's daily life."

Extract from the forward by
Dr. Charles R. Brooks
N.D.R.I, New York

A Transcendental Diary — Volume 5
Covers October 1976 – November 1976

This volume covers Srila Prabhupada's visits to Aligarh, New Delhi, and Chandigarh; and an extended repose at ISKCON's Krishna-Balarama Mandir in Sri Vrindavana-dhama.

During his stay in Vrindavana, one of the greatest challenges to the legitimacy of his preaching arose. ...A collusion of disgruntled parents, misguided lawmakers, and demonic 'deprogrammers' threw down the gauntlet in the first real legal challenge to the existence of ISKCON. And Srila Prabhupada accepted it with alacrity.